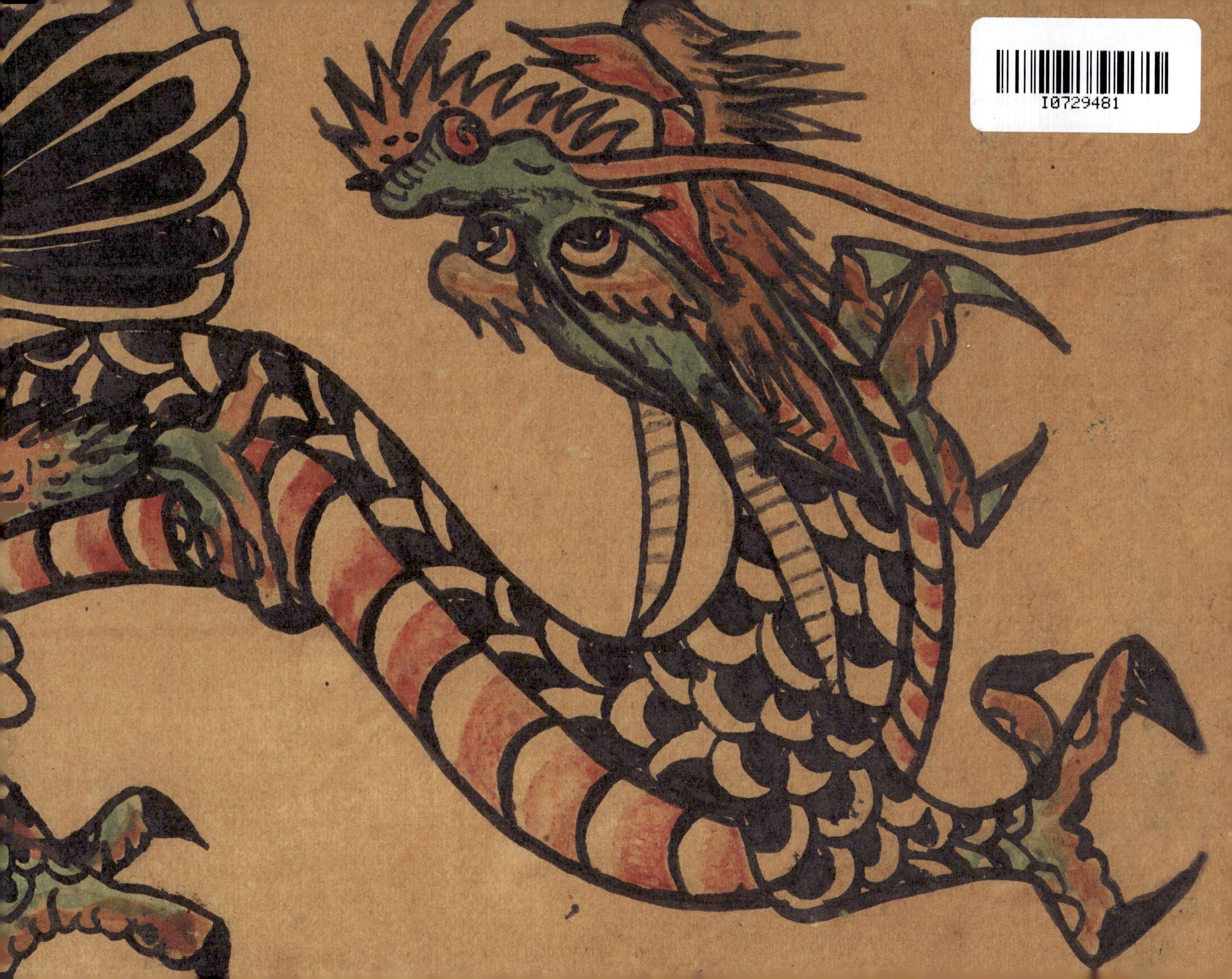
I0729481

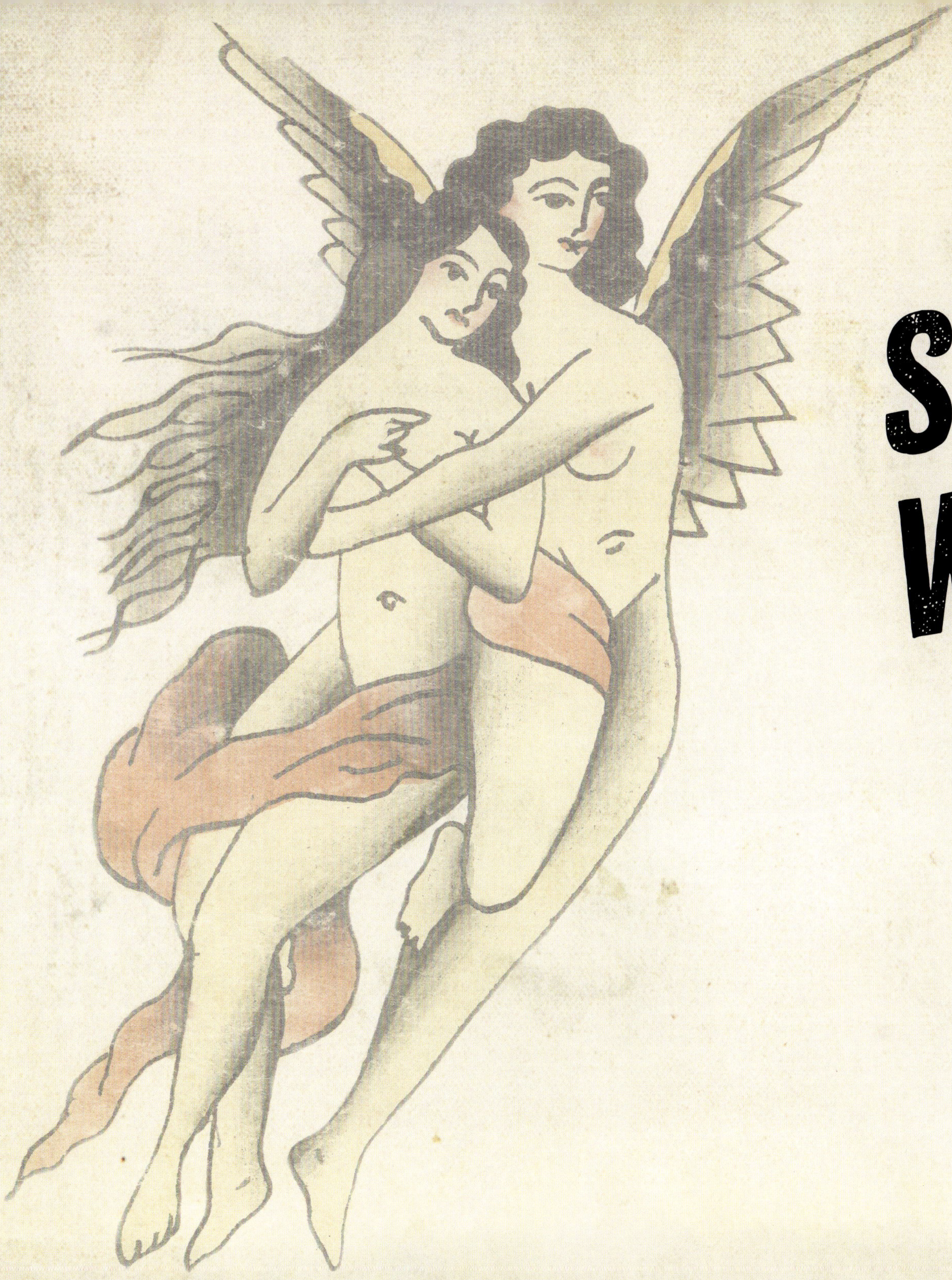

MAUD STEVENS WAGNER

MONA LISA OF AMERICAN TATTOO

ALAN GOVENAR

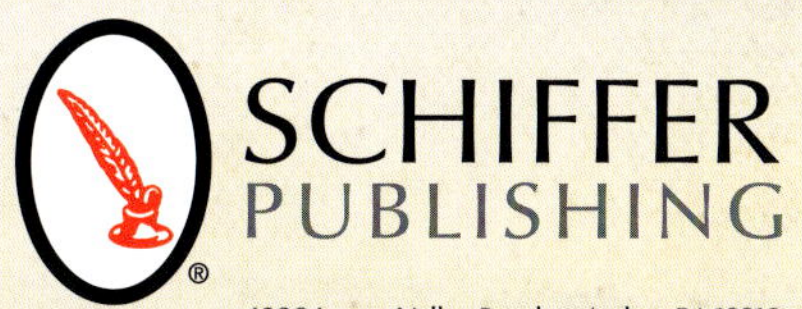

SCHIFFER PUBLISHING

4880 Lower Valley Road • Atglen, PA 19310

Other Schiffer Books by the Author:
Gus Wagner: Globe Trotter and Hand Tattoo Artist, ISBN 978-0-7643-6728-1
Stoney Knows How: Life as a Sideshow Tattoo Artist, 3rd Edition, ISBN 978-0-7643-6400-6
Anne Morgan: Photography, Philanthropy, and Advocacy, ISBN 978-0-7643-6590-4

Cover design by Molly Shields
Type set in Citrus Gothic/Cambria

Photographs, flash, ephemera, artifacts, and scrapbook pages on pages 4-7, 9, 11, 14, 19, 20 (left), 21, 23, 24, 26, 27, 30, 31, 36, 37, 39-56, 58, 59 (bottom), 65-67, 69-78, 80 (left), 81, 82, 90-93, 95-98, 99 (right), 100-102, 104, 106, 107, 108 (right), 109-116, 120-122, 126, ca. 1897–1941, courtesy of the Alan Govenar and Kaleta Doolin Tattoo Collection at the South Street Seaport Museum, New York.
Photograph on page 3, courtesy of Ron Dolecek.
Photographs on pages 12, 13 (left), courtesy of the Tattoo Archive.
Photographs on back cover and pages 18, 22, courtesy of Derin Bray.
Photographs on front cover and pages 15, 16, 17, 20 (right), 28, 29, 32, 64, courtesy of Library of Congress.
Photograph on page 13 (right), courtesy of the Harvard Library.
Photograph on page 59 (top), courtesy of the New York Public Library.
Photographs, flash, and ephemera on pages 1, 8, 10, 25, 35, 38, 57, 60-63, 79, 80 (right), 83, 87, 89, 94, 99 (left), 103, 105, 108 (left), 117-119, 123-125, private collection.

ISBN: 978-0-7643-6930-8
ePub: 978-1-5073-0537-9
Printed in China

Published by Schiffer Publishing, Ltd.
4880 Lower Valley Road
Atglen, PA 19310
Phone: (610) 593-1777; Fax: (610) 593-2002
Email: info@schifferbooks.com
Web: www.schifferbooks.com

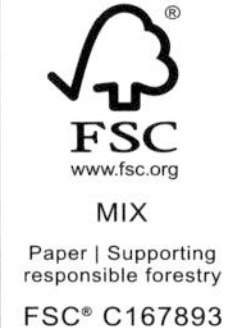

Opposite: Sideshow banner of Maud Stevens Wagner

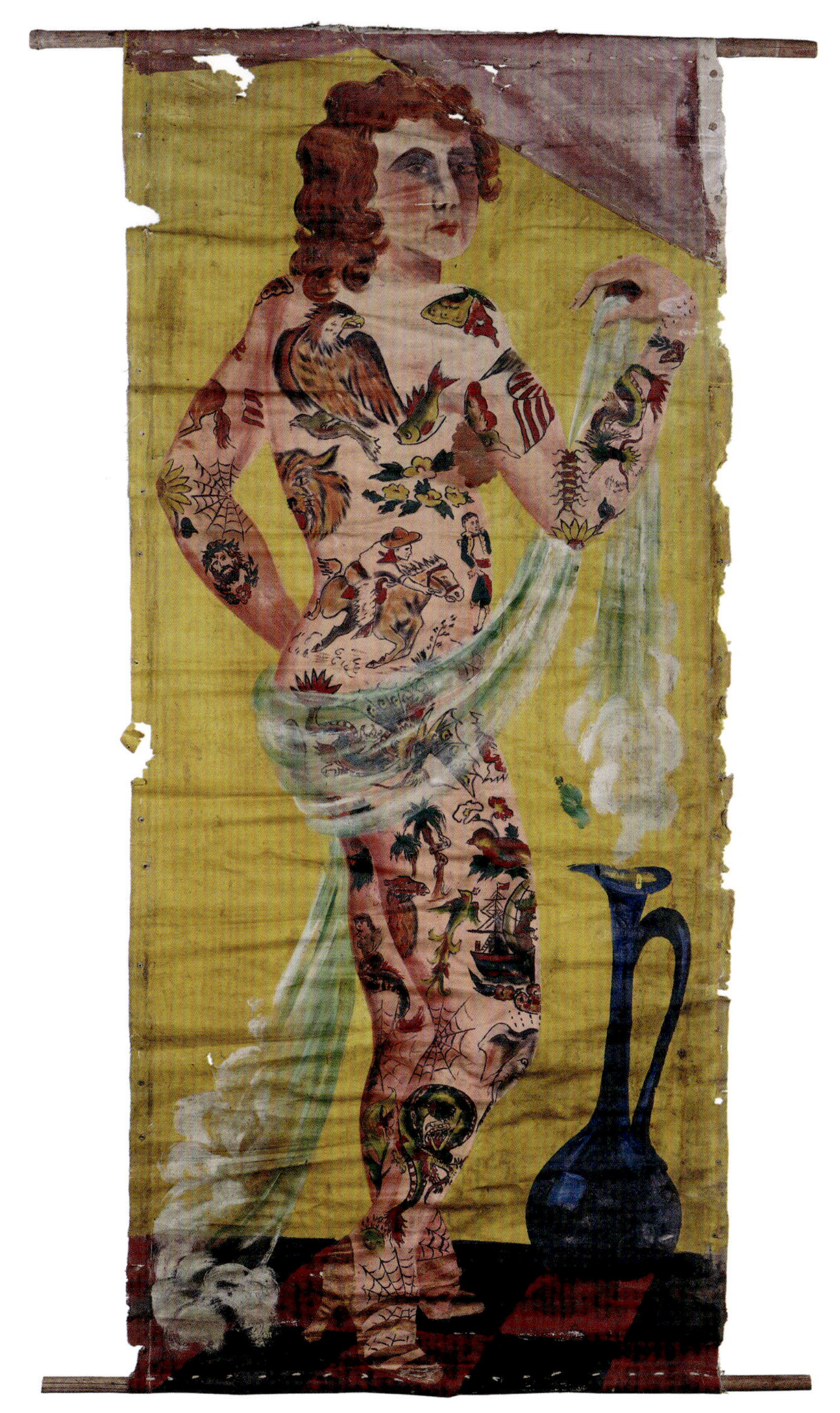

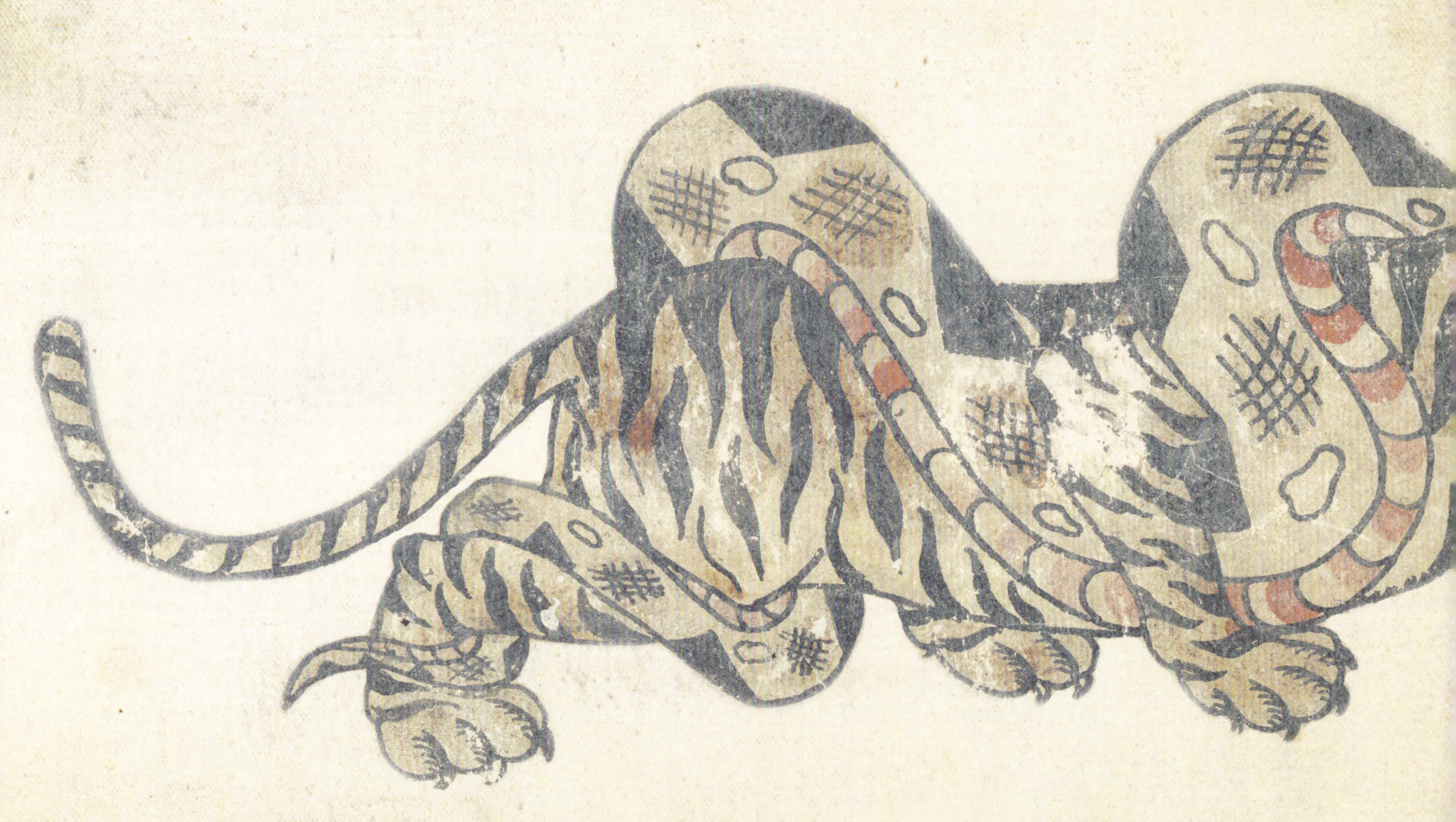

CONTENTS

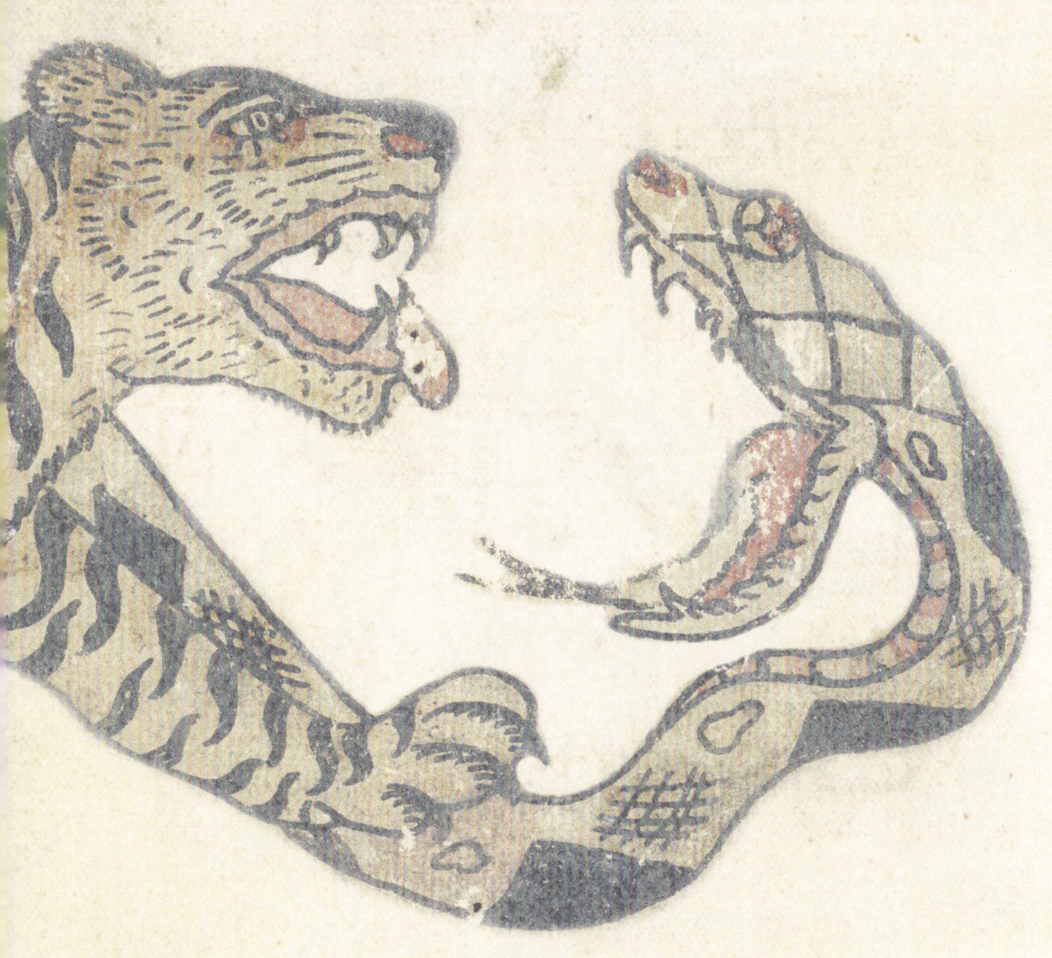

ACKNOWLEDGMENTS

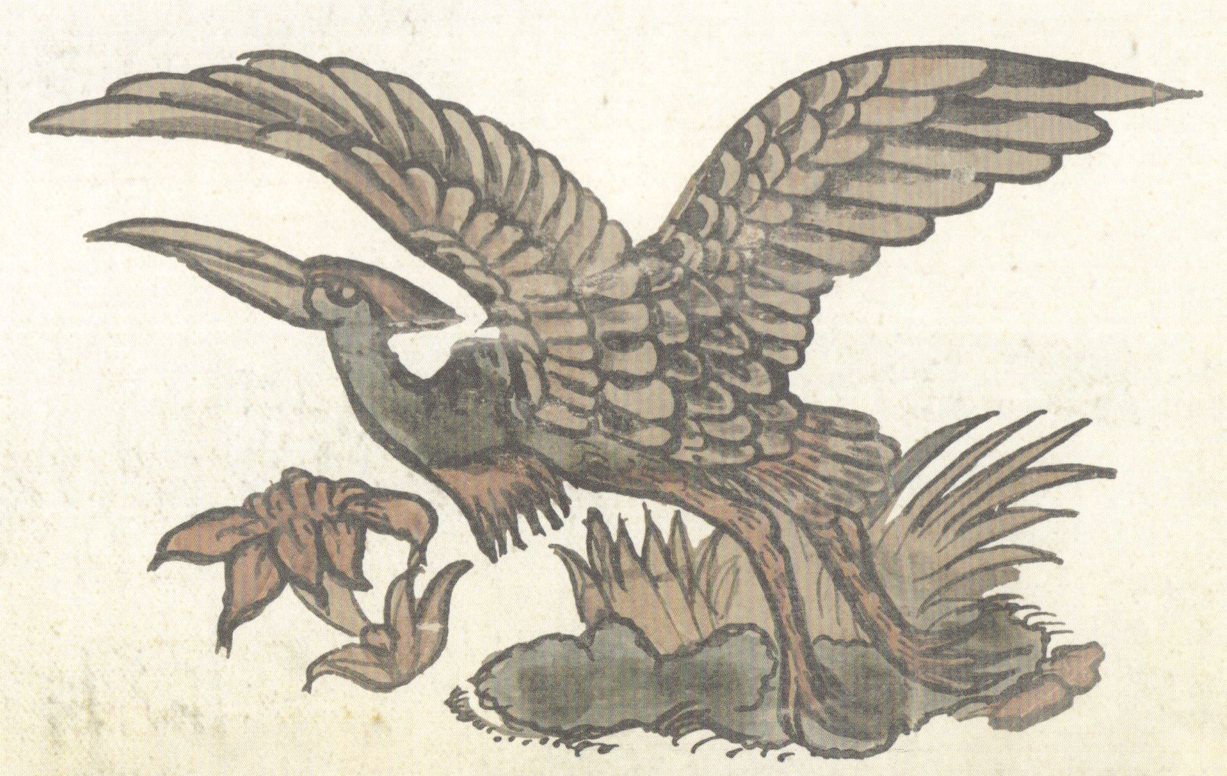

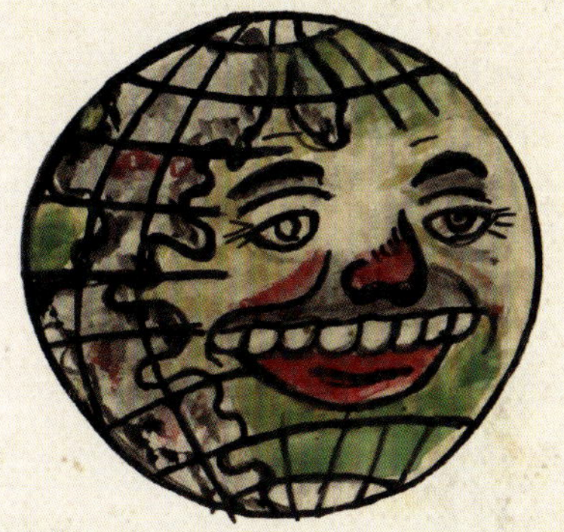

First and foremost, I am grateful to Rockey Reisner for entrusting me with his family treasures, and to my family for believing in my work. Martina Caruso, Director of Collections and Exhibitions at the South Street Seaport Museum, provided scans and documentation and has guided the preservation and conservation of the Alan Govenar and Kaleta Doolin Tattoo Collection. Ed Hardy and Chuck Eldridge offered good counsel as my work advanced. Michelle Myles and Michael McCabe shared their insights into the history of tattooing in New York City. Derin Bray loaned photographs from his collections, and Ron Dolecek made available an image of his vintage sideshow banner of Maud Stevens Wagner. Jason Johnson-Spinos assisted with copyediting and the preparation of photographs and images for publication.

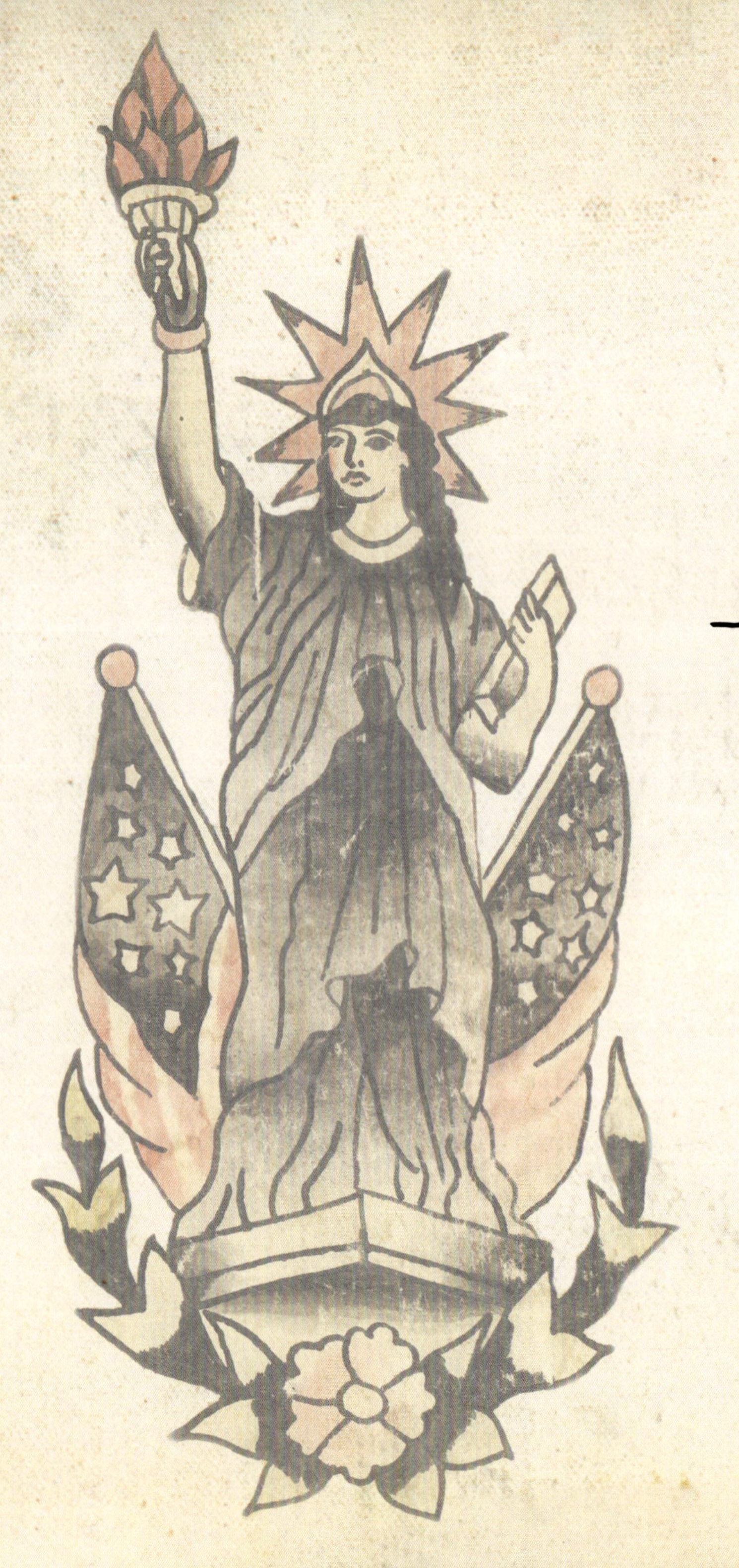

INTRODUCTION

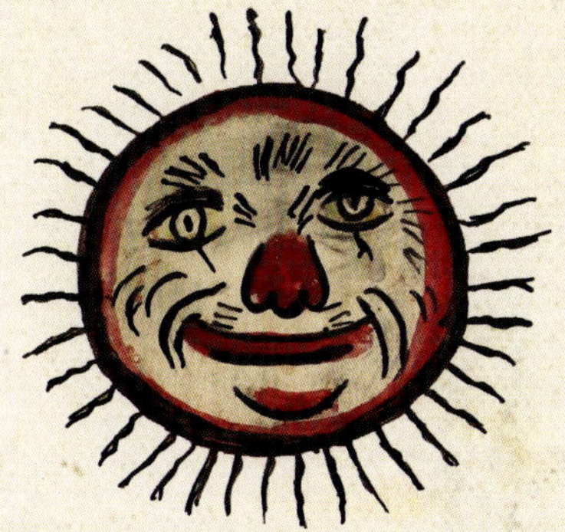

aud Stevens Wagner was an ardent individualist who defied the expectations of the Victorian era—an independently minded young woman who left home to pursue a career of her own making. An acrobat, she exuded an athletic strength with muscular arms and legs, an aerial artist and acrobat on the outdoor stage.

Gus Wagner was a sight to behold, thrusting his chest forward, raising and twisting his arms into a he-man pose, self-assured and proud, whether wearing a loincloth as if he was a tribesman from Borneo or dressed up in the trappings of the Old West to look like Buffalo Bill. Gus was a man of all cultures, a globetrotter, who had traversed the world as a merchant seaman and had hundreds of tattoos that chronicled his travels and adventures.

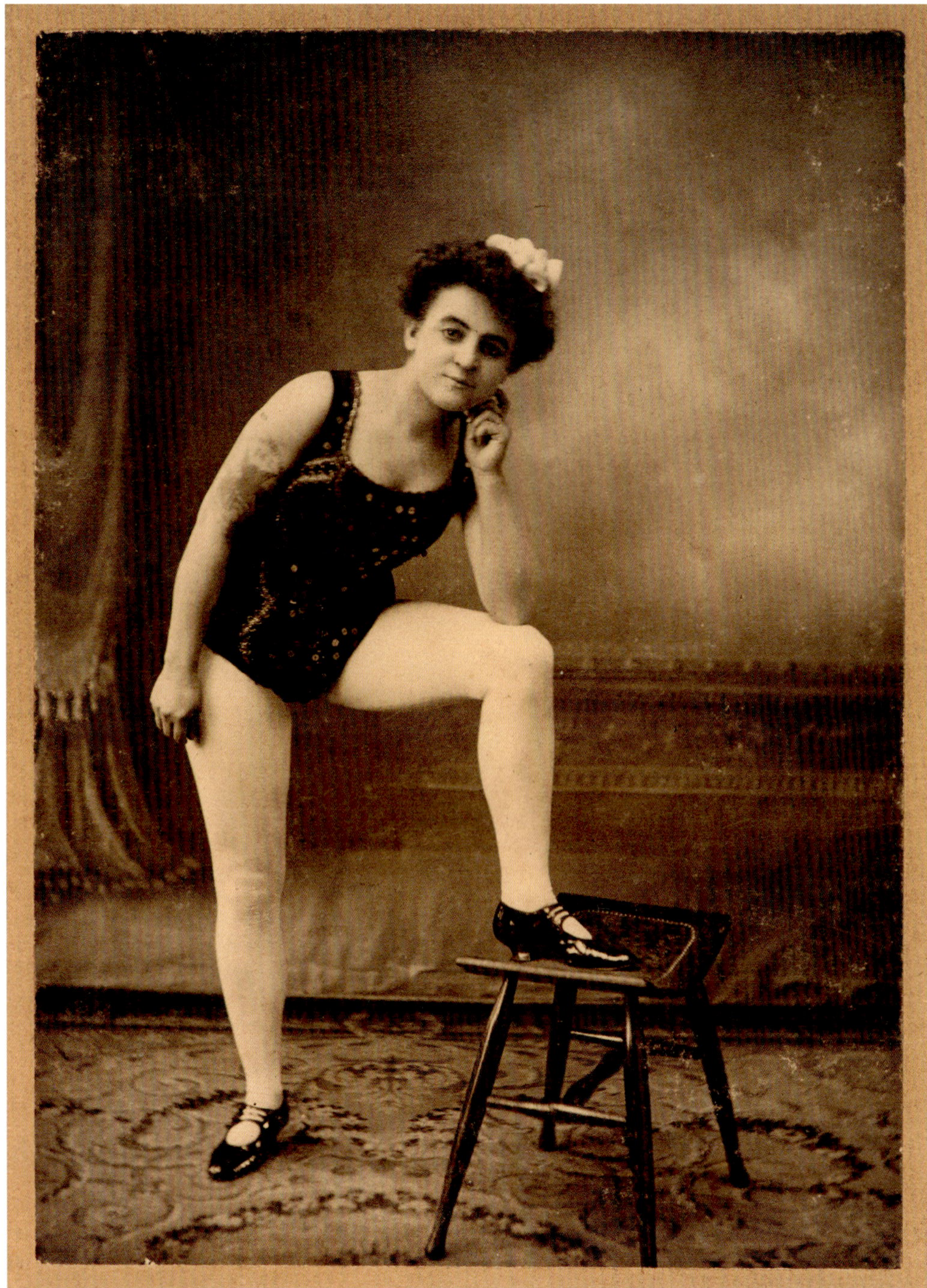

Maud Stevens Wagner, ca. 1904

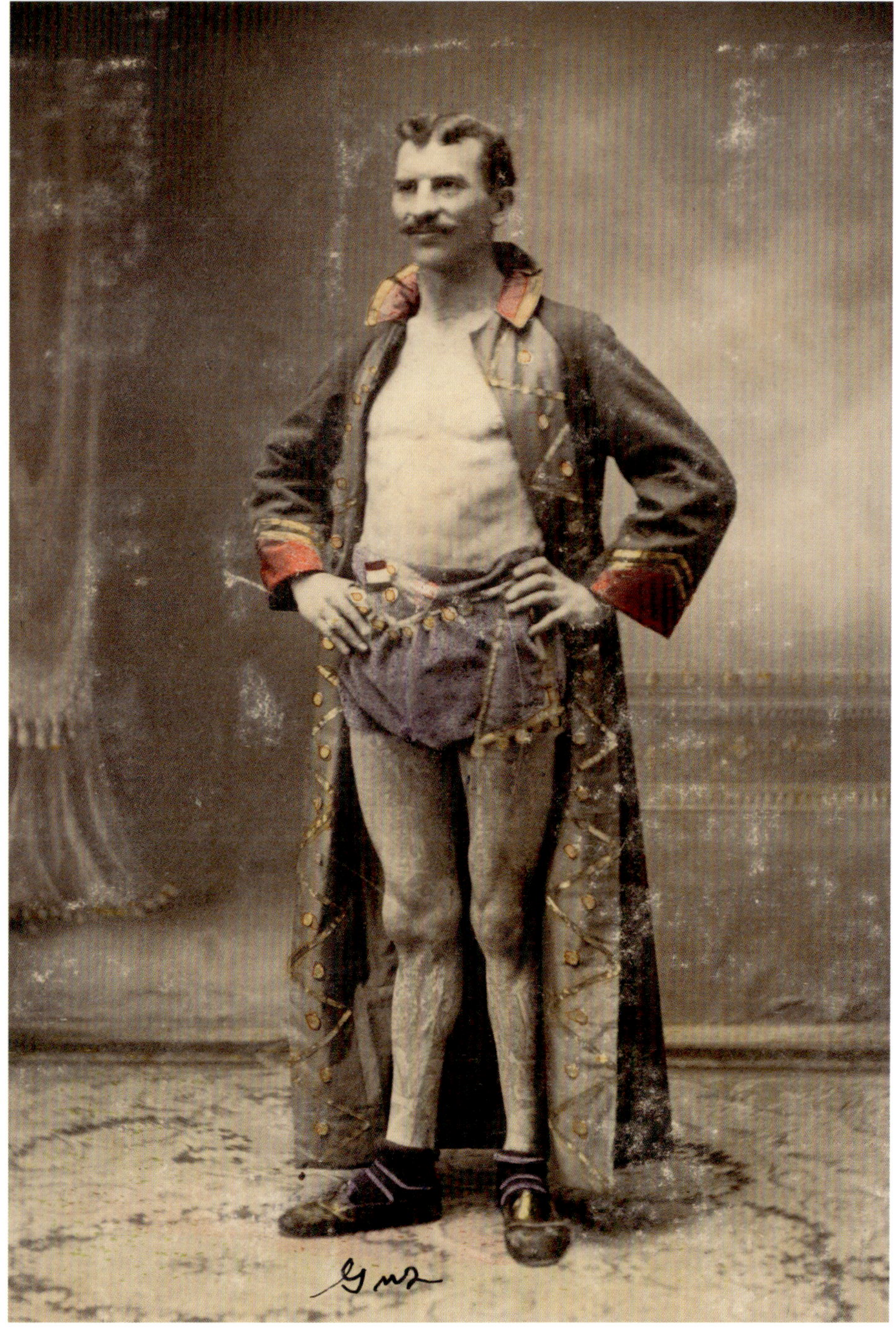

Gus Wagner, St. Louis, Missouri, 1904

When Gus and Maud embarked on their journey as tattooed attractions across the United States in 1907, they were likely inspired by Frank and Annie Howard, who, by the end of the nineteenth century, were the most acclaimed tattooed couple in the Western world. Both born in Rhode Island in the 1850s, Frank and Annie were covered with an encyclopedia of tattoos that echoed the zeitgeist of the era in which they lived and worked. After performing regularly at Austin & Stone's Dime Museum in Boston's iconic Scollay Square, they made two tours with Barnum & Bailey's Greatest Show on Earth in 1888 and 1897. Frank and Annie were consummate entertainers and self-promoters with an unparalleled business acumen that turned their fame into a highly profitable livelihood—tattooing, operating tattoo shops, and selling mail-order tattoo supplies.

Frank Howard, who boasted about the handmade tattoos he made and exhibited, was quick to switch to the electric tattoo machines, first patented by Samuel F. O'Reilly on December 8, 1891. Meanwhile, Gus Wagner saw an opportunity to define his own brand as "Globetrotter and Last of the Hand Tattoo Artists." Gus was not only a sideshow attraction but was the embodiment of the "noble savage," with tattoos that were at once traditional and exotic, aggrandizing his extraordinary trek around the globe. On the outdoor stage, Gus was able to show off his tattoos and act out in ways that may not have been possible as part of the Barnum & Bailey circus.

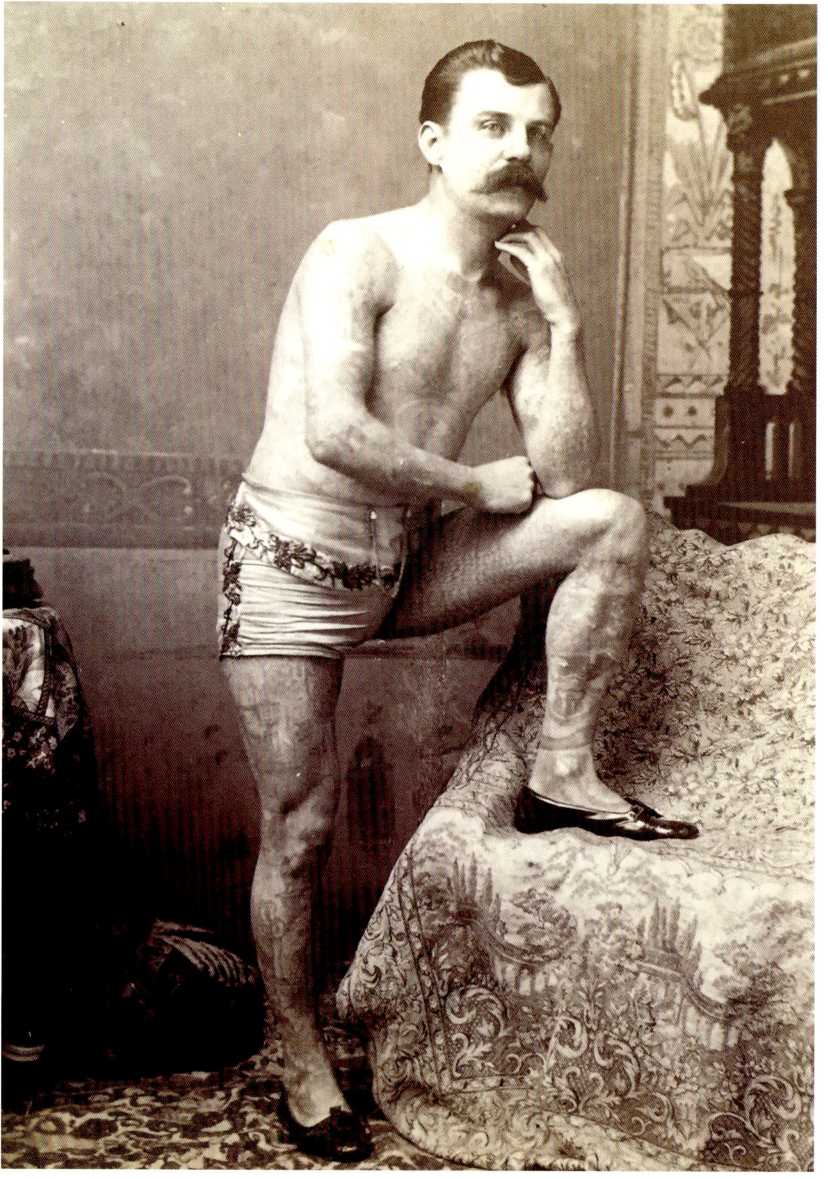

Frank Howard, ca. 1880s

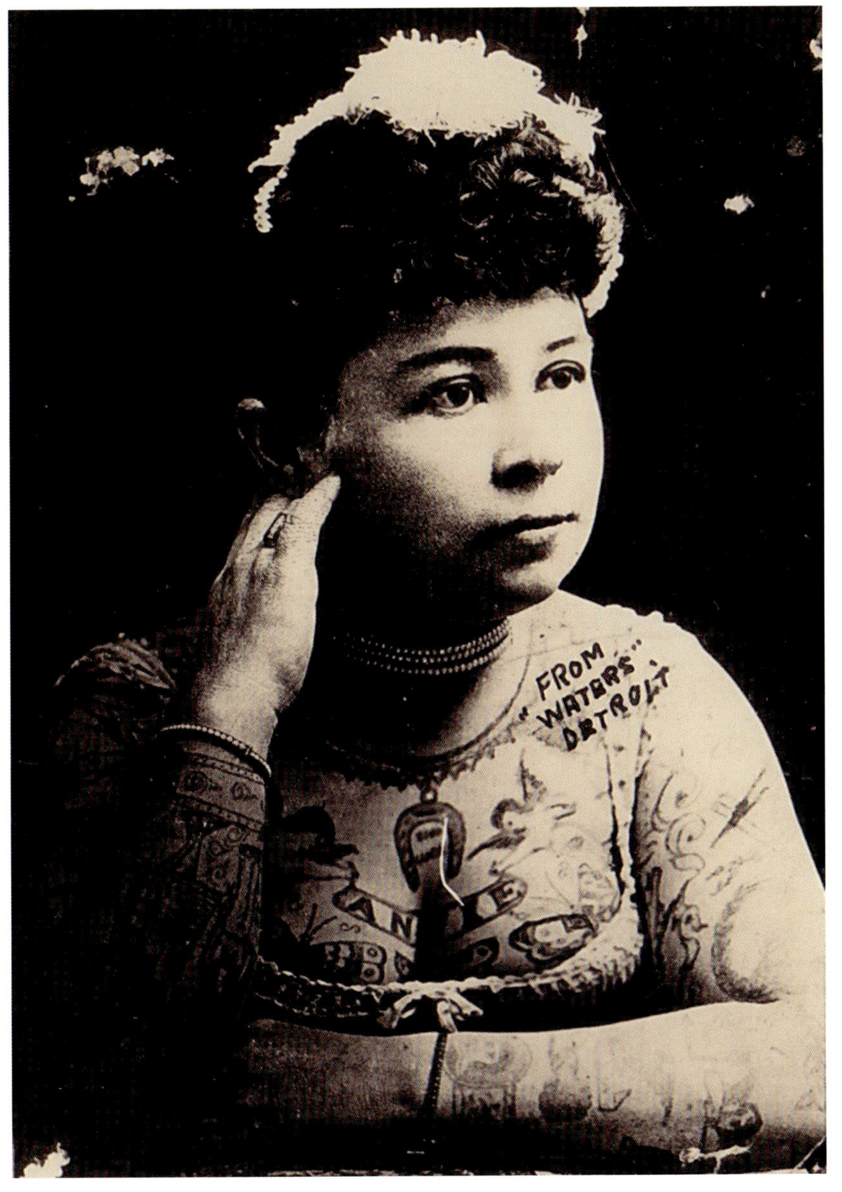

Annie Howard, ca. 1880s

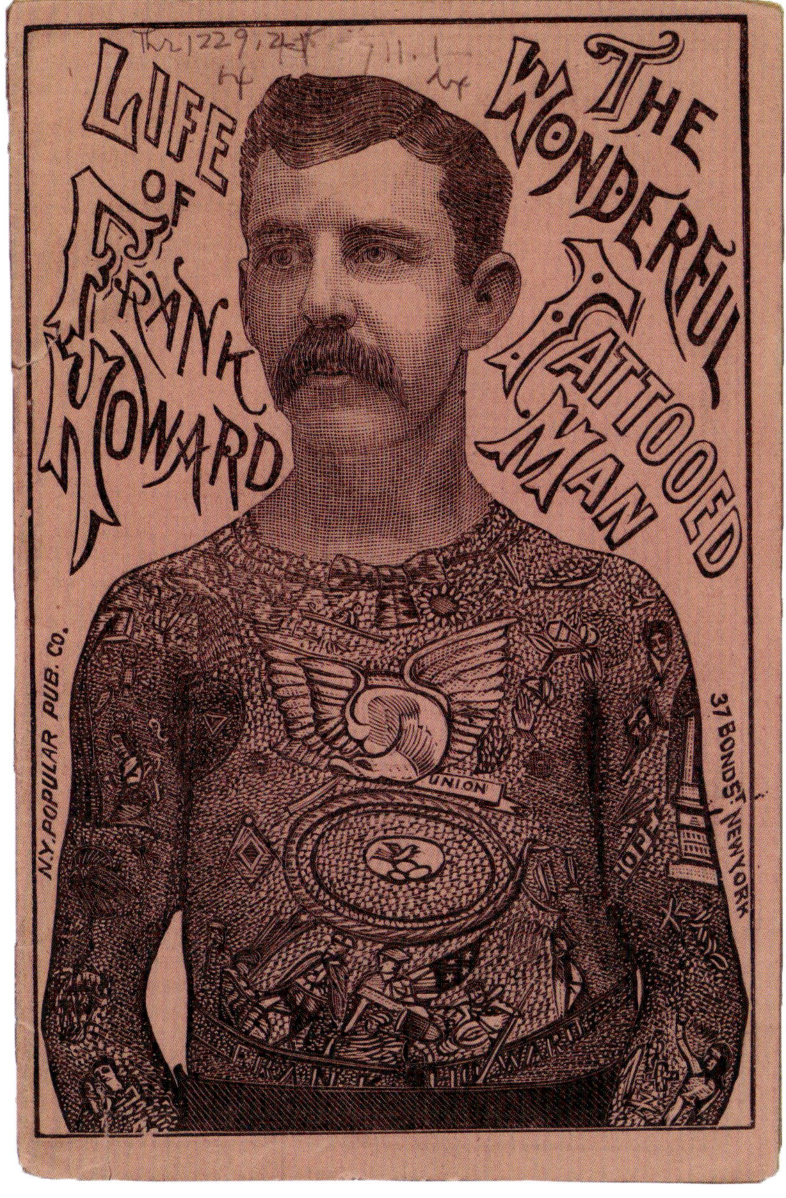

Front cover of Frank Howard's book, *Life of Frank Howard, The Wonderful Tattooed Man*, ca. 1880s

Gus and Maud embraced the circus and carnival sideshow life and were exemplars among the countless men and women who crisscrossed the United States in what were often called "ragbag shows." Together, they brought the excitement of the Big Top into the little-tent shows of small-town America, offering tattoos at affordable prices for working people who might not have otherwise been able to acquire them.

In a 1992 conversation, Patricia "Pat" Waynette Hook, a distant cousin of Gus and Maud's daughter Lotteva Wagner Davis, recalled, "Maud was an artist from the age of eight. Around 'Sycamore Hill' (at Homestead, Kansas) in the evenings she would sew. She taught twice at the normal school in Emporia." She considered going into nursing. Her father, David V. Stevens, was a medical intern during the Civil War, and her uncles John J. and William O. Stevens also "did some doctoring. In the Chicago area she became associated with a Dr. Sweeney. He asked her to marry him. He said she would be in charge of his special appendicitis cases. She said she didn't have enough experience for that. Then he explained that since most people didn't really have appendicitis, he only cut just through the skin and put in a few stitches. He didn't really remove the appendix. Maud couldn't go along with that—so she didn't marry him."

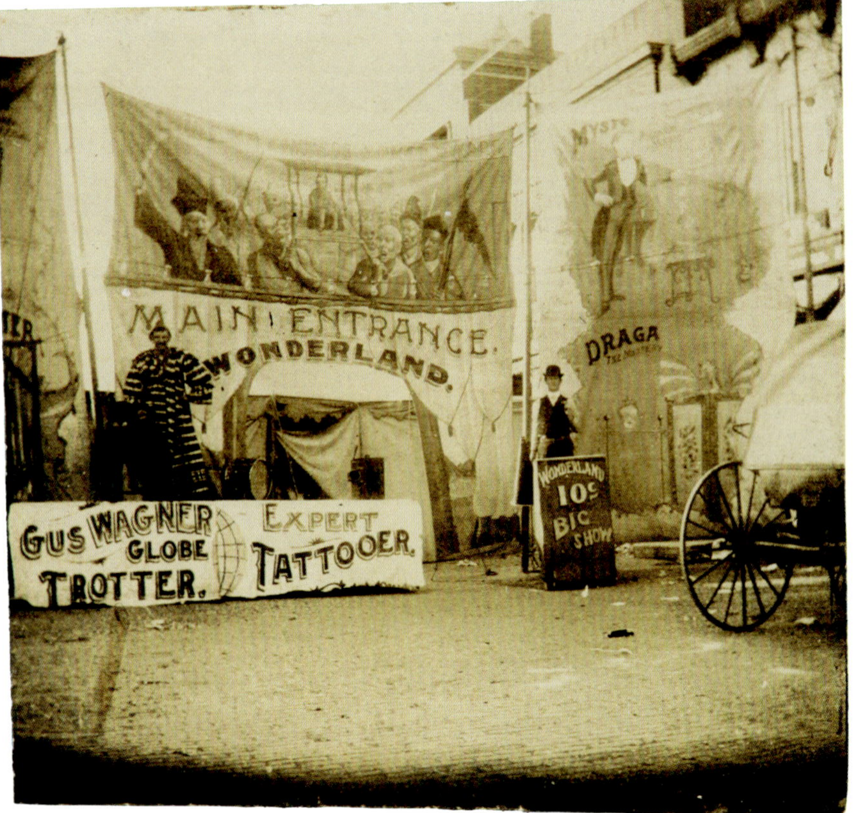

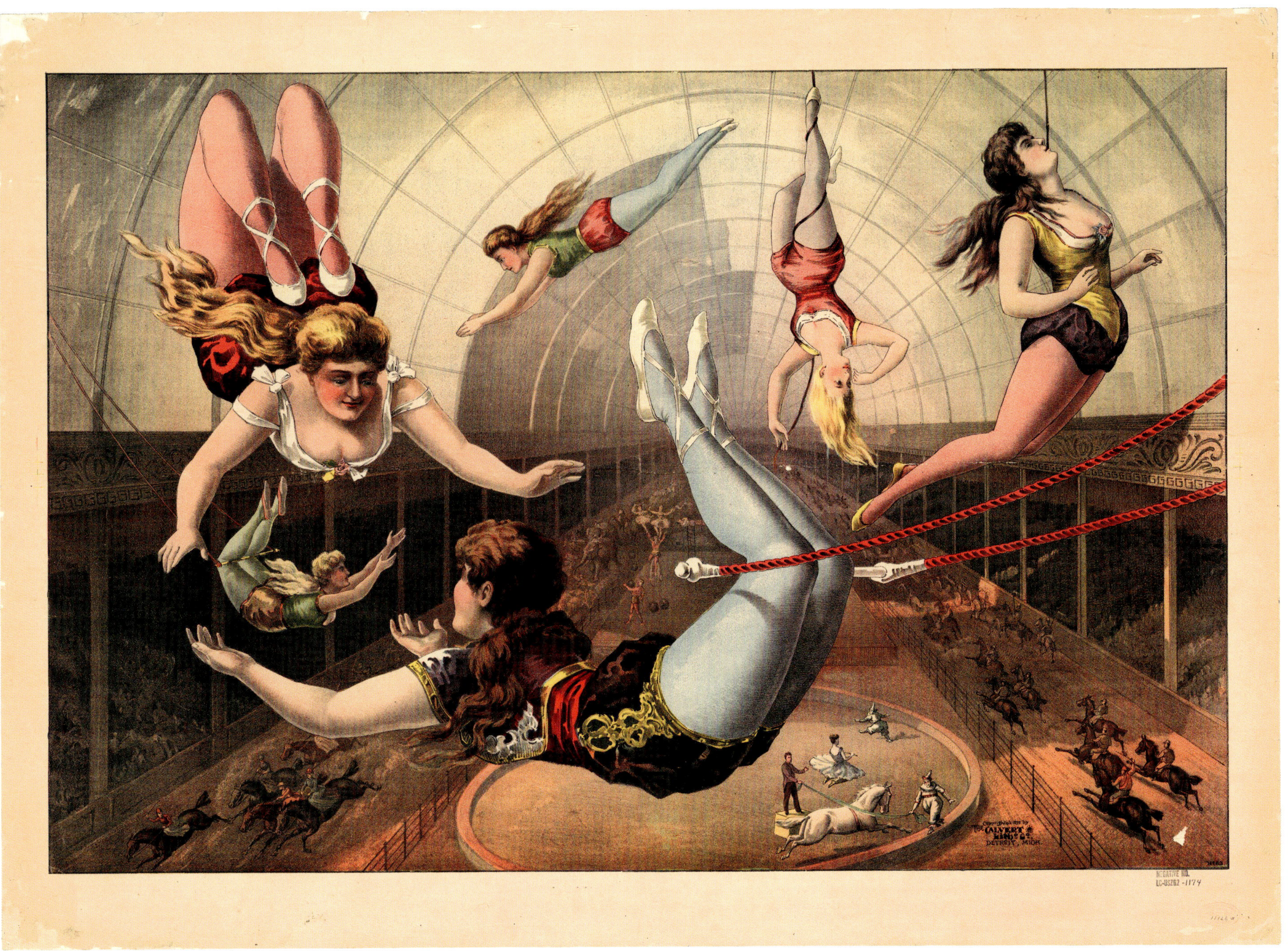

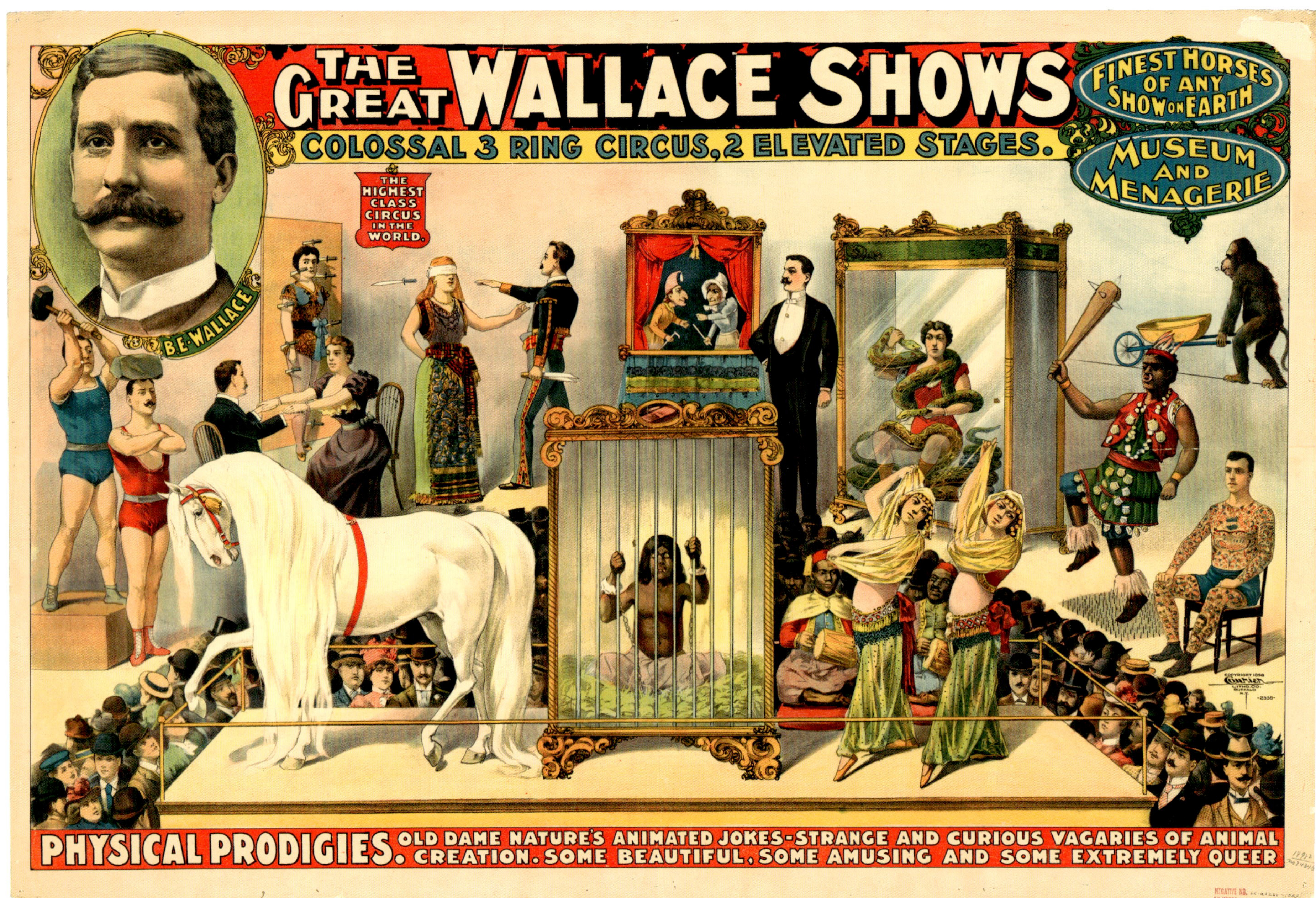

THE GREAT WALLACE SHOWS
FINEST HORSES OF ANY SHOW ON EARTH
MUSEUM AND MENAGERIE
COLOSSAL 3 RING CIRCUS, 2 ELEVATED STAGES.
THE HIGHEST CLASS CIRCUS IN THE WORLD.
B. E. WALLACE
PHYSICAL PRODIGIES. OLD DAME NATURE'S ANIMATED JOKES-STRANGE AND CURIOUS VAGARIES OF ANIMAL CREATION. SOME BEAUTIFUL, SOME AMUSING AND SOME EXTREMELY QUEER

Maud decided to pursue work that utilized her rudimentary medical knowledge and embodied her aspirations to be a performer: "She began to do 'literaries' and to lecture on skulls at Green's Museum. She had a collection of skulls of animals and of humans of different races."

Gus and Maud met or were introduced around 1903, probably after seeing each other on a circus or sideshow stage. One can only imagine Gus, a sturdy thirty-one-year-old man, regaling Maud about his hundreds of tattoos and his globetrotting maritime life before revealing that he was also an artist, having learned the techniques of hand-tattooing in Borneo and Java. No doubt Gus told Maud that, in addition to tattooing and exhibiting himself, he could "double as a contortionist and can also pick up a few dollars now and then tattooing the country boys and girls," boasting, "I'm not in much danger of starving."[2]

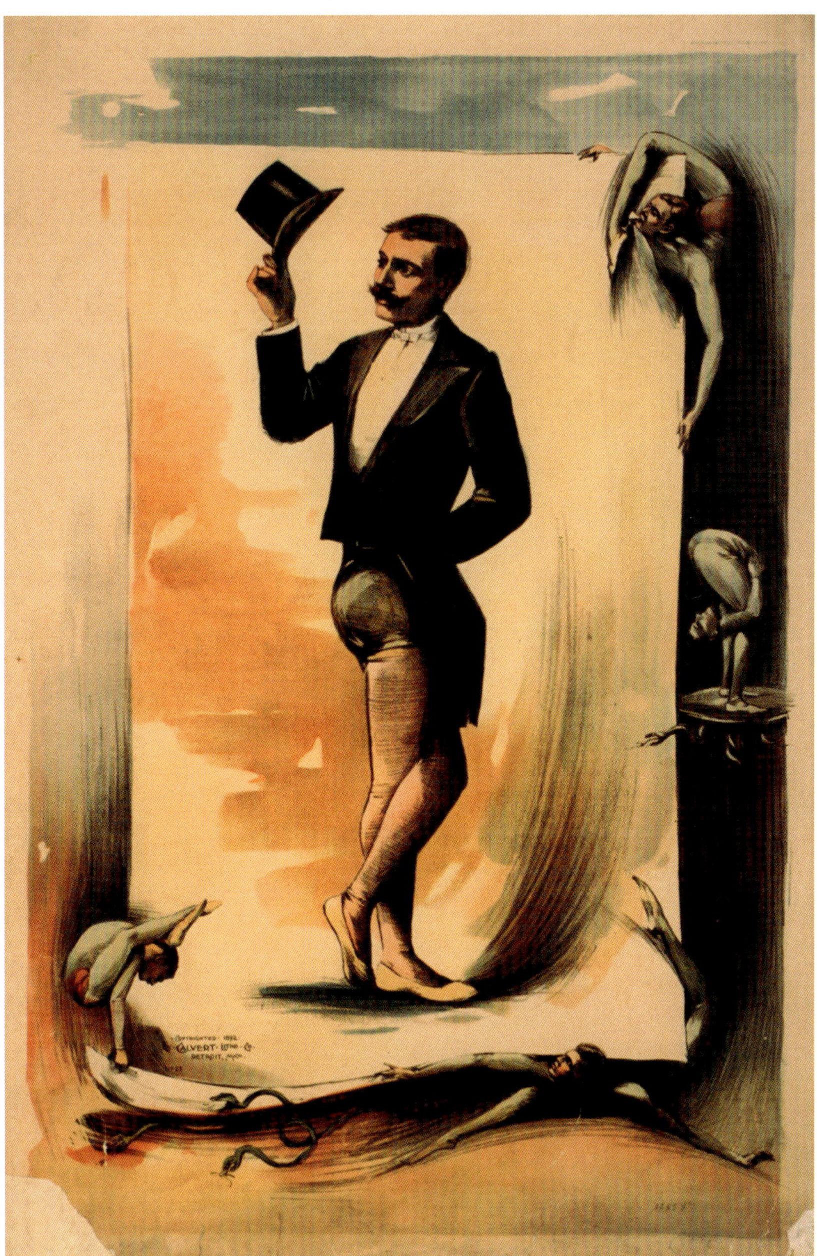

Opposite: Poster for the Great Wallace Shows, published by the Courier Lithograph Company, 1898

Right: Contortionist illustration, ca. 1892

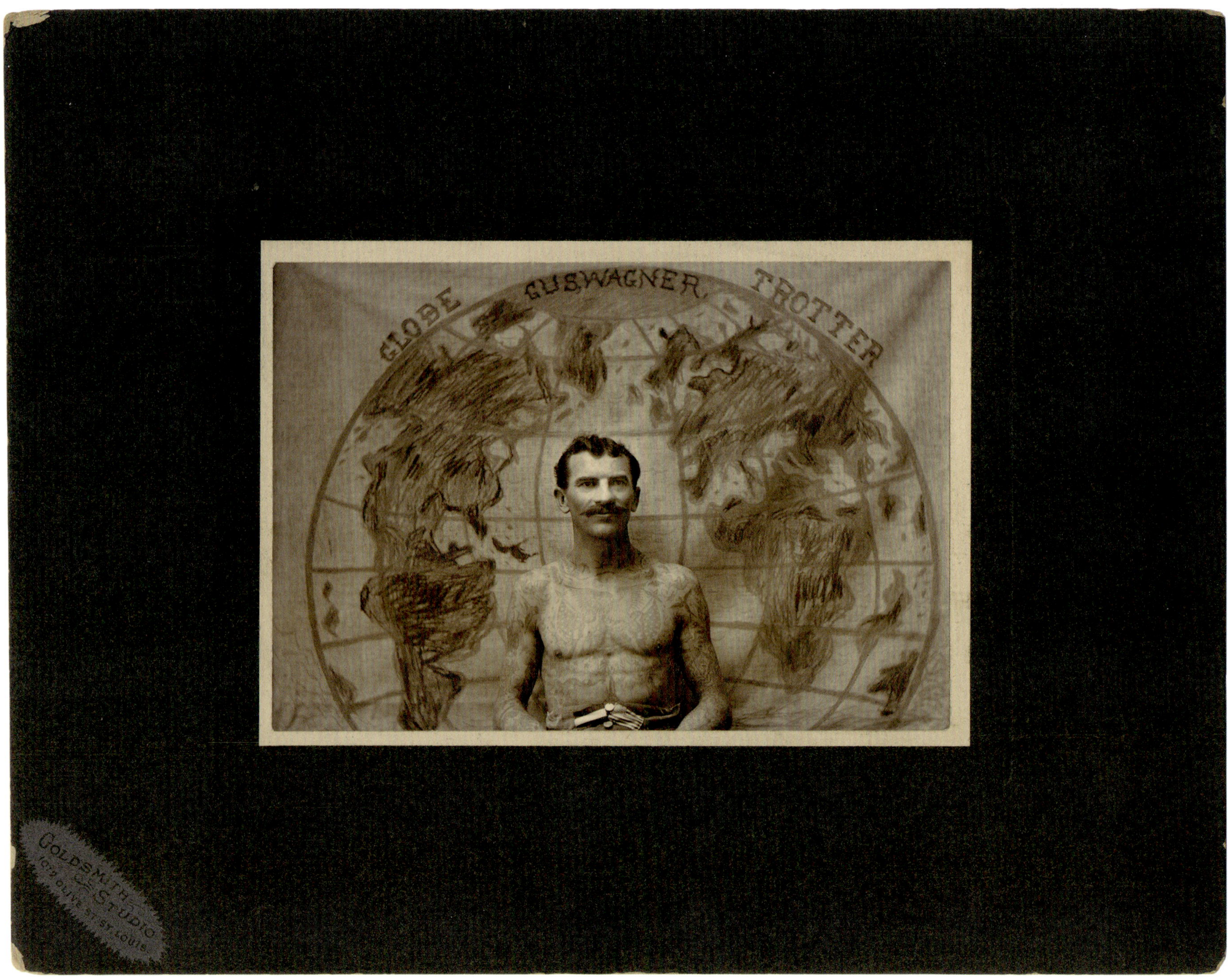

GLOBE   GUS WAGNER   TROTTER
GOLDSMITH
STUDIO
1073 OLIVE ST ST LOUIS

Opposite: Gus Wagner, ca. 1904

Right: Maud Stevens Wagner, February 1904

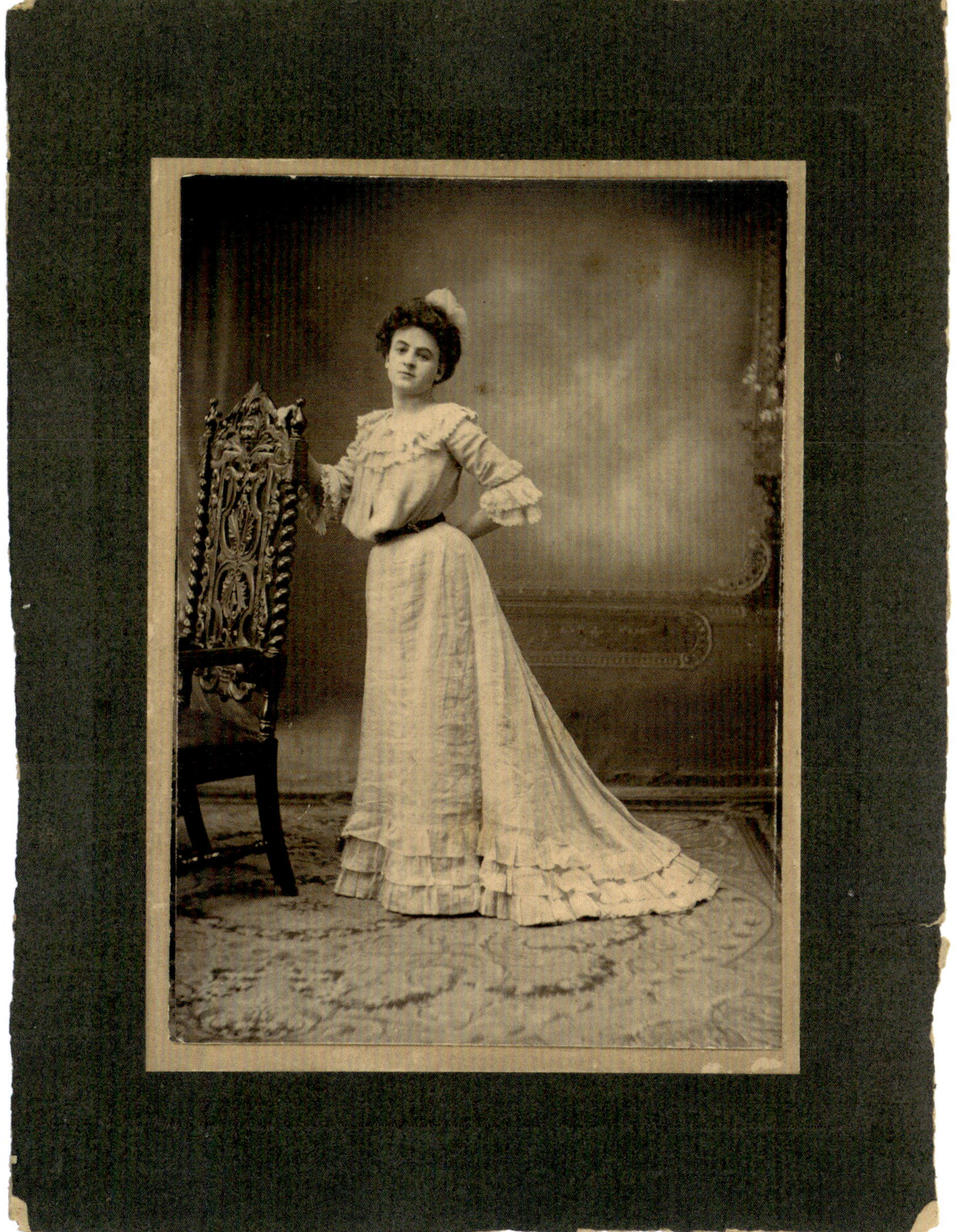

By then, Maud (born February 12, 1877, in Lyon County, Kansas) was twenty-six and a starry-eyed sideshow performer and "lecturer," a barker with her own tales of wonder, perhaps calling out to passersby to buy tickets to see her, Gus, and other acts under the Big Top.

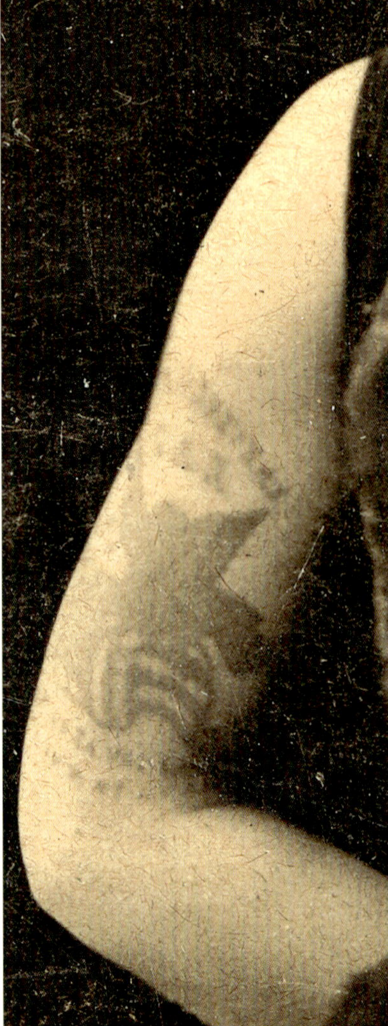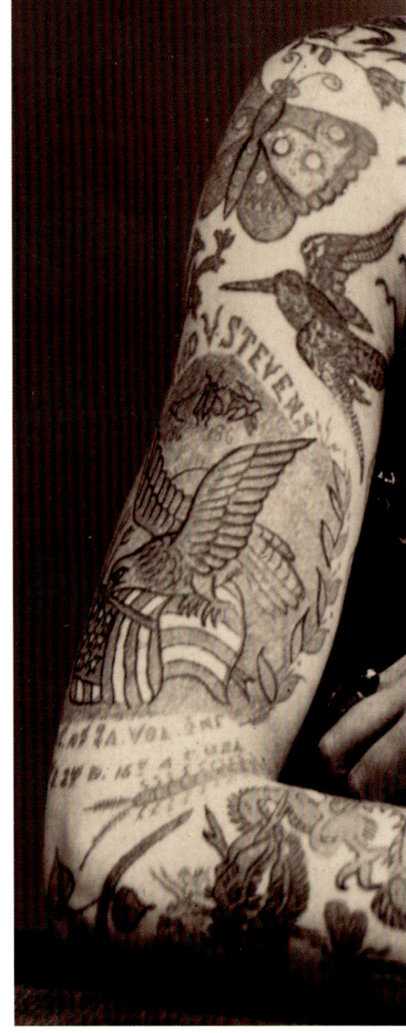

Lotteva remembered in a 1989 interview with Chuck Eldridge of the Tattoo Archive that Maud was lecturing in the kids show and doing her free act also, a high-wire act. And he insisted they get married. He made her quit the aerial work. She thought it over and she said, 'Tell you what, if you'll tattoo me all over and teach me how to tattoo, I'll give up the aerial work." Well, he says, 'That's a deal.' Her first tattoo was her father's military insignia from the Civil War on her right arm. Gus used a machine for that, but she insisted on having the rest done by hand."

The military insignia Maud chose was an eagle and was accompanied by an inscription memorializing her father, David V. Stevens, who, like many in his family, was a wounded veteran of the Civil War. In his pension application in 1896, David V. Stevens recalled: "About 12th or 13th of December 1864 while before Savannah, Georgia I was engaged in cooking breakfast—and my company was in the second line of breastworks south of the Ogeche and Savannah River canal. The enemy discerned our position and commenced shelling. A bomb shell burst within a few feet of my head. I fell to the ground. I think Sgt. Gray helped me up, and we moved up nearer the fortifications. I was company cook and in the discharge of my duty. I never recovered from the deafness . . . I am growing worse as the years multiply."

Left: Maud's right bicep tattoo, before and after other tattoos were added

Opposite: Maud assisting Gus, ca. 1910

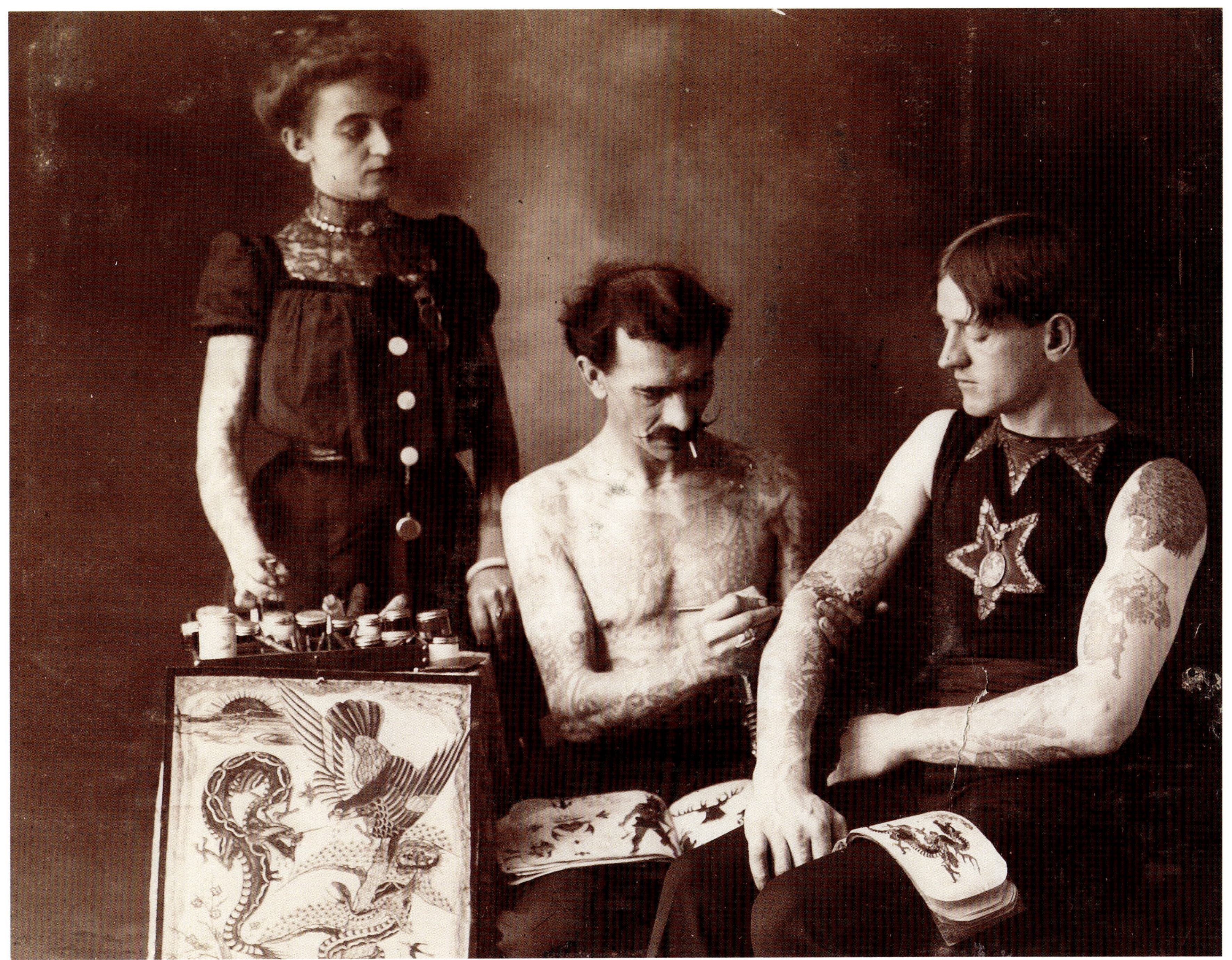

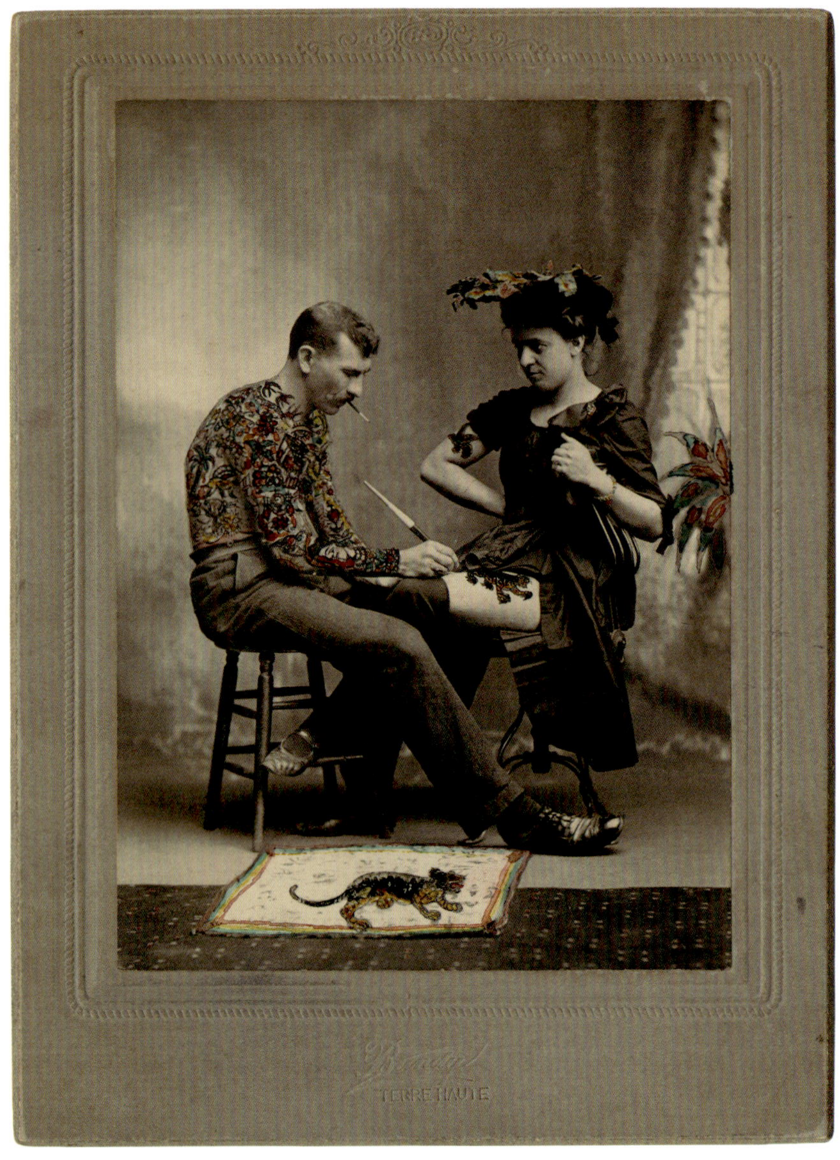

Clearly, David V. Stevens was an inspiration to his daughter, Nora, who changed her name to Maud after she left home to pursue a career as a circus performer but never lost contact with her family. In fact, Dora, Maud's elder sister, joined her.

Both Maud and Dora were tattooed by Gus; Maud between 1904 and 1907, and Dora during the same period, although the extent of her tattoos was not as documented as Maud's. Lotteva told Pat Hook that both Maud and Dora "did shows: The Stevens Sisters in ____. One play was 'The Bluebeards.' Dora later had tattoos all over."

Left: Gus tattooing Maud, ca. 1904

Opposite, top: Maud tattoos Henry Wagner and Gus tattoos Dora Stevens, ca. 1910. *Detail from Gus Wagner's scrapbook*

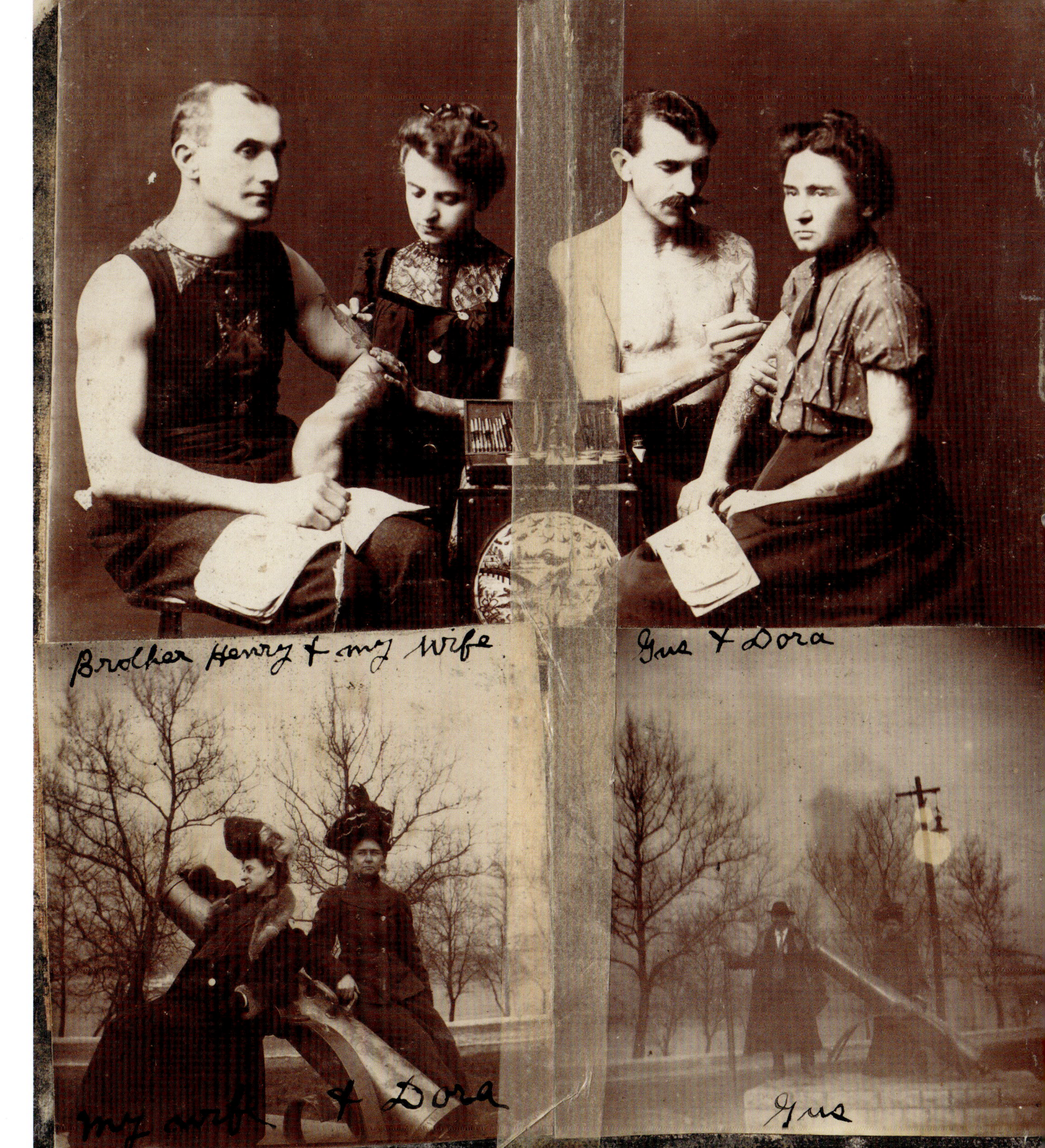

Brother Henry & my Wife.
Gus & Dora
my wife & Dora
Gus

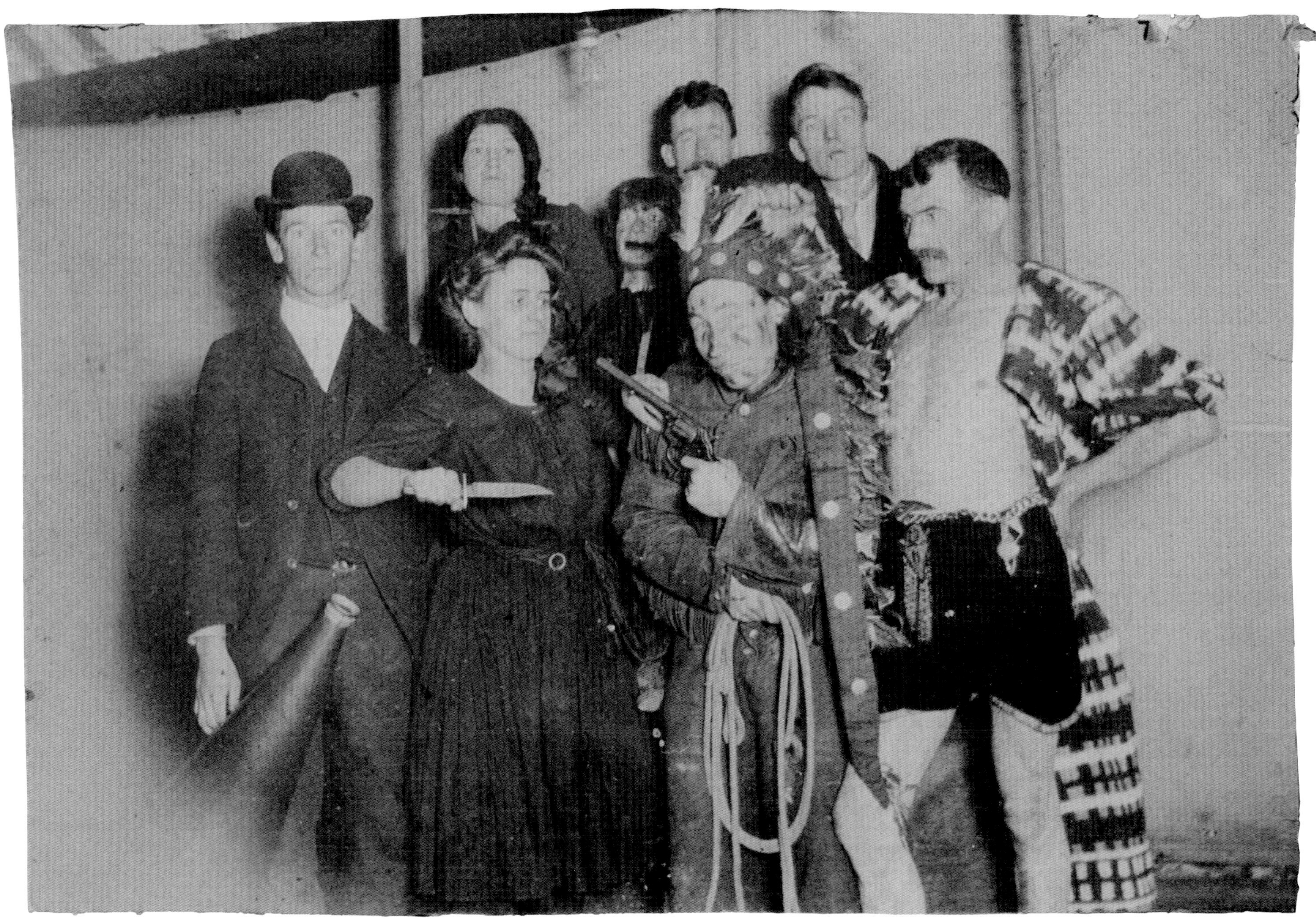

Maud and Gus in a show, 1903.
Detail from Gus Wagner's scrapbook

Genealogical records and newspaper articles compiled by Lotteva have conflicting dates when Gus and Maud were married: in Chillicothe, Ohio, in the fall of 1903, and in St. Louis, Missouri, on October 3, 1904, although in the 1905 state census Maud is listed as "single" and living with her parents in Kansas, where she grew up. Regardless of these date irregularities and the possibility that Gus and Maud were not legally married, it's clear that Maud and Gus were an inseparable couple, who balanced parenting and work, traveling around the country as the Wagner's Traveling Museum, exhibiting themselves, and making tattoos in circus and carnival sideshows, dime museums, and pop-up shops.

grandfather

FAMILY HISTORY RECORD

RECORD No. ______

belonged to Methodist church Lyon Co., KS

HUSBAND **David Van Buran Stevens**
Birthdate 23 June 1838   Birthplace Newark, Ohio   Licking Co.
Deathdate 28 Oct. 1926   Burial Place Homestead Cem., Chase Co., KS   bur. Oct 31 Ernest McKenzie undertaker

Son of Roswell N. Stevens   and (Maiden Name) Elizabeth Vance

Marriage Date 30 Apr. 1867   Place of Marriage Tama Co., Iowa (Toledo)

attended 33rd GAR encampment at Topeka May 27, 1914 for dedication of Memorial Hall "Golden Jubilee"

WIFE Sarah Jane McGee
Birthdate 21 Oct. 1844   Birthplace Delaware, Ohio   near Marion (Union Co., 1860 Claiboure Twp. P.O. Richwood)
Deathdate 26 Mar 1923   Burial Place Homestead Cem., Chase Co., KS   bur. Apr. 7
a brother I. N. McGee at Ponca City, Okla 1949

Daughter of: George McGee   and (Maiden Name) Huntingdonshire, England ?

SP 369.3 K13 33-20 p.85 and Pp. 49-78 address, parade, etc.

David's obit, also Dora's & Gus Wagner's obit / 1850 Morrow Co., Ohio, / 1860 Marion Co., Ohio /

Data Obtained from: Tama Co., Iowa mar. rec.; Census: 1856 Iowa, 1872 Cowley Co.?, 1875 Lyon Co., KS; 1880 Lyon Co., 1900 Chase Co. KS Tama Co.   1925 Chase Co., 1915 Chase Co. Homestead Twp.

Additional Date:
Other Marriages   to KS 1869
Places of Residence   by 1897 a resident of Homestead in Chase Co., KS; post office – Clements
Military Service   Co. C 10th Iowa Inf. Civil War enrolled 5 Jan '67   "C–10" GAR unit
Occupations   Farmer
Other Information   Father, Roswell, lived with them from 1870's till his death in 1888 Lyon Co., KS

CHILDREN	BIRTH		DEATH		MARRIAGE		
	Date	Place	Date	Place	Date	Place	To Whom
Dora	Jan 17th 1869	Iowa	30 June 1949	St. Marys Hospital Emporia, KS / Funeral at Friends Church, Homestead	still single 1900 / " " 1925		remained single
mother N. Maud	Feb. 1877	Kansas	30 Jan 1961	Bur. Homestead Cem.	Fall 1903 Chillicothe, Ohio / Oct. 3, 1904 at St. Louis on her obit.	single on 1905	Gus Wagner 1910– dau. Lotteva Wagner b. 1910 California

Genealogical record compiled by Lotteva Wagner Davis

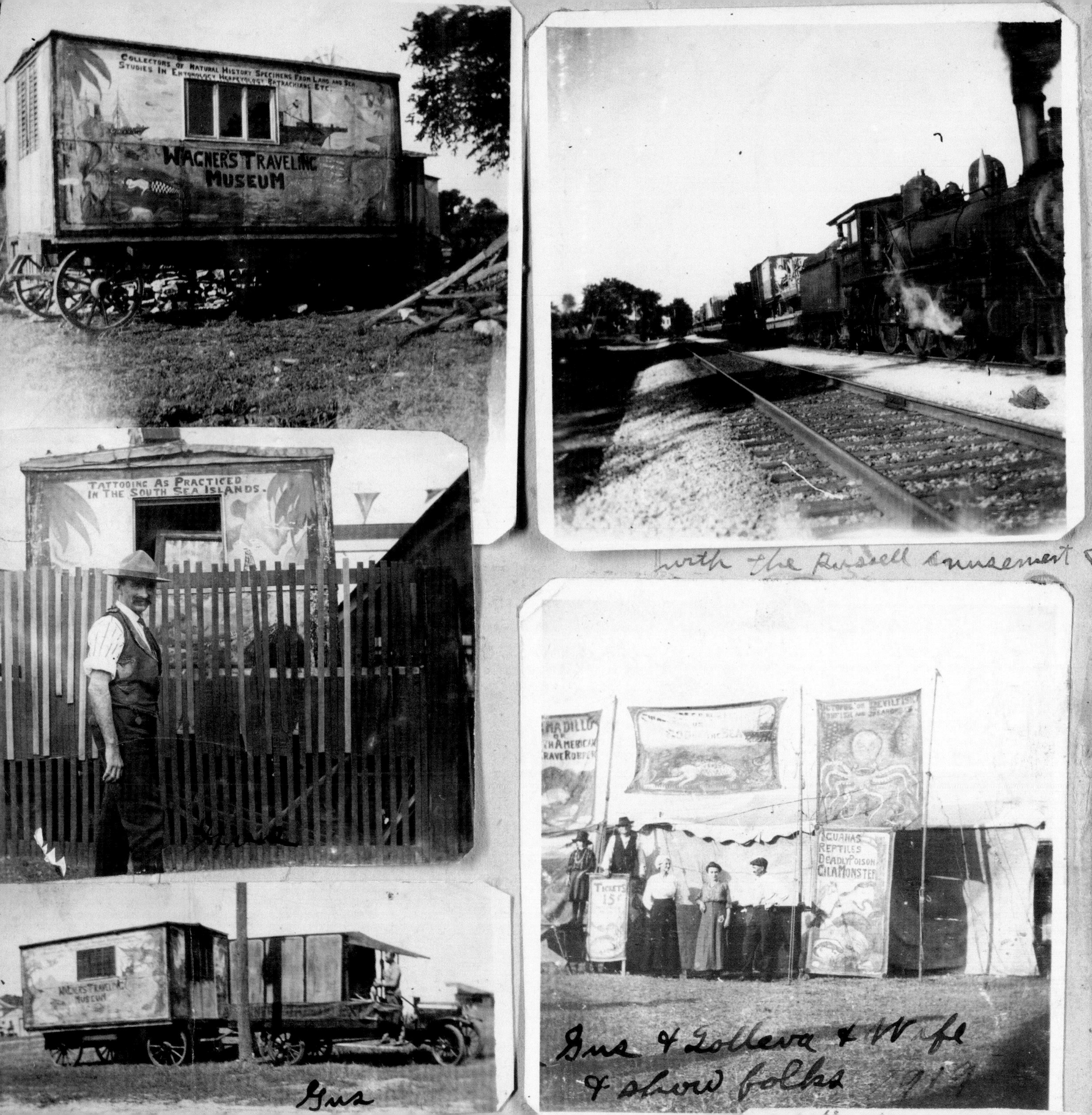

Left: *Detail from Gus Wagner's scrapbook, ca. 1919*

Opposite: *Gus and Maud, Santa Barbara, California, 1907.*
Detail from Gus Wagner's scrapbook

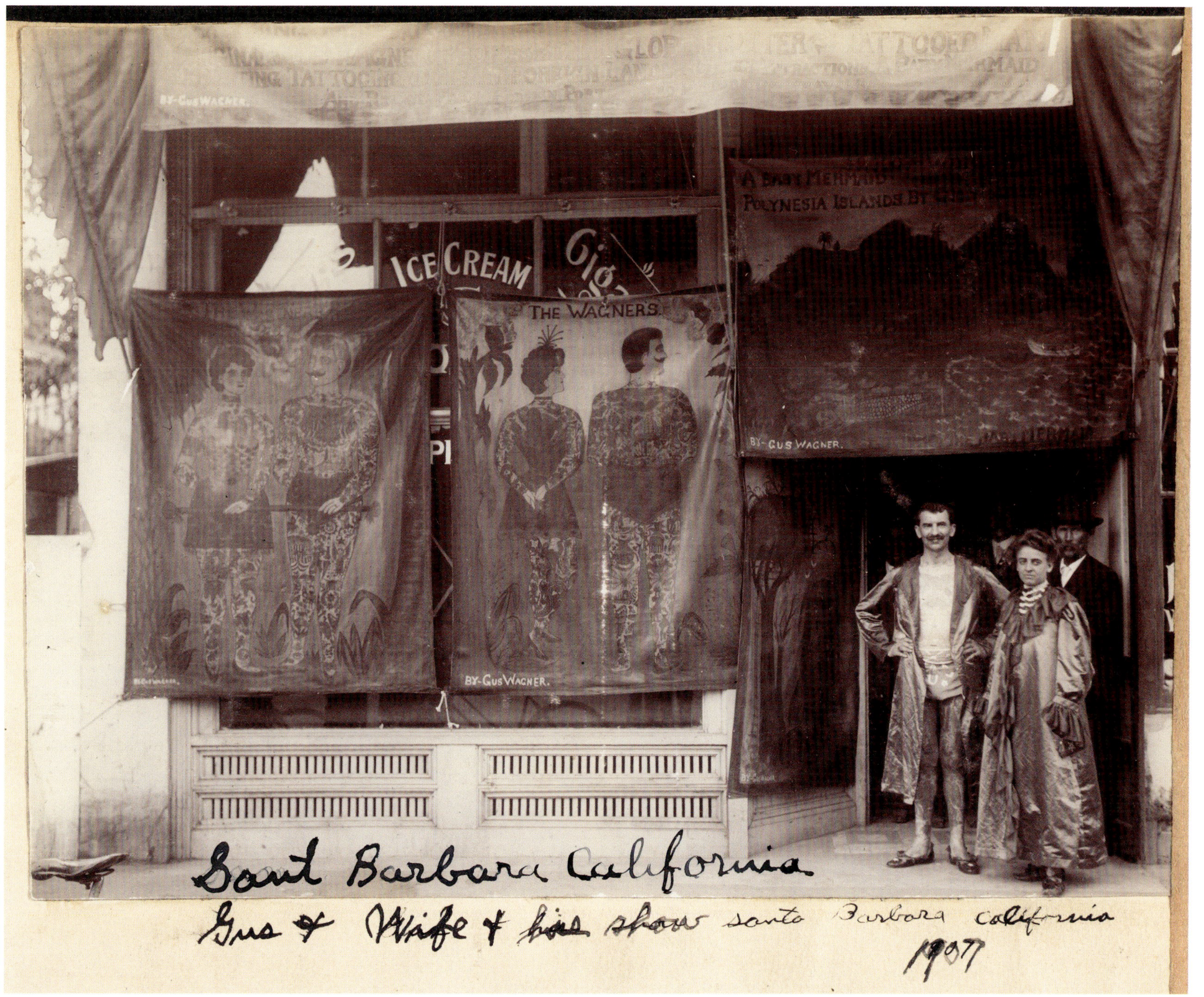

Sant Barbara California

Gus & Wife & his show santa Barbara california 1907

At the Louisiana Purchase Exposition, also known as the St. Louis World's Fair, held in St. Louis, Missouri, from April 30 to December 1, 1904, Gus and Maud were a sensation. The St. Louis World's Fair had a global focus and extolled the virtues of Western imperialism. Financed by local, state, and federal funds totaling $15 million (equivalent to $488,555,556 in 2022), the St. Louis World's Fair included more than sixty countries and forty-three of the then forty-five American states and attracted about 19.7 million visitors.

Below: View from the Ferris wheel southeast over the Japanese garden and "Jerusalem" to Festival Hall, St. Louis World's Fair, 1904, stereograph

Opposite, top: The Pecan Horse, Mississippi Exhibit, Horticultural Building, St. Louis World's Fair, 1904, stereograph

Opposite, bottom: The Great Ferris Wheel, St. Louis World's Fair, 1904, stereograph

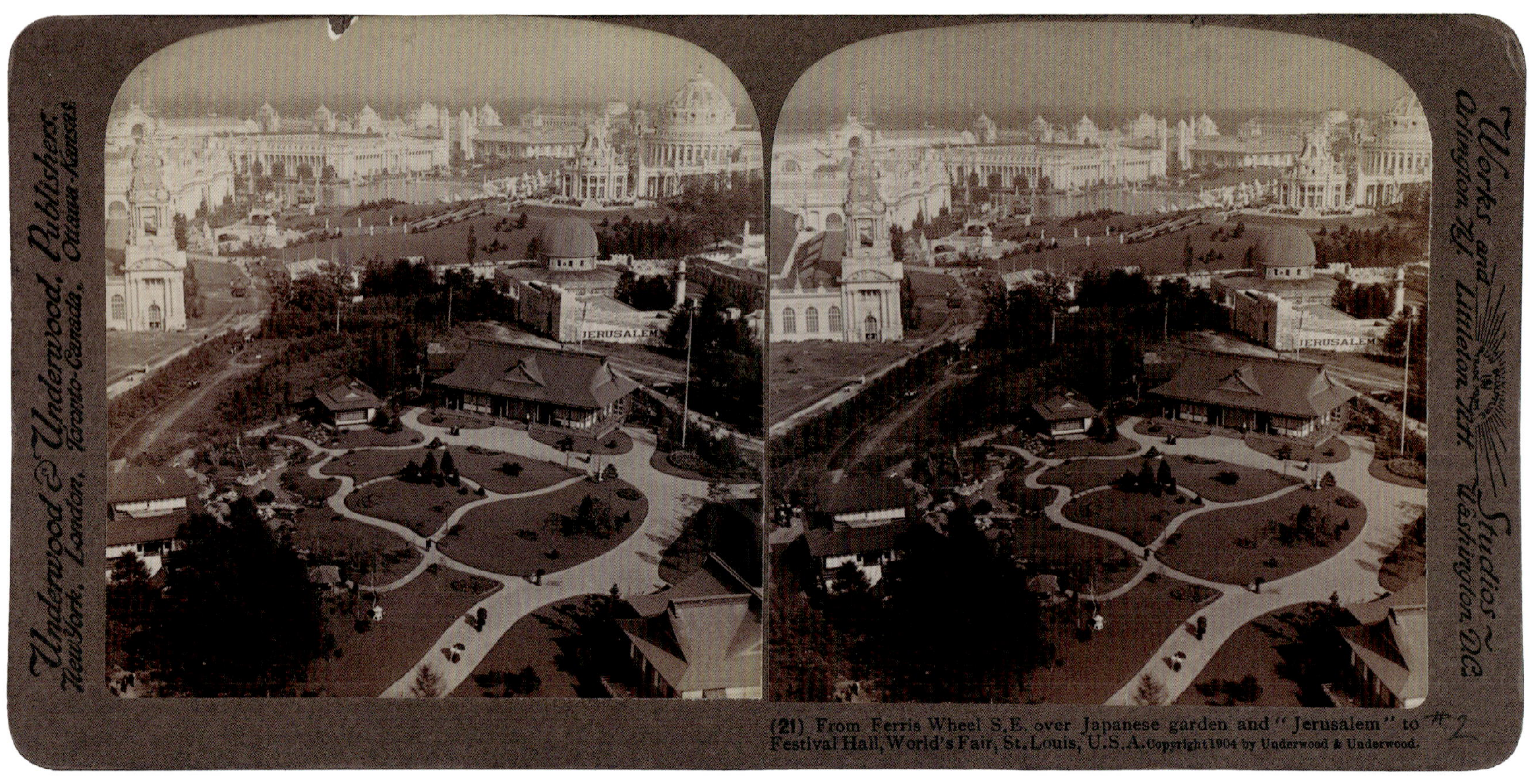

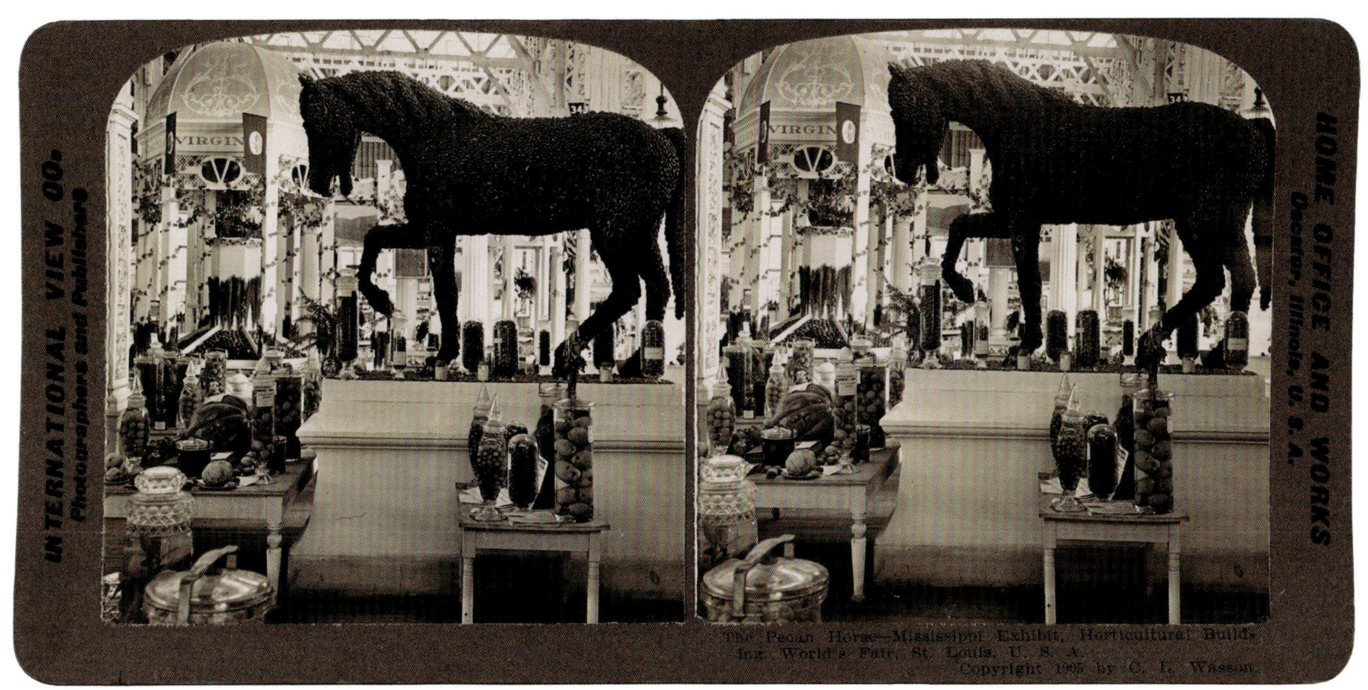

The Pecan Horse—Mississippi Exhibit, Horticultural Building, World's Fair, St. Louis, U. S. A. Copyright 1905 by C. I. Wasson.

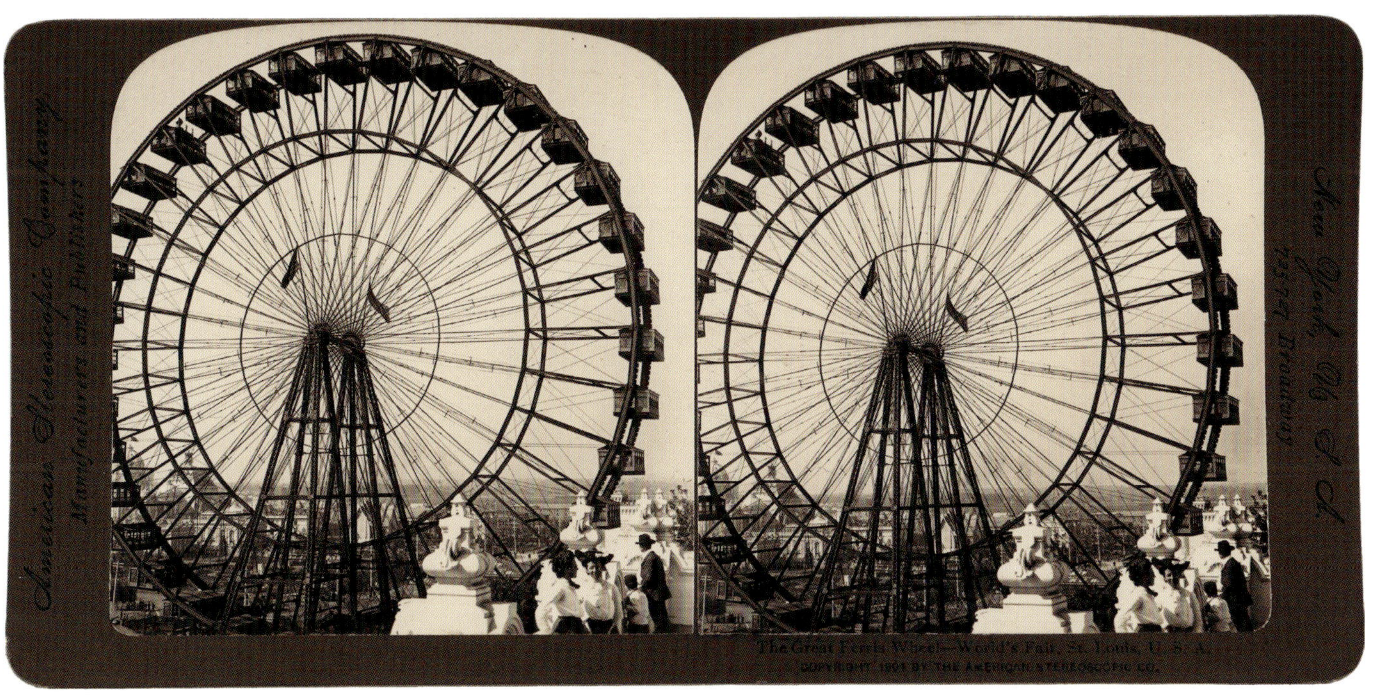

The Great Ferris Wheel—World's Fair, St. Louis, U. S. A. Copyright 1904 by the American Stereoscopic Co.

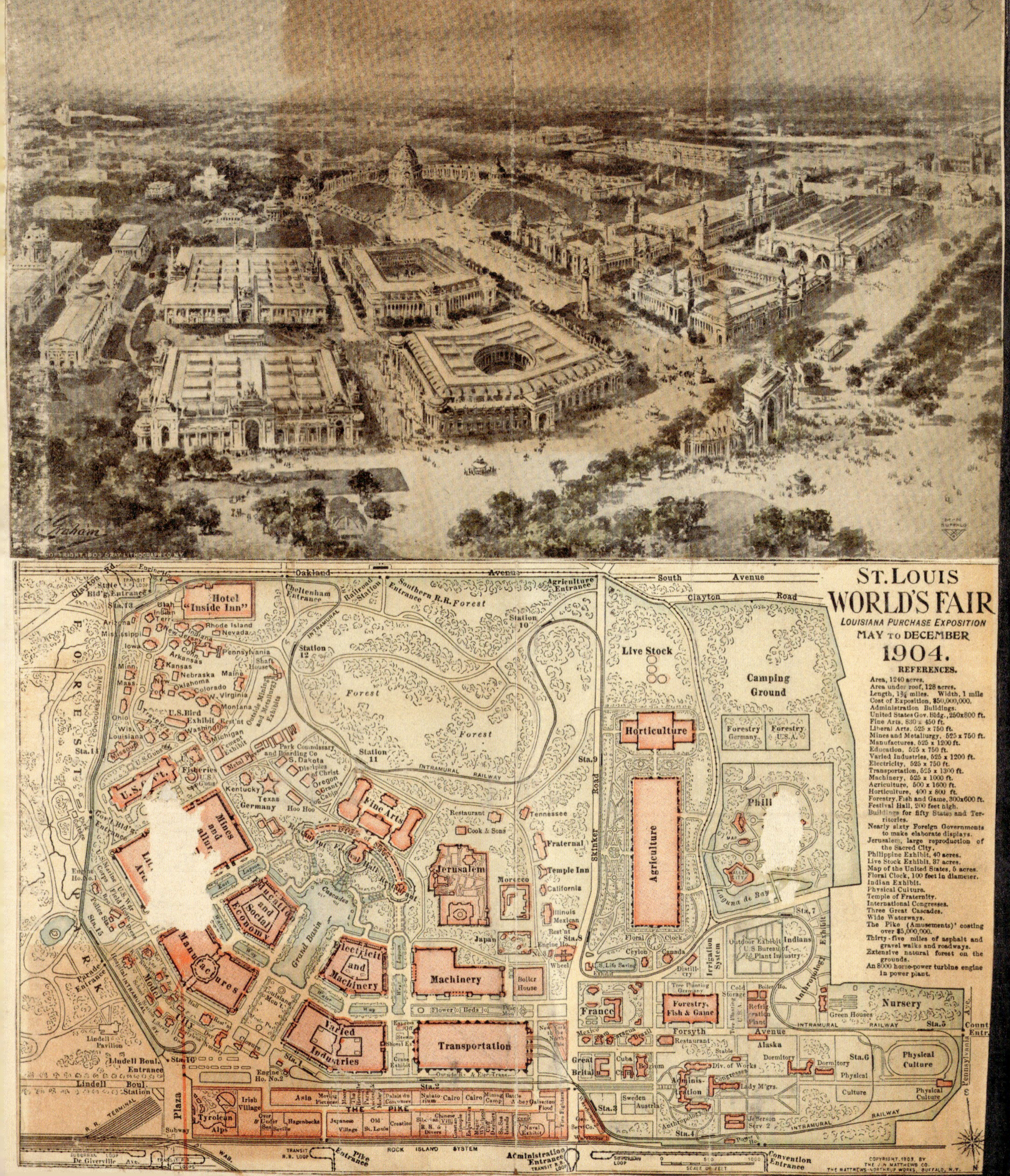

Left: St. Louis World's Fair ephemera, 1904
Page from Gus Wagner's scrapbook

Opposite: Pages from Gus Wagner's scrapbook

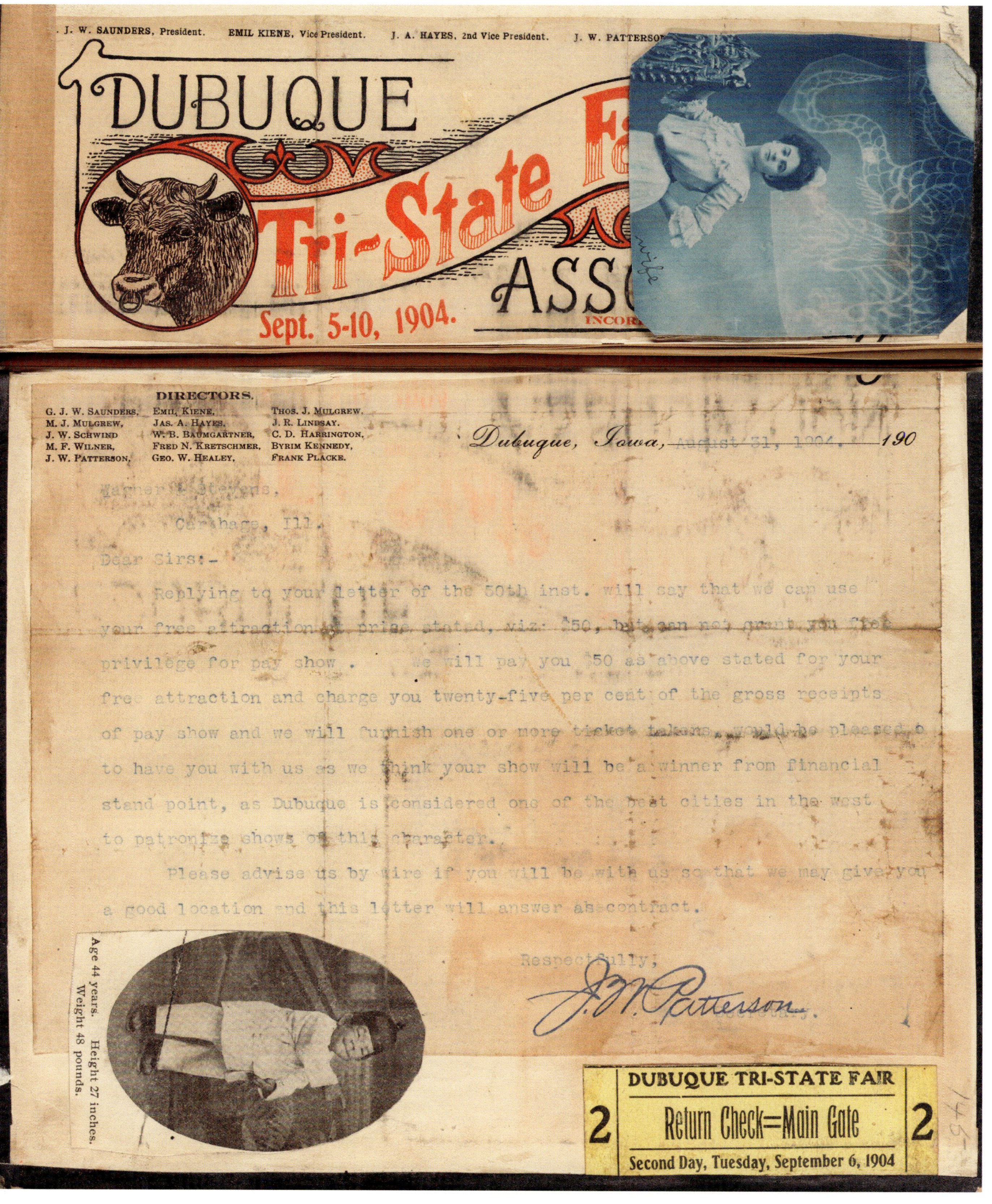

DIRECTORS.

G. J. W. SAUNDERS,   EMIL KIENE,   THOS. J. MULGREW,
M. J. MULGREW,   JAS. A. HAYES,   J. R. LINDSAY,
J. W. SCHWIND   W. B. BAUMGARTNER,   C. D. HARRINGTON,
M. F. WILNER,   FRED N. KRETSCHMER,   BYRIM KENNEDY,
J. W. PATTERSON,   GEO. W. HEALEY,   FRANK PLACKE.

Dubuque, Iowa, August 31, 1904. 190_

Warner & Stevens,
Carthage, Ill.

Dear Sirs:-

Replying to your letter of the 30th inst. will say that we can use your free attraction at price stated, viz: $50, but can not grant you the privilege for pay show. We will pay you $50 as above stated for your free attraction and charge you twenty-five per cent of the gross receipts of pay show and we will furnish one or more ticket takers, would be pleased to have you with us as we think your show will be a winner from financial stand point, as Dubuque is considered one of the best cities in the west to patronize shows of this character.

Please advise us by wire if you will be with us so that we may give you a good location and this letter will answer as contract.

Respectfully,
J. W. Patterson.

Age 44 years.   Height 27 inches.
Weight 48 pounds.

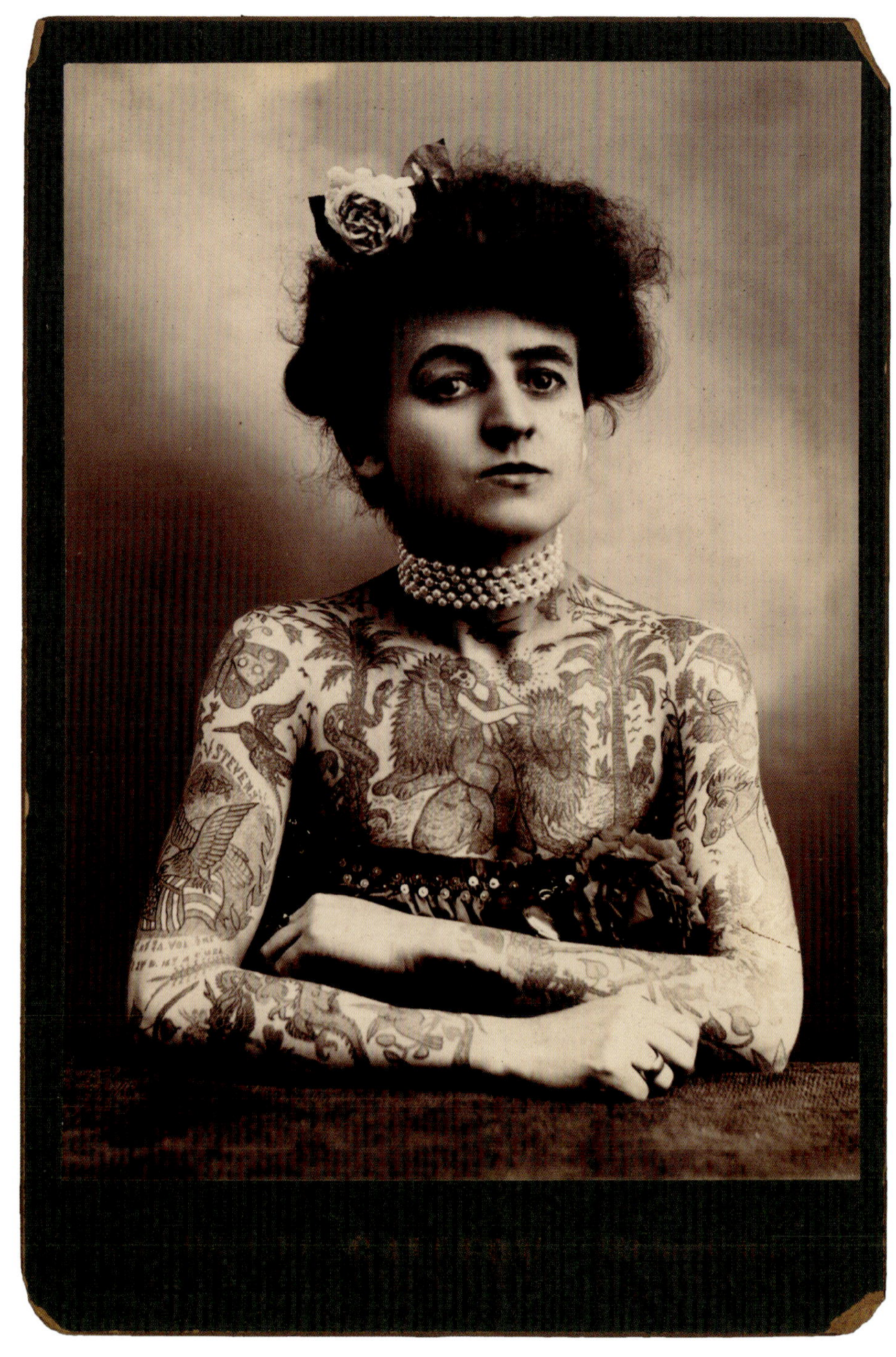

Maud Stevens Wagner, ca. 1907

In a 1907 studio portrait, made at The Plaza Gallery in Los Angeles, Maud Stevens Wagner sits with an enigmatic gaze that brings to mind the Mona Lisa. She leans forward, focused on the camera lens in front of her, a rose pinned loosely in her hair. She appears confident and proud, quietly seductive in the way she displays the glory of her tattoos, accentuating four strands of pearls around her neck, her cleavage barely visible above the top of her frilly circus gown. Maud's eyes are penetrating, her chin raised, and her arms in repose on the table in front of her. Recognizing the significance of this photograph, Gus sent a print to the Library of Congress, and over the years, it has become iconic, establishing Maud as one of the most beautiful tattooed women of her time.

The artist and madame, the wife, are themselves two of the finest galleries of the tattooing art to be found.

Madame, while liberally decorated on every available spot except the face and hands, has far fewer pieces in her collection. For one reason she is smaller and another is she began her collection only eight years ago when Herr Wagner himself made the first drafts for a decorative system which now has spread "to even the toes." That last, it seems, is quite out of the ordinary in tattooing galleries, like the possession of an original da Vinci. She has twelve colors on her body, the limit of the tattooist's art.

Excerpt from "One Art Not on the Bum in Kansas City," newpaper clipping, n.d. in Gus Wagner's scrapbook

Maud Stevens Wagner, San Antonio, 1918

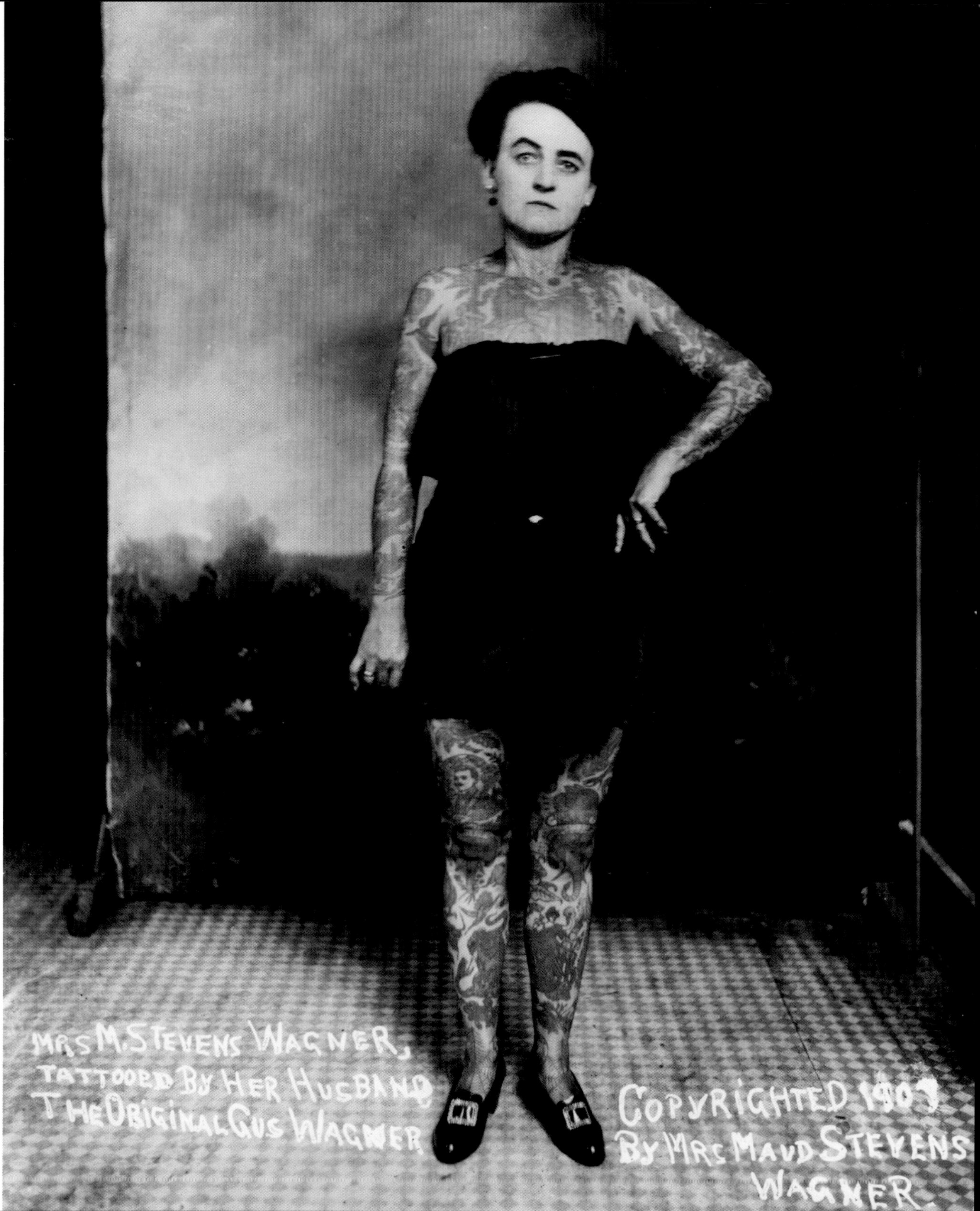

Left: Pages from Gus Wagner's scrapbook

Opposite: Maud holds Lotteva while Gus is tattooing, ca. 1910.
Detail from Gus Wagner's scrapbook

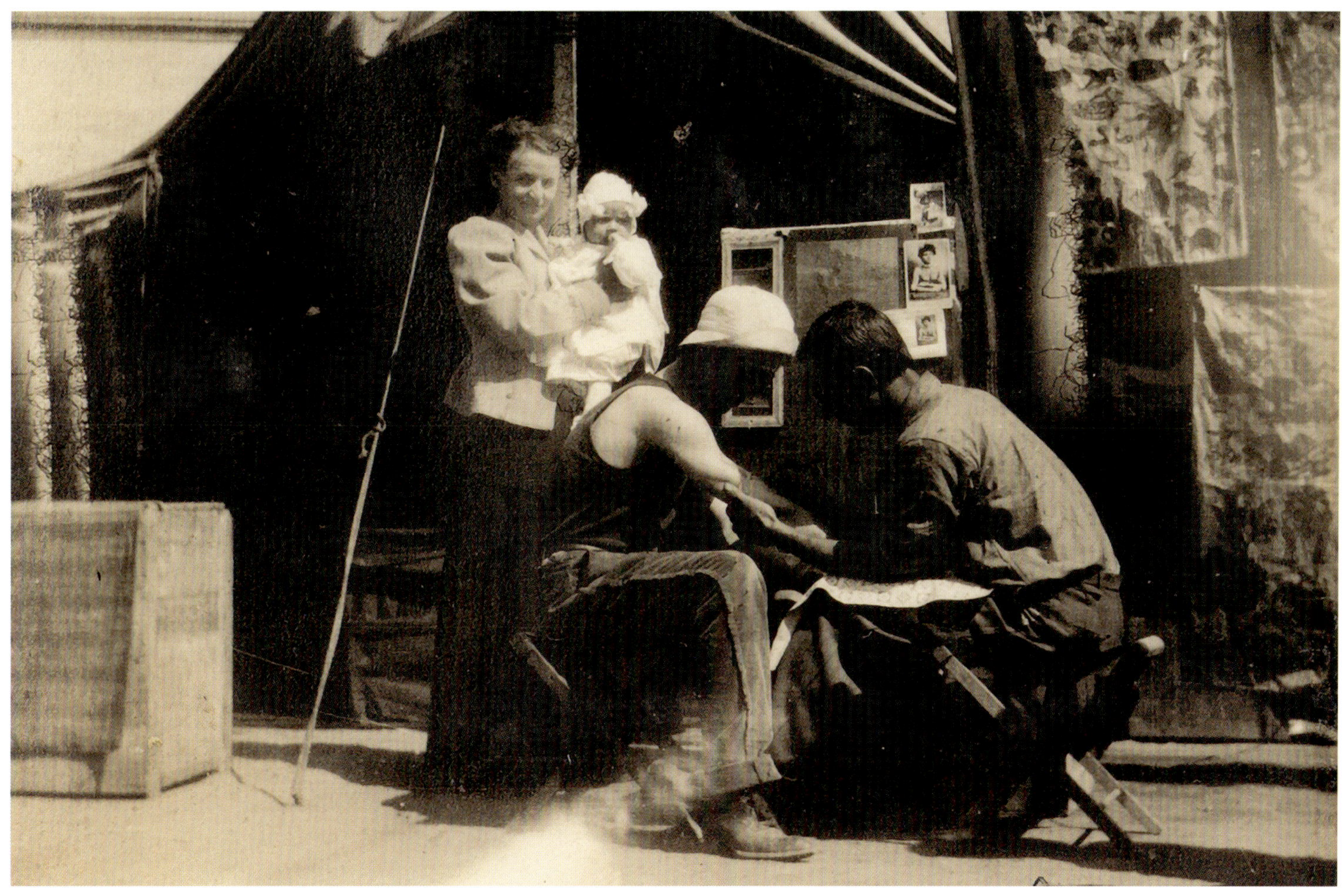

In 1908, Maud gave birth to her first child, Sarah Jane, who died when she was a month old. Lotteva said, "She was born at Homestead. Maud said she would never have another baby there. She got childbed fever. Their cows were dry. Guernsey sent over some milk, but it was sour. The baby died. The doctor had Maud only drink her herb tea."[3]

Two years later, on March 12, 1910, Maud gave birth to a second daughter, Lotteva, in Los Angeles "in a rooming house, operated by a woman called 'Aunty Days.' Maud ordered a big meal after the birth and they said she would never eat it, but she did."[4]

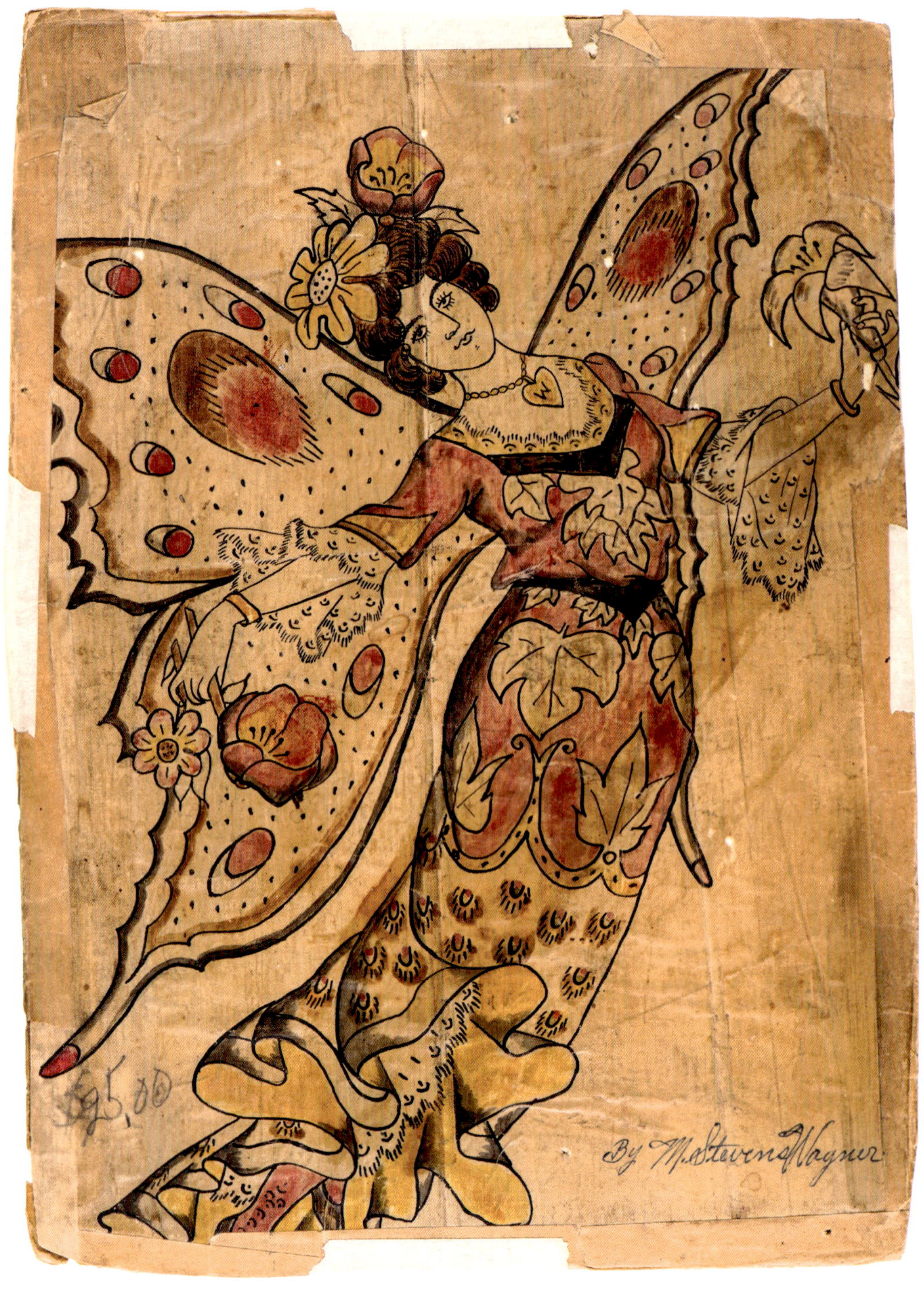

Flash by Maud Stevens Wagner

While Maud is often acclaimed as the first woman tattoo artist in the United States, it is likely that others preceded her. One painting, presumably a flash sheet, signed M. Stevens Wagner was framed by Lotteva and kept in her personal collection. No photographs featuring tattoos she made have been found. One can only wonder which of the tattoos appearing in the snapshots contained in the scrapbook of her husband, Gus Wagner, were made by her.

Regardless of the extent of her tattooing, Maud was unique. She was a performance artist on the sideshow stage and a loving mother, in addition to being a collector of the unusual and absurd, explaining once to Lotteva that she "had a copperhead (snake) which she had 'fanged herself,'" advising her that "it is very difficult to fang a copperhead because the fangs are small, and the snake usually bleeds to death."[5]

Right, top: Maud's business card
Detail from Gus Wagner's scrapbook

Right, bottom: Detail from Gus Wagner's scrapbook

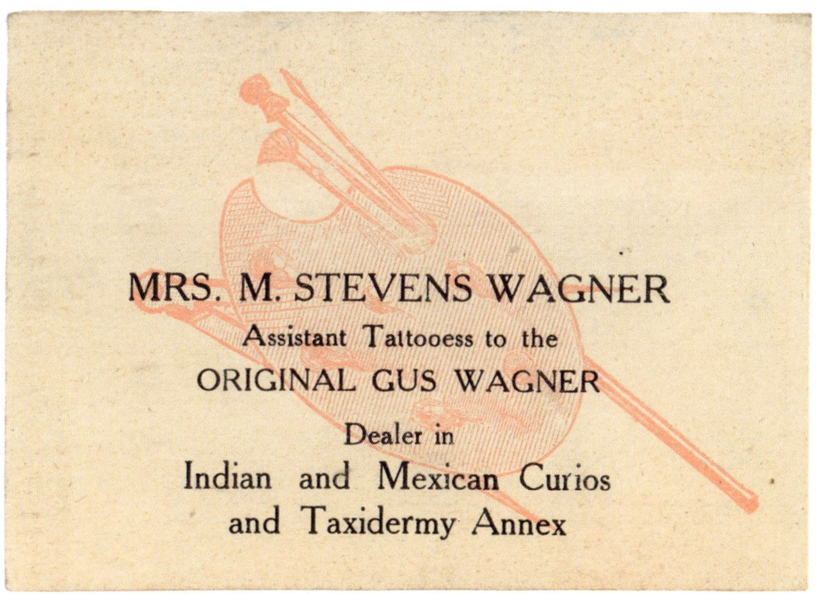

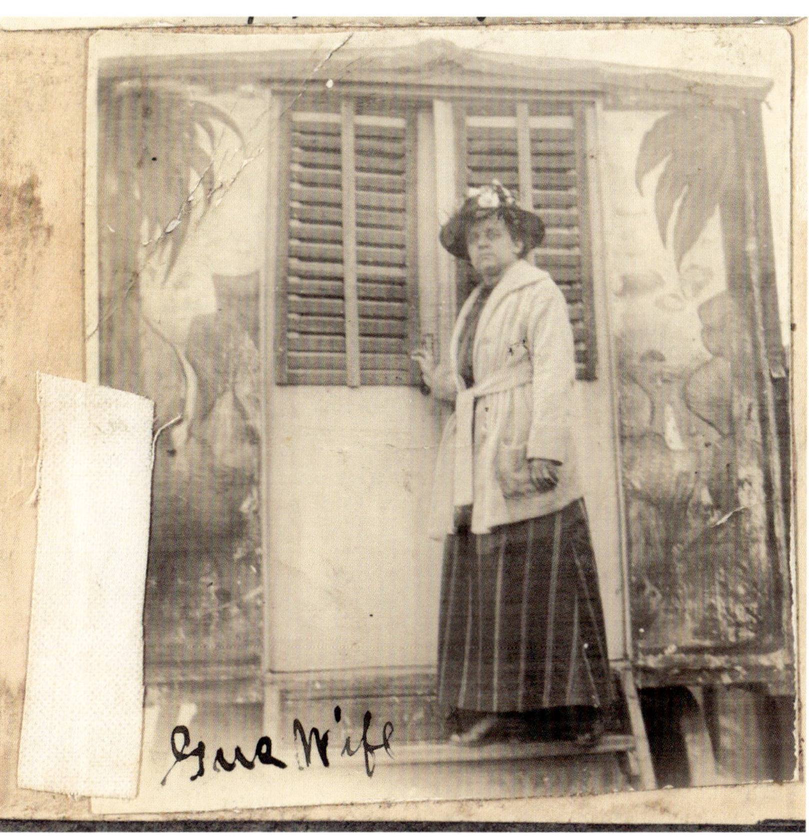

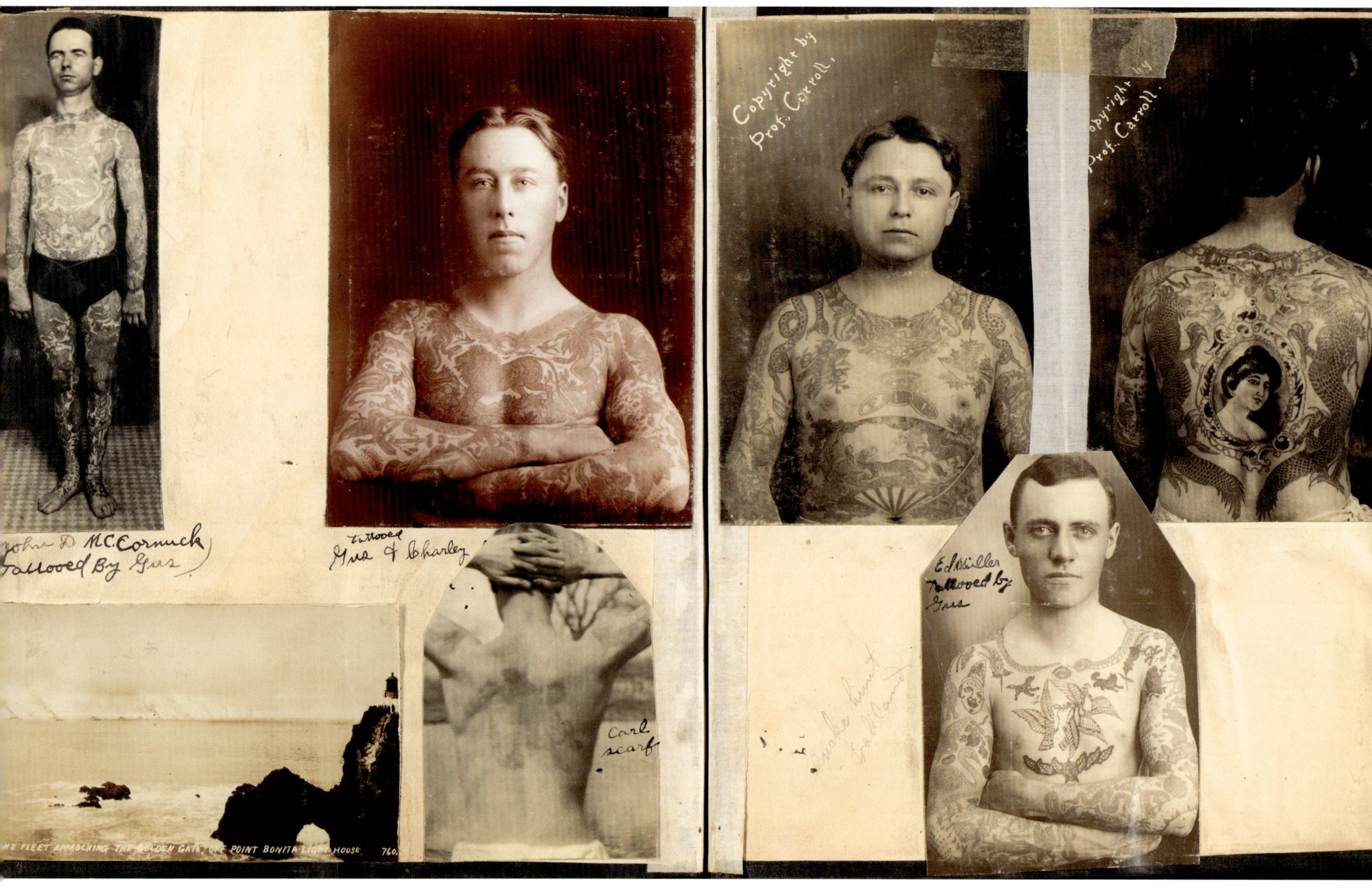

Pages from Gus Wagner's scrapbook

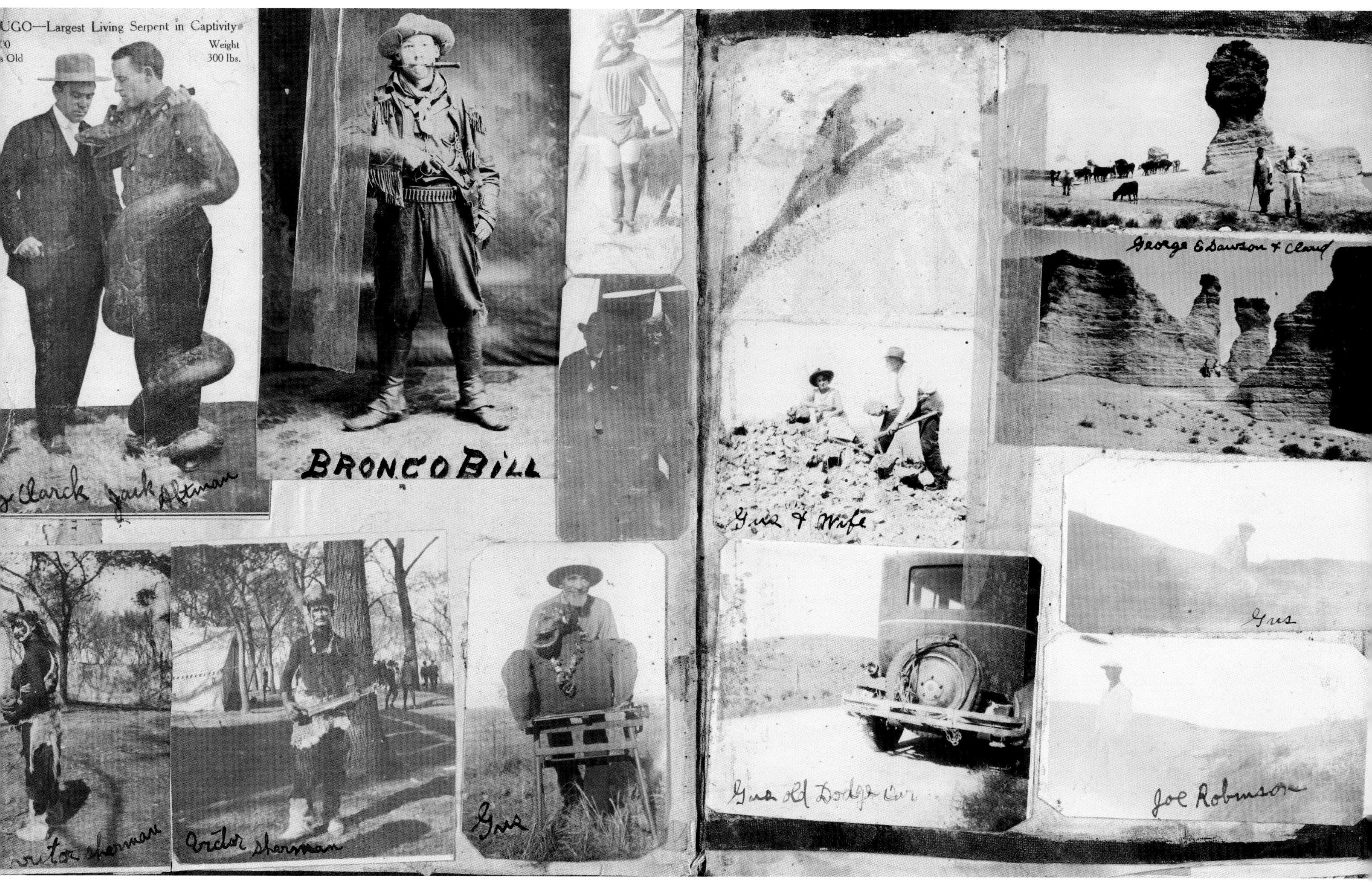

Pages from Gus Wagner's scrapbook

Over the years, Gus nurtured a lifelong fascination with rare and exotic species of animals, snakes, and lizards and corresponded with biologists at the Smithsonian Institution, the Instituto Vital Brazil, and the Southern Biological Supply Company in New Orleans, among others. Gus collected these animals, as well as curios, via mail order and his forays around the world. Gus took great pride in keeping his "pets" alive, and when they died, he trained himself to become a taxidermist. He often featured his stuffed and mounted creatures in sideshow exhibits and sometimes sold them in roadside stands, along with his woodcarvings and other memorabilia.

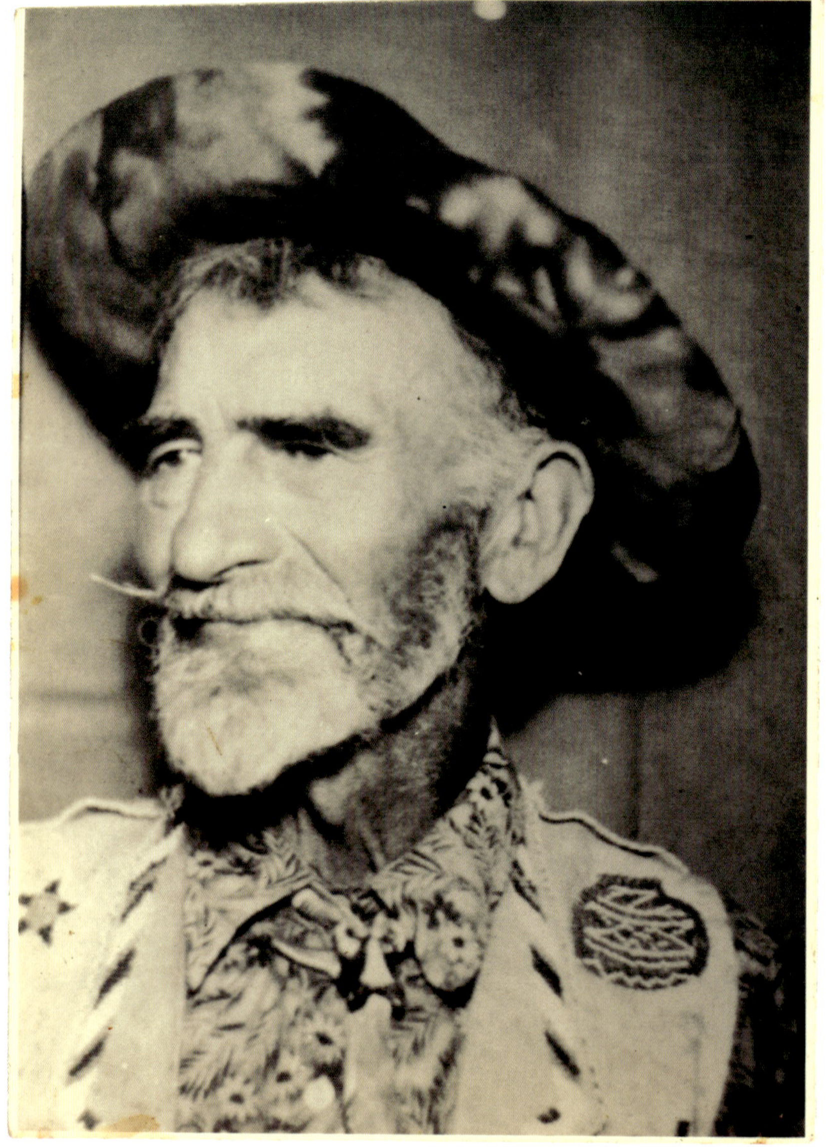

Portrait of Gus Wagner wearing a hat, 1938

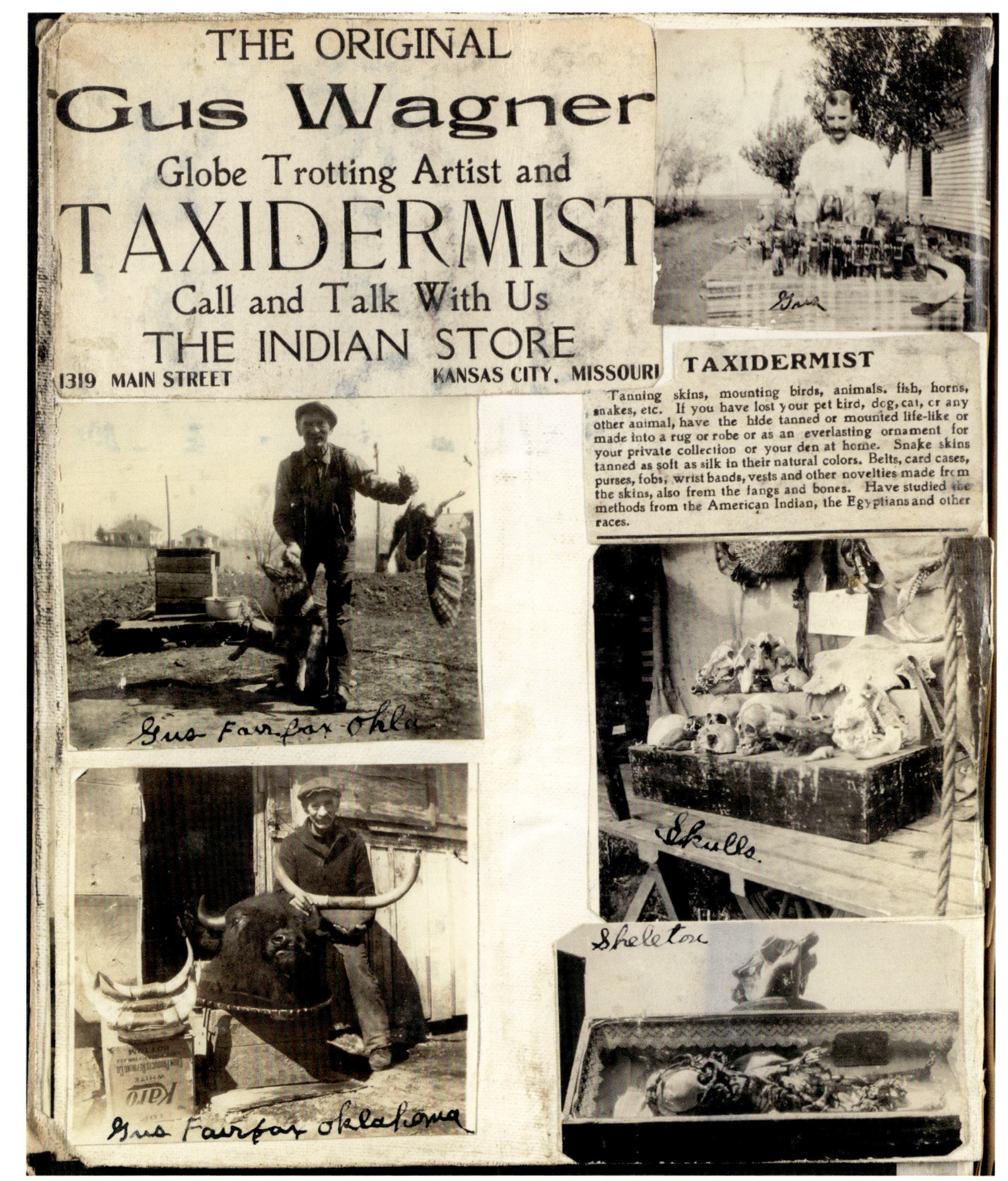

Page from Gus Wagner's scrapbook

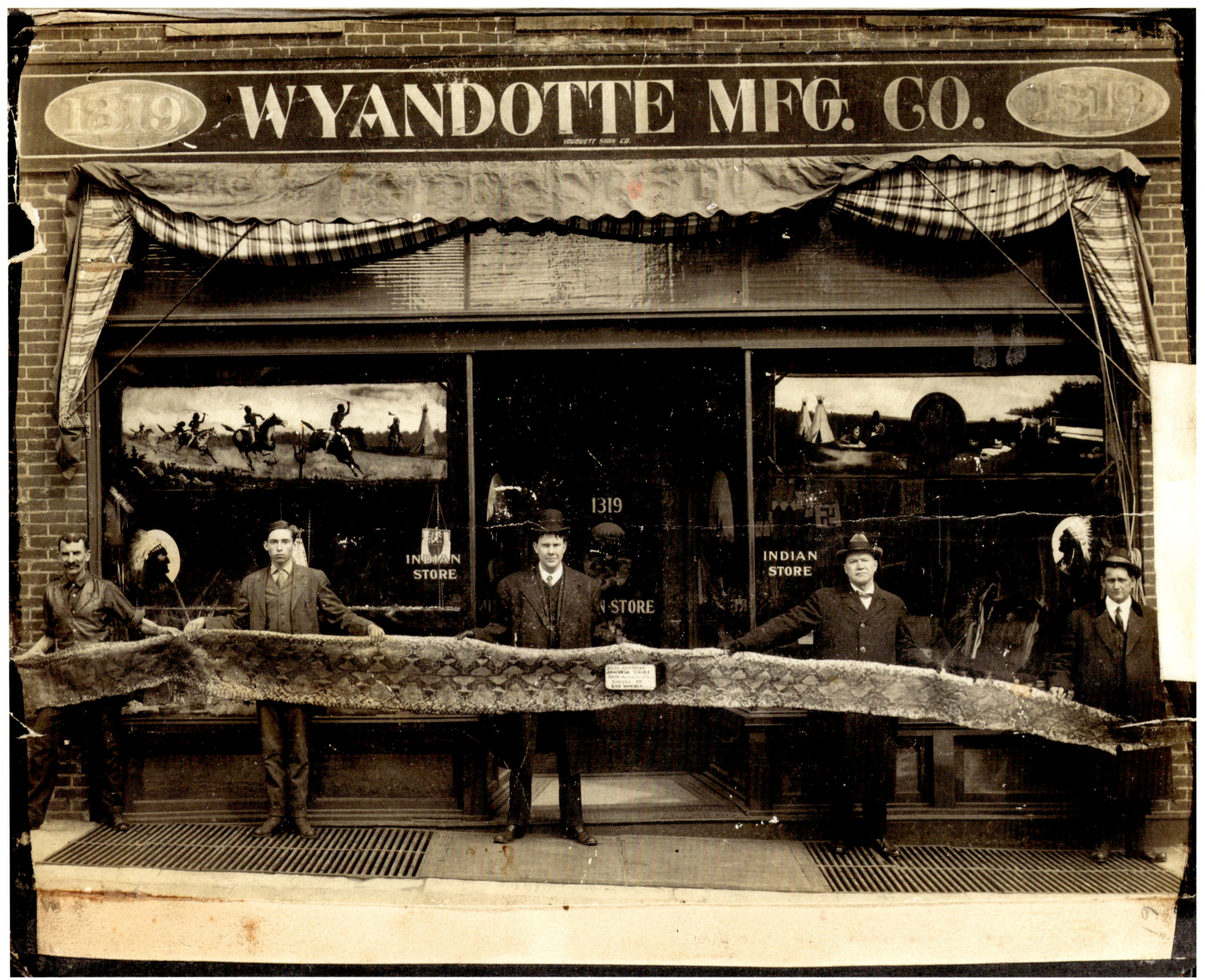
1319
WYANDOTTE MFG. CO.
1319
1319
INDIAN STORE
INDIAN STORE

Huge Reptile Captured By Gus Wagner

Gus Wagner, former Marietta man and a brother of Capt. Henry Wagner of the Marietta Fire Department, is one of the heroes of a big snake hunt staged some months ago on the plains of Kansas where he and a companion captured an East Indian python, a huge reptile that is believed to have escaped some years ago from a circus. Lem Laird, a sturdy Kansan, shared honors with Wagner in capturing the snake believed by many to have been the largest reptile ever taken in the United States.

The snake was lassoed by the two men and was hitched to a tree where the tightening noose about its neck finally strangled it to death, then its skin and skeleton were preserved by the two hunters.

Wagner is well known in Marietta where he spent his early life. He is a native of the Devol's Dam neighborhood. He visited relatives here a year ago last Summer and Fall and at that time was conducting a museum show making county fairs in this section of the country. He is a resident of Harper, Kansas, and the following story of the snake's capture is from the columns of a newspaper published in that town:

MANY STORIES

There have been many stories told of late about large snakes having been seen in the vicinity of the Chikaskia River and Dead Man's Lake, north of Harper, Kans. There has been much excitement and worry among the farmers in that neighborhood. Some claim to have lost young calves, pigs and chickens because of the ravages of the monster reptile. These raids on young farm stock, it is claimed, have been going on for several years, and recently it was the good fortune of two men to solve the mystery of "the demon of Dead Man's Lake." The two men are Lem Laird and Gus Wagner. Mr. Laird lives north of Harper a few miles, and is a well known naturalist, and a man experienced with reptiles, and at the time Mr. Wagner was his guest. Mr. Wagner is a globe-trotter and naturalist.

Stories were again circulating about the giant snake having made another raid on a farmer's stock along the Chikaskia River, and hearing of the excitement, the two naturalists scented the possibility of the trail of big game. Thus it was Laird and Wagner one murky morning, late in October 1930, set out for the Chikaskia River and Dead Man's Lake, in quest of the monster that was terrorizing the farmers.

TRAMP MANY HOURS

For hours the naturalists tramped along the banks of the Chikaskia River, through slough grass, waist

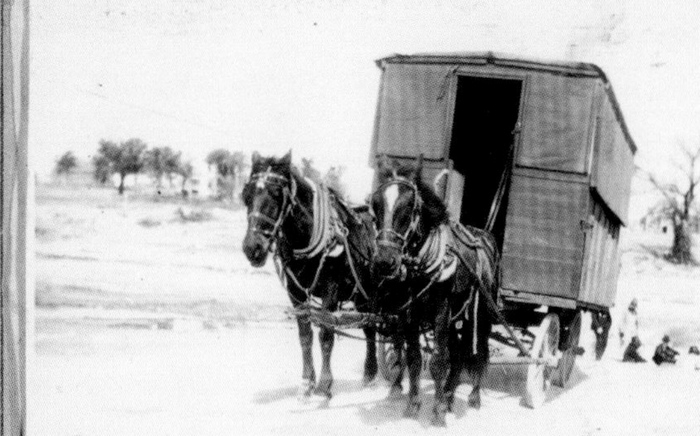

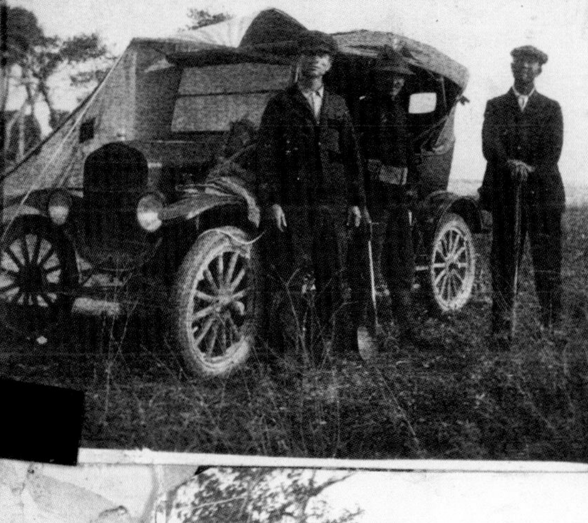

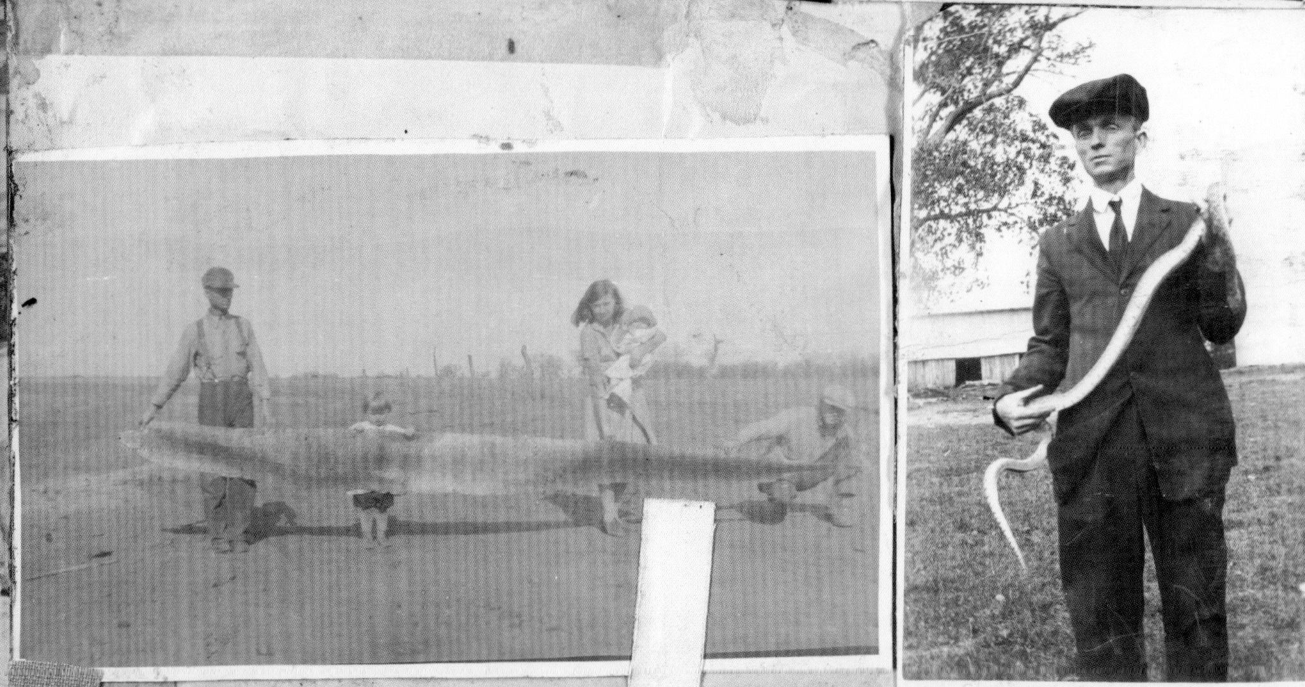

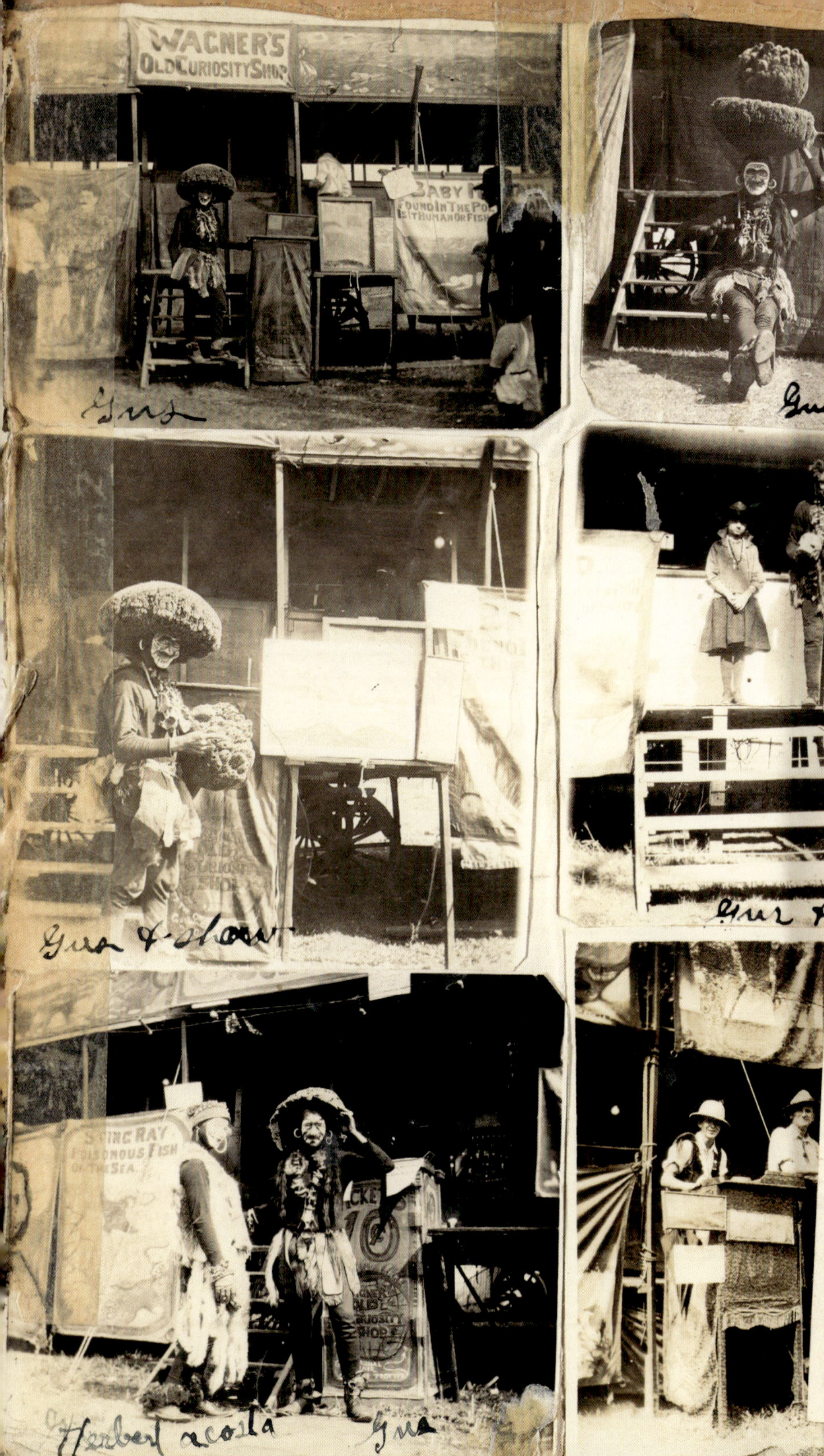

Rattlesnakes Hold No Terror for Wagner

Veteran Carnival Man Fondles the Poisonous Reptiles Like Little Girls Play With Dolls

In front of the Republican-Gazette office last Thursday afternoon before a group of pop-eyed spectators a man picked up a lively rattlesnake, pried the snake's mouth open and felt of the wicked fangs, then with a match extracted some of the poison from the snake's mouth and put it into his own. Later this man, who wields such an uncanny influence over rattling reptiles, allowed one of the rattlers to thrust its tongue against the ball of his eye—and neither the snake nor the man exhibited any ill effects from the ghastly performance.

The snake charmer is Gus Wagner, now with the Brodbeck Carnival Company. Wagner was on vacation last week, and he spent the time in Gove county hunting rattlesnakes to add to his collection. With him were Amos Chitty of Kansas City, Mo., and M. W. Laird of Harper, Kansas. This man Laird, so Wagner tells us, has a regular snake farm at Harper and does a wholesale business of supplying shows and museums with these crawling vermin.

Wagner and his companions picked up eight good rattlesnake specimens on their hunt in Gove county last week. This is an off-season, they tell us—rattlesnakes stay too close to their holes in dry weather—or they'd have secured many more for their collection. Wagner doesn't give all his attention to snakes; he has gathered insects, scorpions and other species of the lower order for purposes of exhibition, at one time having 3,-000 insects and 2,000 scorpions in his possession.

Wagner showed at the Gove County Fair here a number of years ago, and the trip to Gove City Thursday was to say hello to some of the folks he met here at that time.

Frank George and family

Left: Page from Gus Wagner's scrapbook

Opposite: Pages from Gus Wagner's scrapbook

October 13, 1919.

Mr. Gus Wagner,
Route #1,
Clements, Kansas.

Dear Sir:

The two young snakes which you were kind enough to send us sometime ago arrived in good shape, and proved very interesting, especially the young cottonmouth with a white tail. I don't recollect having seen one so plainly marked as that before. It shows pretty well how closely the cottonmouth and the copperhead are related, the latter also having light tips to the tails when quite young. Can you tell from which locality the mother snakes of both species came?

With regard to the horned toad, I can only say that I don't believe that the bite of it will produce hydrophobia. The thing does not seem probable, and I have never heard of it. My experience with the horned toad is very much like yours. Your kind offer to send us any of them is appreciated, but we have at the present time all the horned toads that we need from localities from which you are likely to have specimens.

We have not published any book giving colored plates with names of North American snakes, nor has any such work ever been published to my knowledge since Holbrook's work in 1842. The nearest approach to it would be Ditmar's Reptile Book, published some years ago by Doubleday, Page & Co., New York City.

The only dealer from whom you can buy snakes like the anaconda, etc., that I know of is Louis Ruhe, 248 Grant Street, New York City.

Yours truly,

L. Stejneger

Head Curator,
Dept. of Biology.

Mr. Gus Wagner,

C/o General Delivery,

Shiner, Texas.

Dec. 5, 1916.

Dear Sir:

I have your letter of Dec. 1st, and must say that I think you had a pretty narrow escape. Gila Monsters are, as a rule, dangerous pets to have about, and I am surprised that you did not know any better.

A good many people disbelieve that the Gila Monster's bite is poisonous, but as a matter of fact, the poison is a very dangerous one, and if it gets into the blood, it seems to be difficult to eliminate or counteract. I do not know of any effective antidote. The best treatment is to follow the general directions in case of snake bite. Remember one thing - the poison glands are situated in the lower jaw near the front and not in the upper jaw at the posterior end of the mouth, as in the snakes; nor does the Gila Monster inject its poison the way the snakes do. The Gila Monster simply closes its mouth over the wound and hangs on like a bulldog. The poison is thus given time to soak into the body, and in this way is taken into the

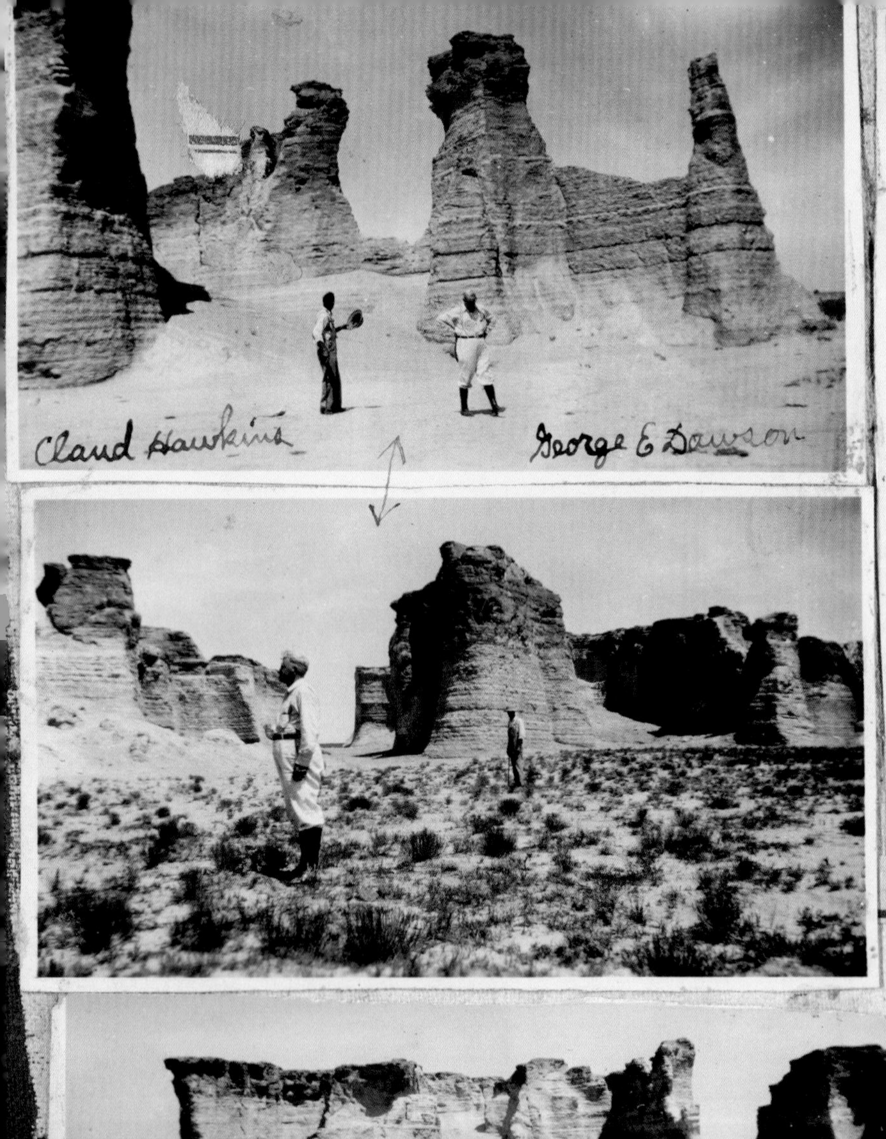

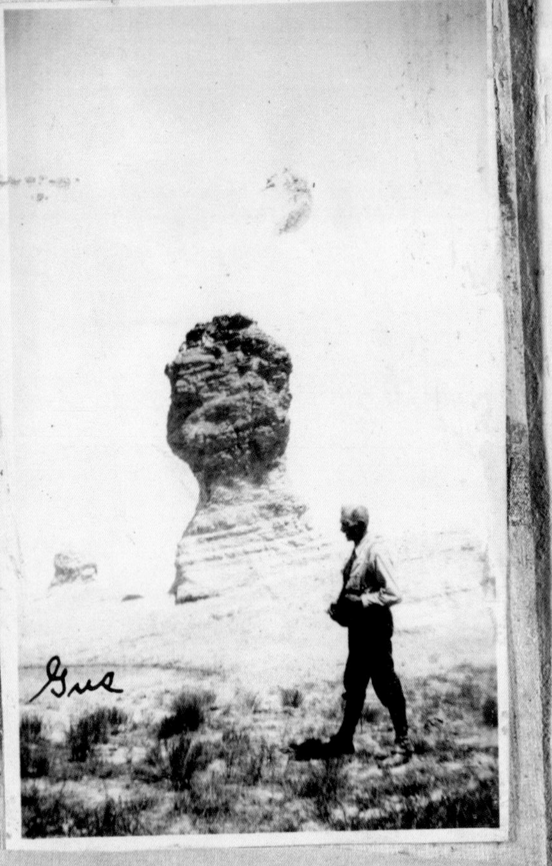

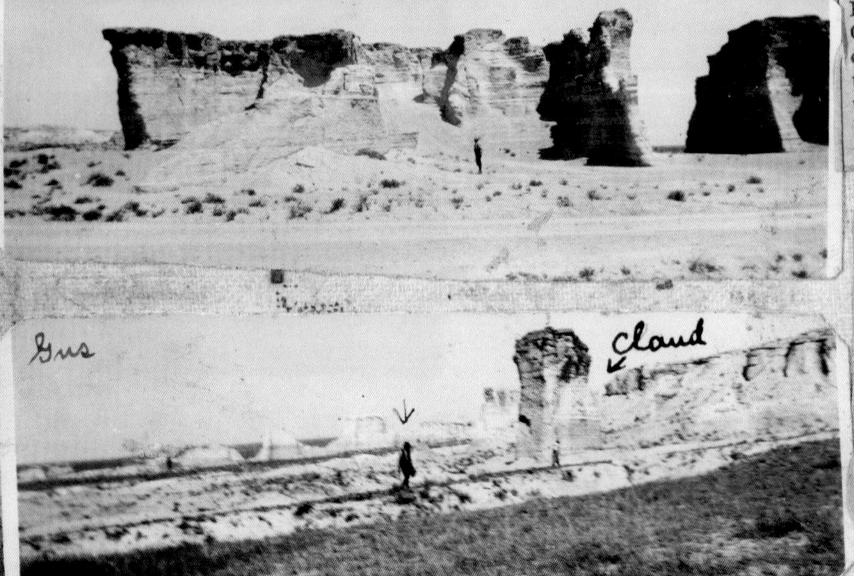

GOVE COUNTY REPUBLICAN-GAZE

Gus Wagner, globe trotter and rattlesnake man, accompanied by Geo. E. Dawson president of the Clements State Bank and C. W. Hawkins president of the Chase County Historical Society, spent several days of this week in Gove county in quest of specimens of petrification, and curios. They visited the Pyramids, Castle Rock, and other places.

Some Indian relics have been received by Dr. D. C. Schaffner, head of the Geology department at the College of Emporia, from Mr. Gus Wagner, who lives at Clements. Mr. Wagner spends most of his time collecting Indian relics, fossils and various geological specimens, and has an extensive private collection. Among the specimens sent to the College were two stone hoes, scrapers, one hammer stone, and one sandstone grinder.

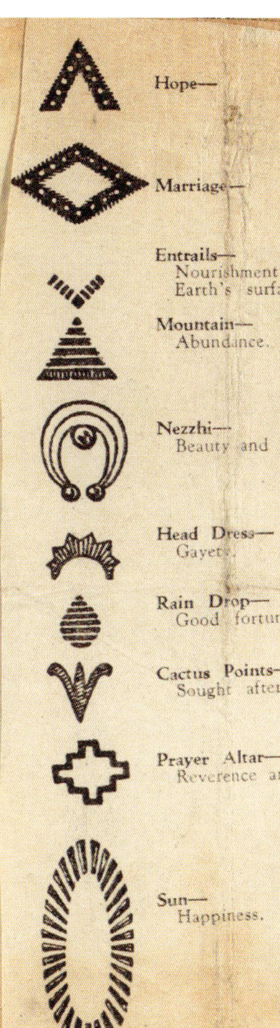

Clements Men Find Rare Indian Relics In the Ozarks

Special to The Gazette:

Clements, June 24—Sweltering in the dense forest undergrowth in the foothills of the Ozarks was the vacation chosen by Claude Hawkins, Clements relic collector. Mr. Hawkins and Gus Wagner have just returned from a 7-day visit in the Boston mountains, a branch of the Ozarks, where they sought prehistoric Indian museum specimens. Mr. Wagner is collecting for commercial purposes and Mr. Hawkins was endeavoring to find new relics for his already well-stocked private collection. According to Mr. Hawkins, the field near Fort Smith, Ark., is the only place in that section where black flint relics may be found. The black flint is rarely found in any other part of the United States.

Collect Hundreds of Pieces.

Together the men collected between 350 and 400 specimens, including mortars, grinders or pestles, axes, hoes, knives, spears, arrow heads, bird points, spades and blades.

Mr. Hawkins became interested in Indian relics in 1928 and has been working on a collection since that time. He values his present collection, classified and cased, at over $2,000. This includes material from Temple Mound, Spiro, Okla., and pottery once belonging to the Arkansas Cherokees as well as local findings. As a life member of the Kansas State Historical society, Mr. Hawkins has a government permit to open Indian mounds seeking museum specimens.

Chase county was supplied with a high grade of flint which the Indians used extensively," said Mr. Hawkins, "there are several rich Indian fields yielding many beautiful artifacts. Perhaps the best camp site in this country is located on the Roniger brothers' farm near Bazaar."

Collects Fossils Also.

In addition to his Indian relics, Mr. Hawkins has several samples of fossils and petrified wood. As rated by the Geological society, Rochester, N. Y., these are about 200,000,000 years old. Other case display antiques are from Mexico, China and Japan, along with a brilliant scarf from Egypt and an ivory necklace from India. He also has an ancient double-burner brass lamp, a brass-topped coffee mill, a spinning wheel, and a fluting or pleating iron.

PRESENTS INDIAN RELICS TO COLLEGE OF EMPORIA

Gus Wagoner, of Clements, has presented the geology department of the College of Emporia, with a number of very interesting Indian relics. Included in the gift was two stone hoes scrappers, a hammer stone and one stone grinder.

Mr. Wagoner has for a long time been interested in Indian relics and fossils and various geological specimens. He has collected these for years and has a large collection.

He is still collecting but such things are not as easily found now as they were in the early years.

While Maud and Gus wanted to raise their daughter as a Christian, they were often rebuffed: "Once they went to church and the preacher apologized for the fact that he had to let 'show people' in. But he said, all had to be allowed in. He lost his job over it, and Maud was very hesitant about the church after that."[6]

Researchers have scoured the landscape to find out more about Maud and Gus, and maybe that's what they intended. Perhaps they wanted to remain mysterious and mystifying, exerting a control over what people thought and imagined. Maud and Gus were ahead of their time. Skin was their medium, but the values and aesthetic vision they embraced were unparalleled. At the height of their careers, Maud and Gus established the Wagner Amusement Company and expanded their work to become promoters of street fairs, carnivals, and expositions. In one advertisement, they stated, "We control the best to be had in Midway Attractions on the Coast today and are constantly seeking New Attractions."

Gus and Maud's days together are a love story, where details are few. But photographs, ephemera, and the enduring devotion of their daughter Lotteva attest to the magic of their lives on the road as a family, making a home wherever they chose. Together, the Wagners were a very unconventional family, devoted to one another, with a shared vision in their pursuit of the untold possibilities of the American Dream.

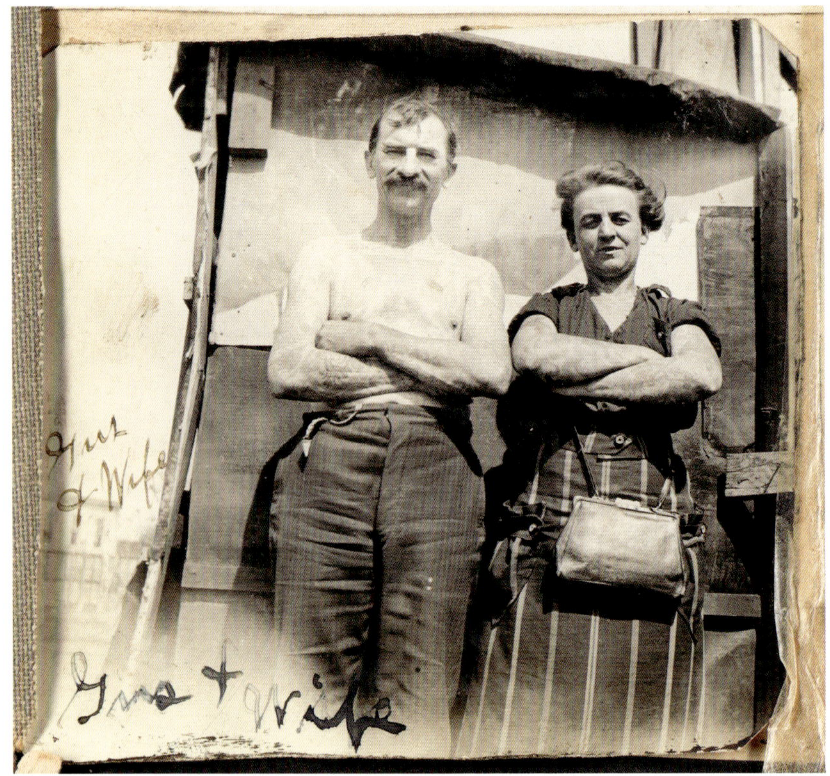

Above: Detail from Gus Wagner's scrapbook

Opposite: Page from Gus Wagner's scrapbook

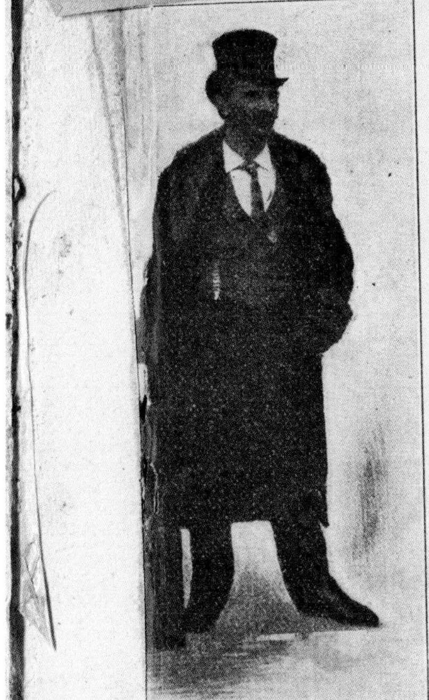

MARIETTA LEADER

Dec. 10, 1902.—Mr. Gus Wagner, the world-known globe trotter and tattoo artist, departed today for Newark, O. Several gentlemen in Marietta have their arms entirely covered and some tattooing on their bodies, and even the society leaders visited the tattooist.

The ✠ Wagner Amusement Company
PROMOTERS OF
Street Fairs, Carnivals, Expositions, Et

Have to our credit 18 years in the Show Business throughout The United States, Canada, South Africa, Australia, New Zealand and The Orient

We control the best to be had in Midway Attractions on the Coast today, and are constantly seeking New Attractions

Write us for Open Time, our Methods of Boosting your City, Lodge or Enterprise whatever it may be. ∴ Can give Reference if required

ST. LOUIS POST DISPATCH

Dec. 8, 1904.—If there is any fun in the tattoo business Gus Wagner ought to know it. Besides being a professional tattooer, Wagner is a professional contortionist, a globe trotter, a graduate from the stoking hold of a merchant vessel, a showman, and altogether an interesting personage. A Post-Dispatch reporter saw him at work yesterday—a stick in his mouth used as a palette from which with a needle, with a needle he jigjagged upon the surface of the young man's arm, he took the different colors of pigments he was using in manufacturing a most wonderful representation of a lodge seal, together with the young man's initials

DELEWARE JOURNAL AND HERALD

July 21, 1903.—Mr. Gus Wagner, who recently arrived in Delaware, is now located on West Williams street, He is skilled in the art of tattooing, and to him Marietta papers have devoted columns of interesting description regarding his tours around the world.

THE KANSAS CITY TIME

Dec. 11, 1905.—At 16 East Sixth street lives Gus Wagner and his wife, tattoo artists, who have in the last nine months tattooed 2,206 persons in Kansas City. Wagner is himself a solid mass of tattooing. On his breast is the history of his life; on his back is a history of America; on each arm a romance of the sea; on one leg a history of Japan; and on the other a history of China. His wife has j[illegible] with tattoo designs.

WHEELING NEWS

27, 1902—(Special).—The illustration is the like[ness] [o]ne of the greatest globe trotters in the country, [W]agner, who has sailed on every ocean open [to com]merce. He returned to Marietta where he was bo[rn] [i]n 1872, last May, and is spending the summer with [his] mother. He has 264 designs of tattooing in eight different colors upon his skin as shown in the above picture. He is skilled in the art of tattooing, having learned the art from the natives of Borneo, Java, India, New Zealand, China, Japan and Polynesia Islands. Following [is a] brief description of his trip around the world:

WAGNER'S ❧ TRAVELING ❧ MUSEUM
FEATURING
"Mrs. Gus Wagner" and the original "Gus Wagner"
THE MOST ELABORATELY TATTOOED PEOPLE IN THE WORLD
— ALSO —
"A BABY MERMAID"
"THE HUMAN - HEADED OCTOPUS"
THE PETRIFIED HEAD OF A
"TATTOOED MAORI CHIEF"
FROM NEW ZEALAND.

And many other Interesting Curiosities from every quarter of the Globe. We combine two shows in one

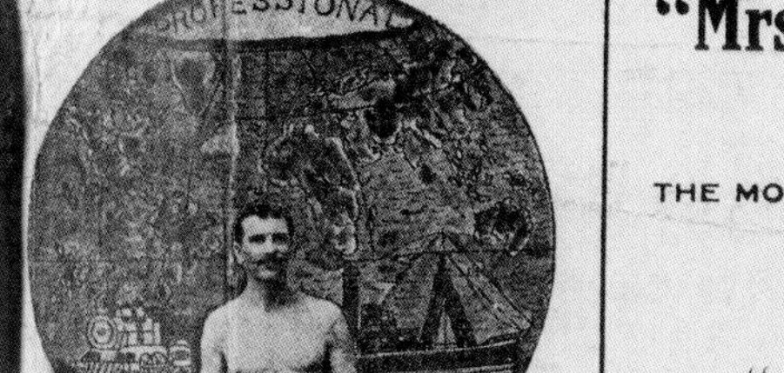

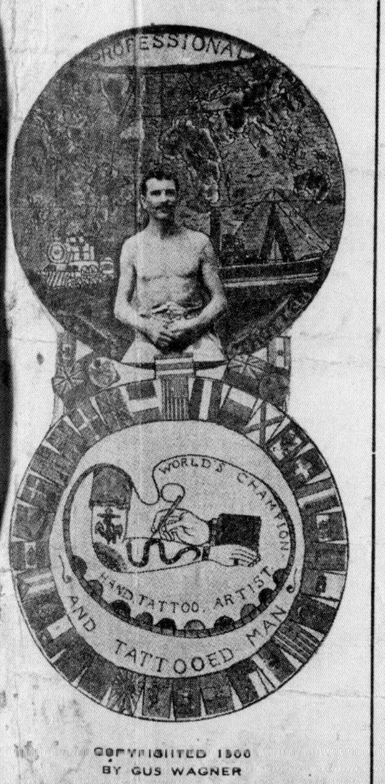

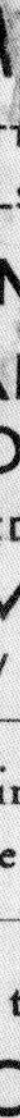

Under the Management of the Original, Gus Wagner

"GLOBE TROTTER AND TATTOOED MAN

Positively nothing to offend the Most Fastidious.   We cater to Ladies, Gentlemen and Child[ren]

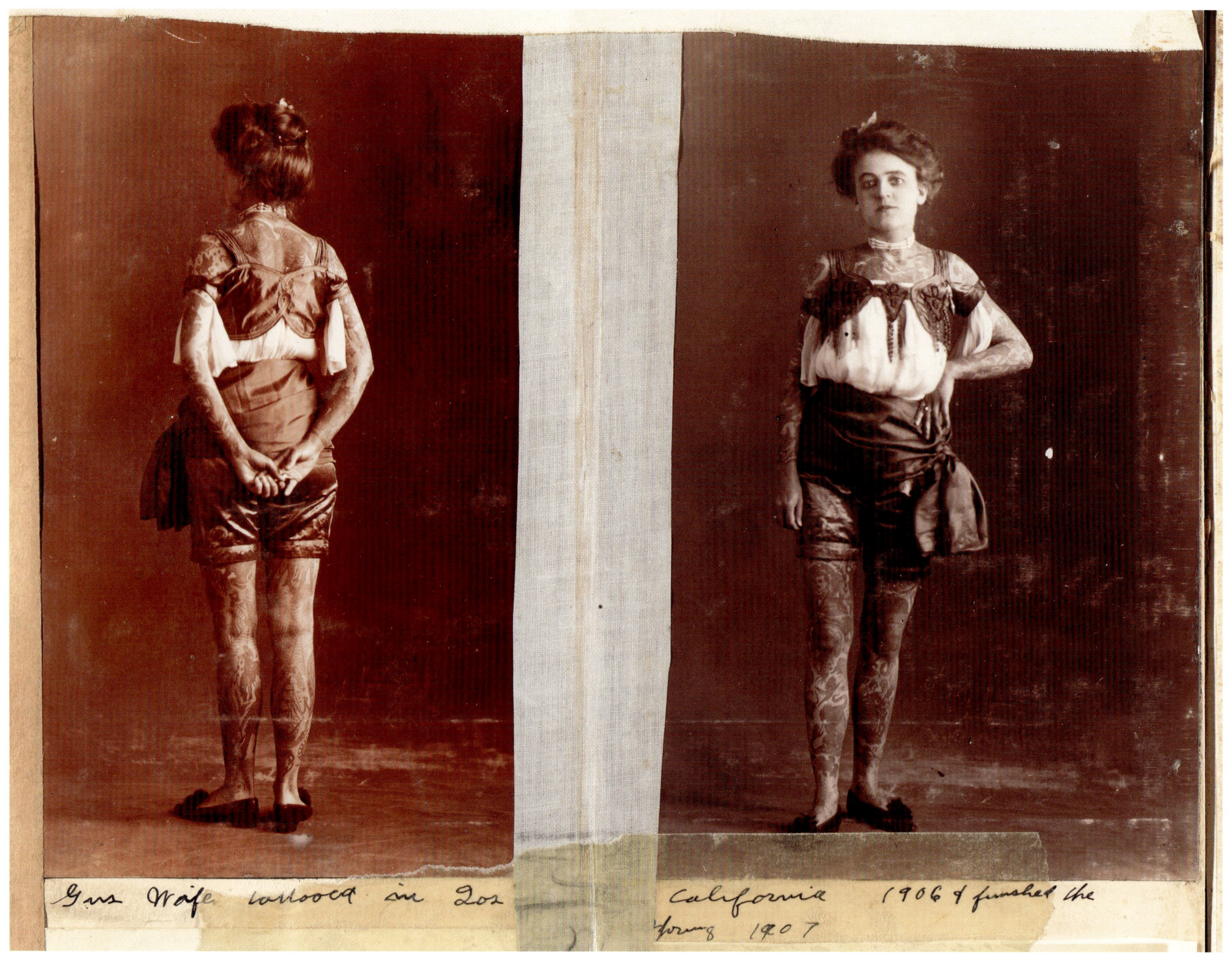

Gus Wife tattooed in Los ... California 1906 & finished the
young 1907

Opposite: Detail from Gus Wagner's scrapbook

Right: Maud Stevens Wagner, Kansas City, Missouri, 1906

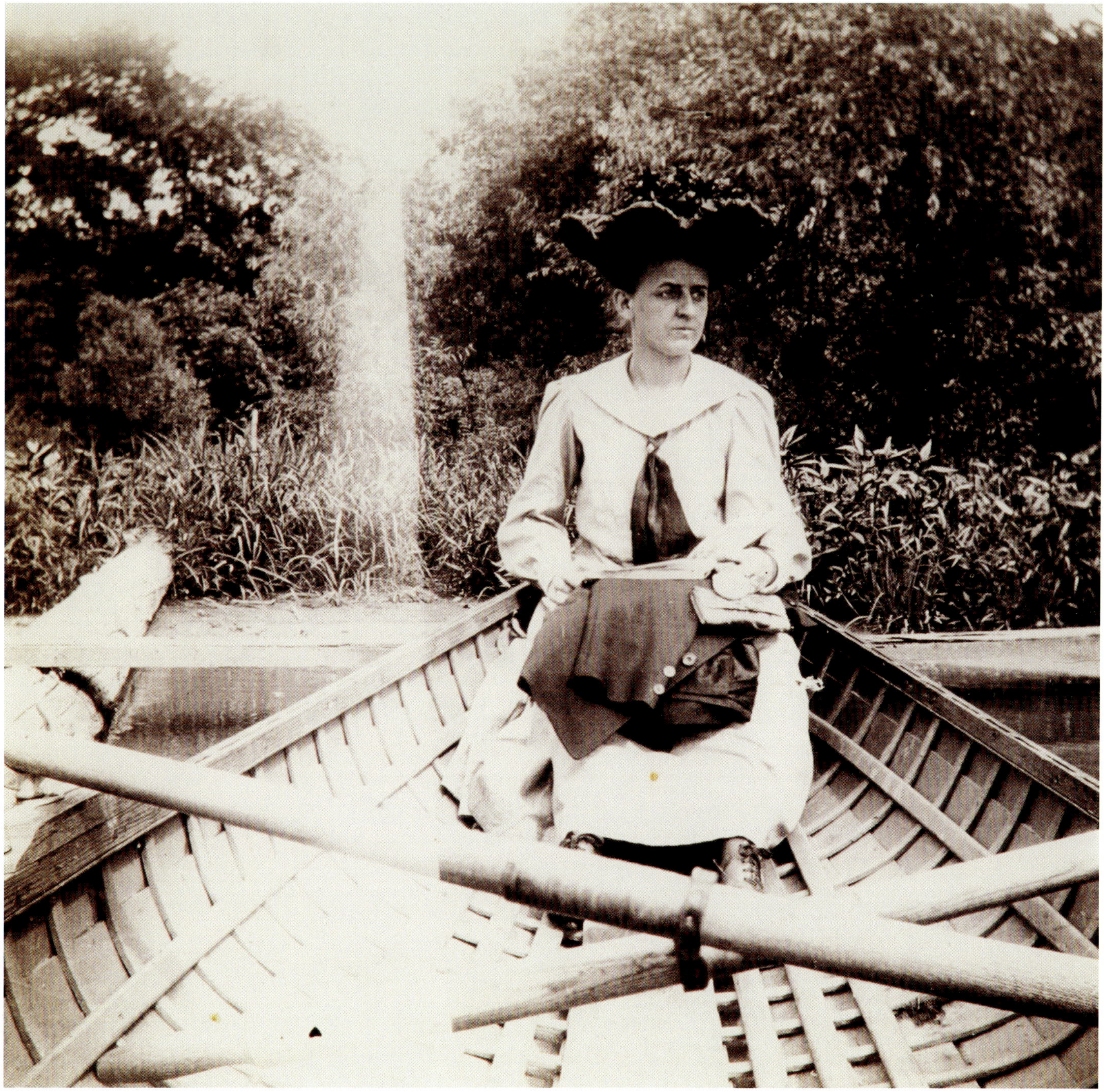

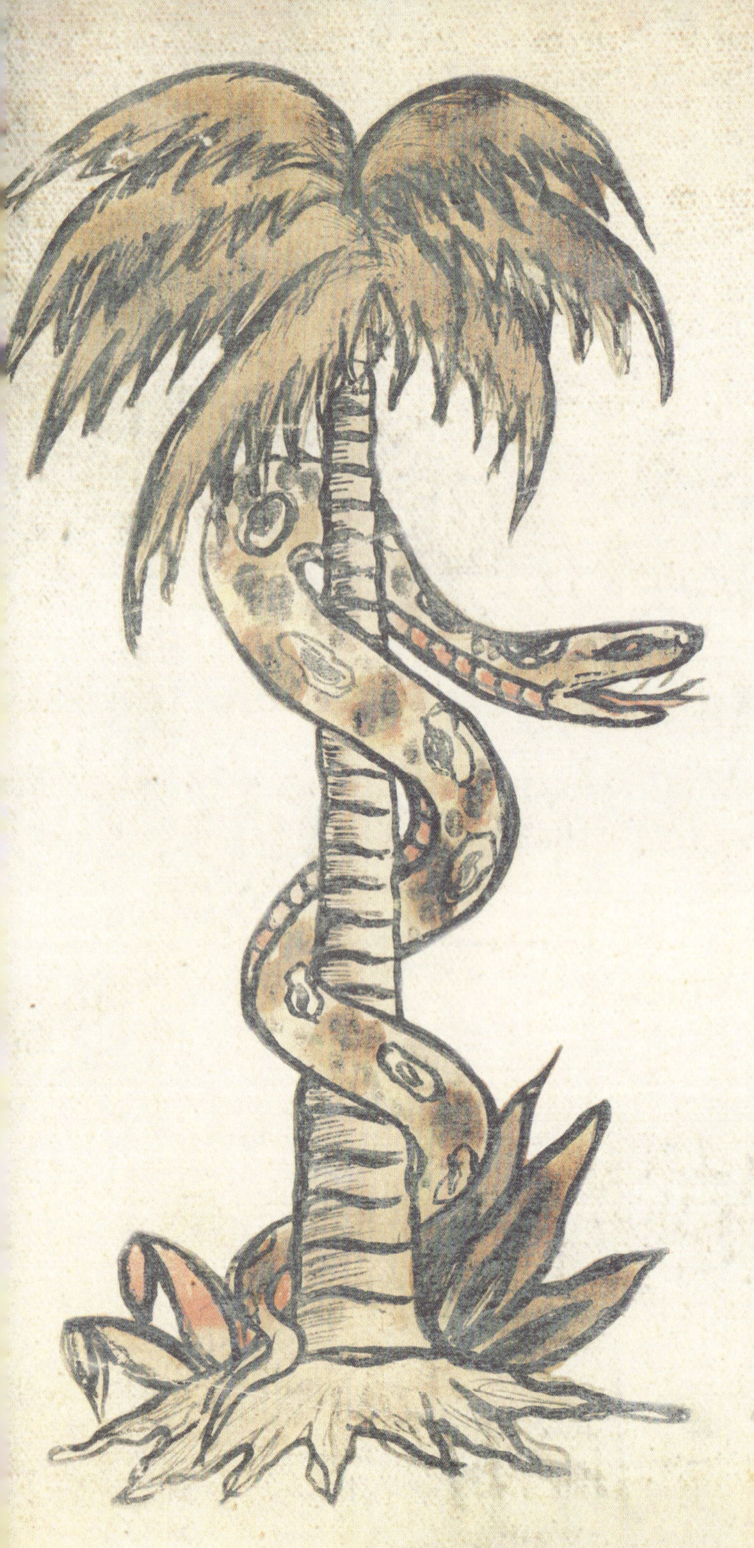

ORAL HISTORY: LOTTEVA WAGNER DAVIS

INTERVIEWED BY CHUCK ELDRIDGE
EDITED BY ALAN GOVENAR

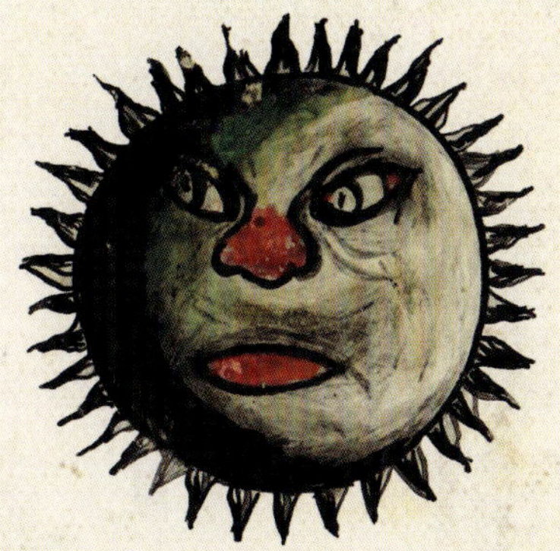

Gus Wagner traveled all over and got all kinds of tattoos and got completely covered. To run this long story short, he come back to this country and started tattooing again. He made a trip out west to Cripple Creek. Spent a night in a tree because the timber wolves were after him. He went out there and worked in logging camps and one thing and another, tattooing and working. Then he went back to Ohio and then he went to the St. Louis World's Fair, which was in 1904. The World Exposition, which is what they really called it.

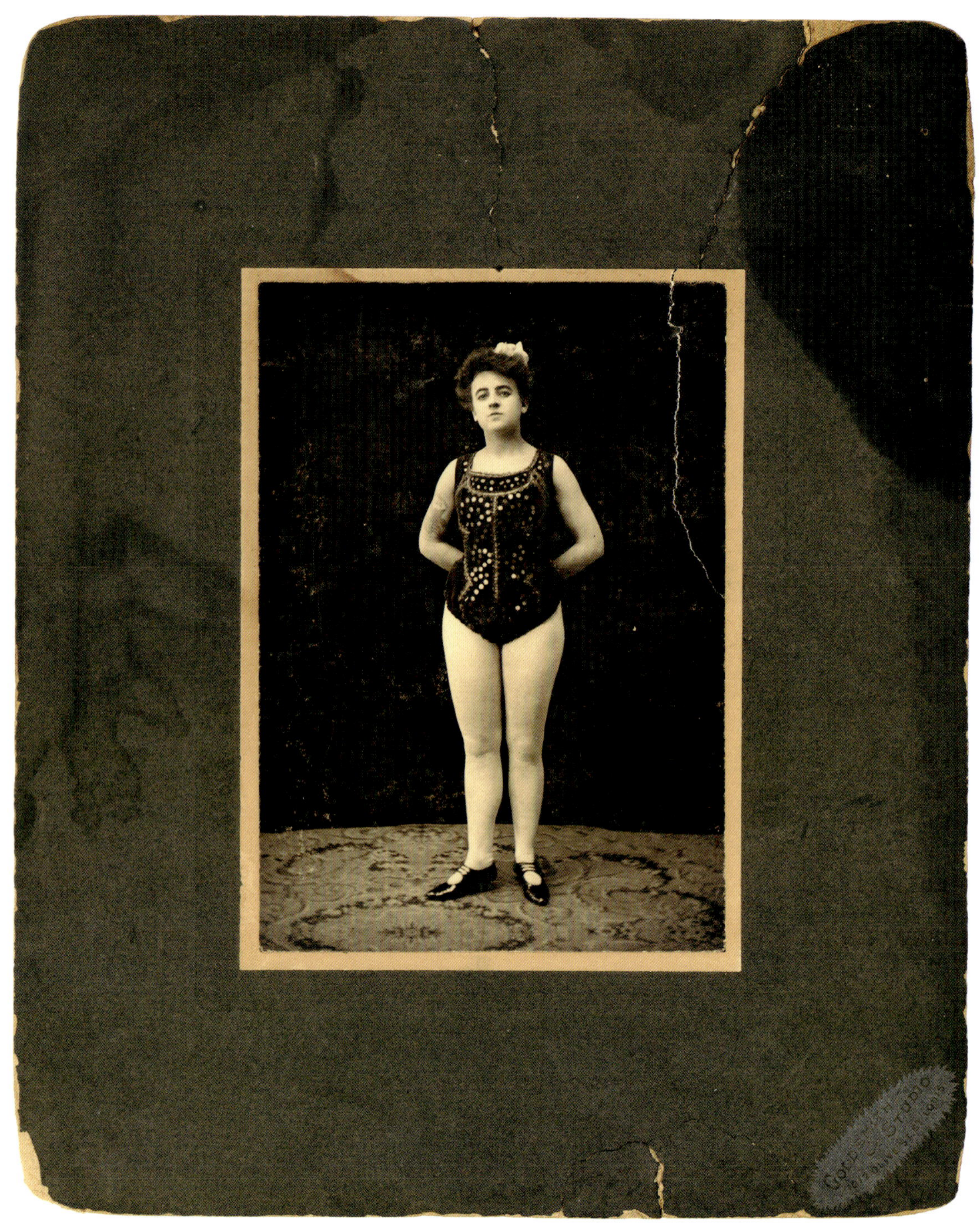

There my mother, Maud Stevens, was an aerial artist and working in the kids show. The kids show was like a sideshow. And Gus went to work in the sideshow at the world's fair, tattooing. And [after they got to know each other,] he insisted they get married. He made her quit the aerial work. She thought it over and she said, "Tell you what, if you'll tattoo me all over and teach me how to tattoo, I'll give up the aerial work." Well, he says, "That's a deal." And sent her sister Dora a wire and she come to St. Louis, and Gus and Maud got married.

Opposite: Maud Stevens in leotard and stockings, ca. 1904

Right: Maud's older sister Dora Stevens, age nineteen, ca. 1888

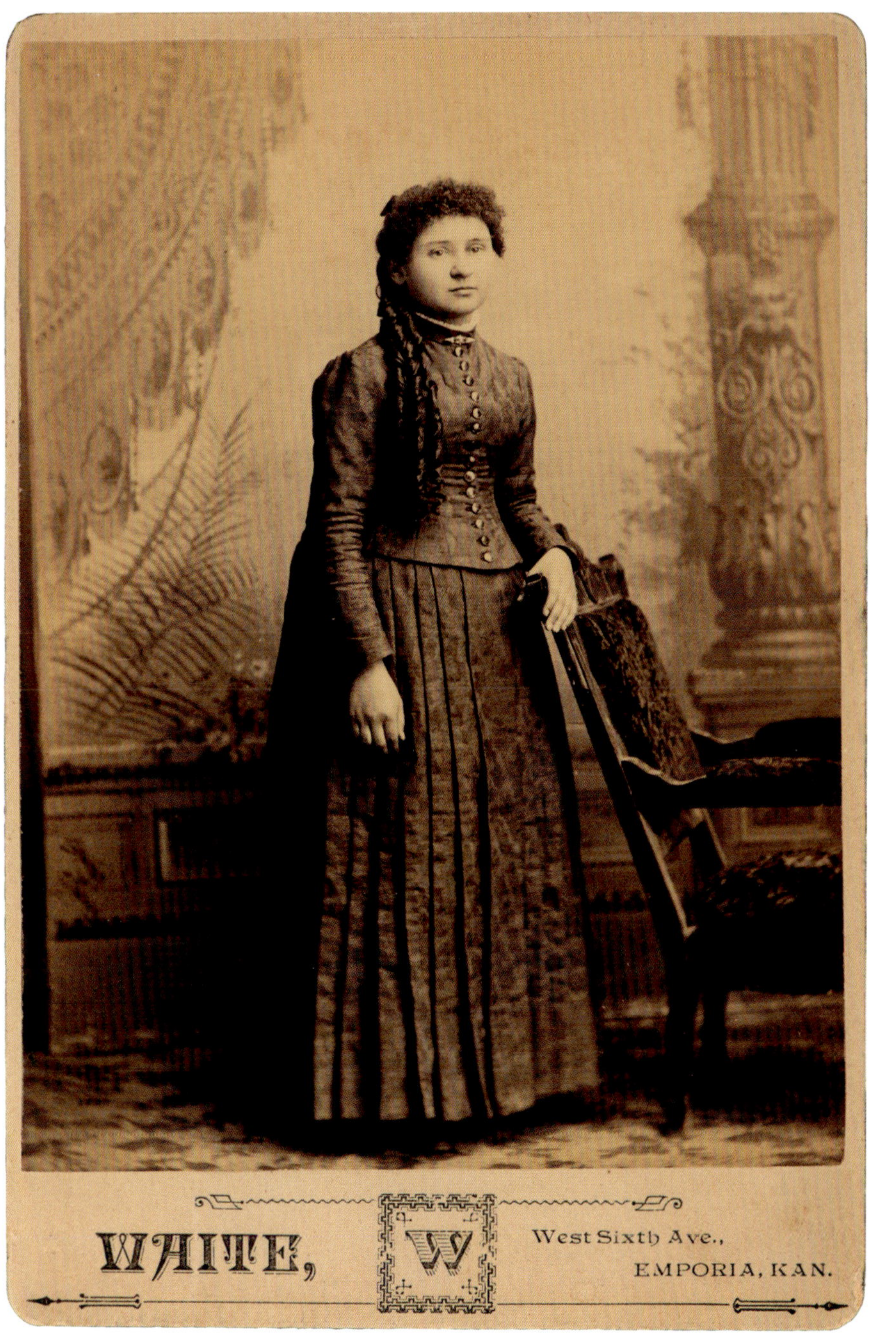

KANSAS CITY
PENNY AMUSEMENT PARLOR
AND SHOOTING GALLERY.

❋ ❋ ❋

545 MAIN STREET.

W. T. GREEN, PROP,

KANSAS CITY, MO. _Dec 4_ 190_5_

To Whom it may concern

Mr Gus Wagoner has been in my place of buisness Tattooing for the past nine months. I have found him to be quiet industrious honest and a man of good habits Anything you may do for him will be highly appreciated by me.

W. T. Green

Deputy License Inspector of Kansas City Mo.

also prop. of Penny Amusement Parlor

545 Main st. K. C. Mo.

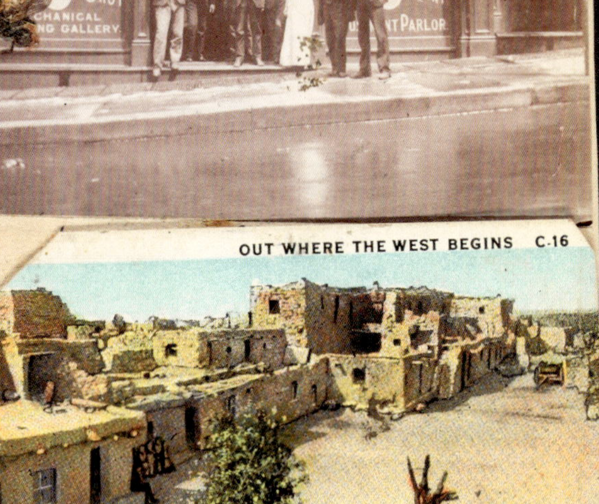

OUT WHERE THE WEST BEGINS
By ARTHUR CHAPMAN

OUT where the hand-clasp's a little stronger,
Out where the smile dwells a little longer,
That's where the West begins.
Out where the sun shines a little brighter,
Where the snows that fall are a trifle whiter,
Where the bonds of home are a wee bit tighter,
That's where the West begins.

Out where the skies are a trifle bluer,
Where friendship ties are a little truer,
That's where the West begins.
Out where a fresher breeze is blowing,
Where there's laughter in every streamlet flowing,
Where there's more of reaping and less of sowing,
That's where the West begins.

Out where the world is still in the making,
Where fewer hearts with despair are breaking,
That's where the West begins.
Where there's more of singing and less of sighing,
Where there's more of giving and less of buying
And a man makes friends without half trying,
That's where the West begins.

© J. R

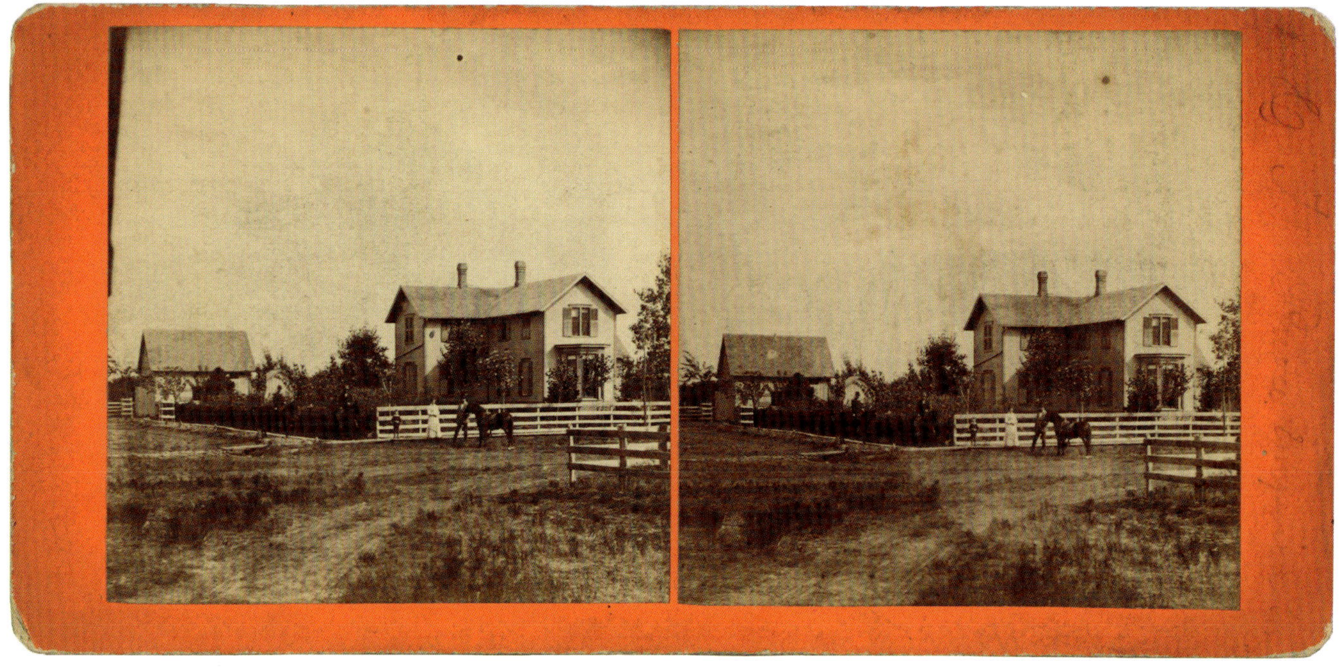

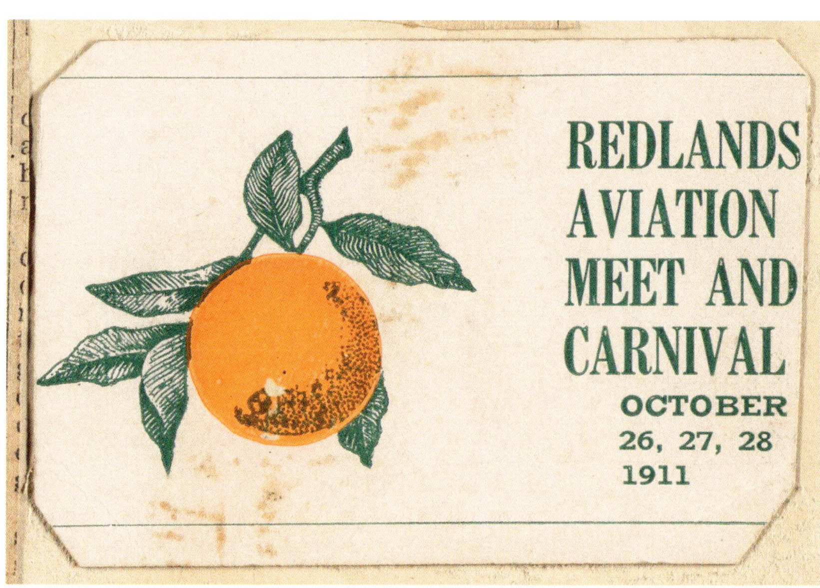

From St. Louis, they traveled. They come home to the ranch in Kansas; that's where she was partly raised on a cattle ranch up 35 miles north of El Dorado, up in the hills. They come up there, worked that winter in Kansas City, had a tattoo shop. The next year, I think it was, they went to California. And they were out there eight years. And I was born 1910. While they were out there, they had the first jumping-horse merry-go-round on the Pacific coast. They had a small carnival with free acts. Mama went to the second aviation meet held in America, held in Redlands, California. They had Paul and his balloon ascension. They had the Wright brothers and the Stevens brothers in there.

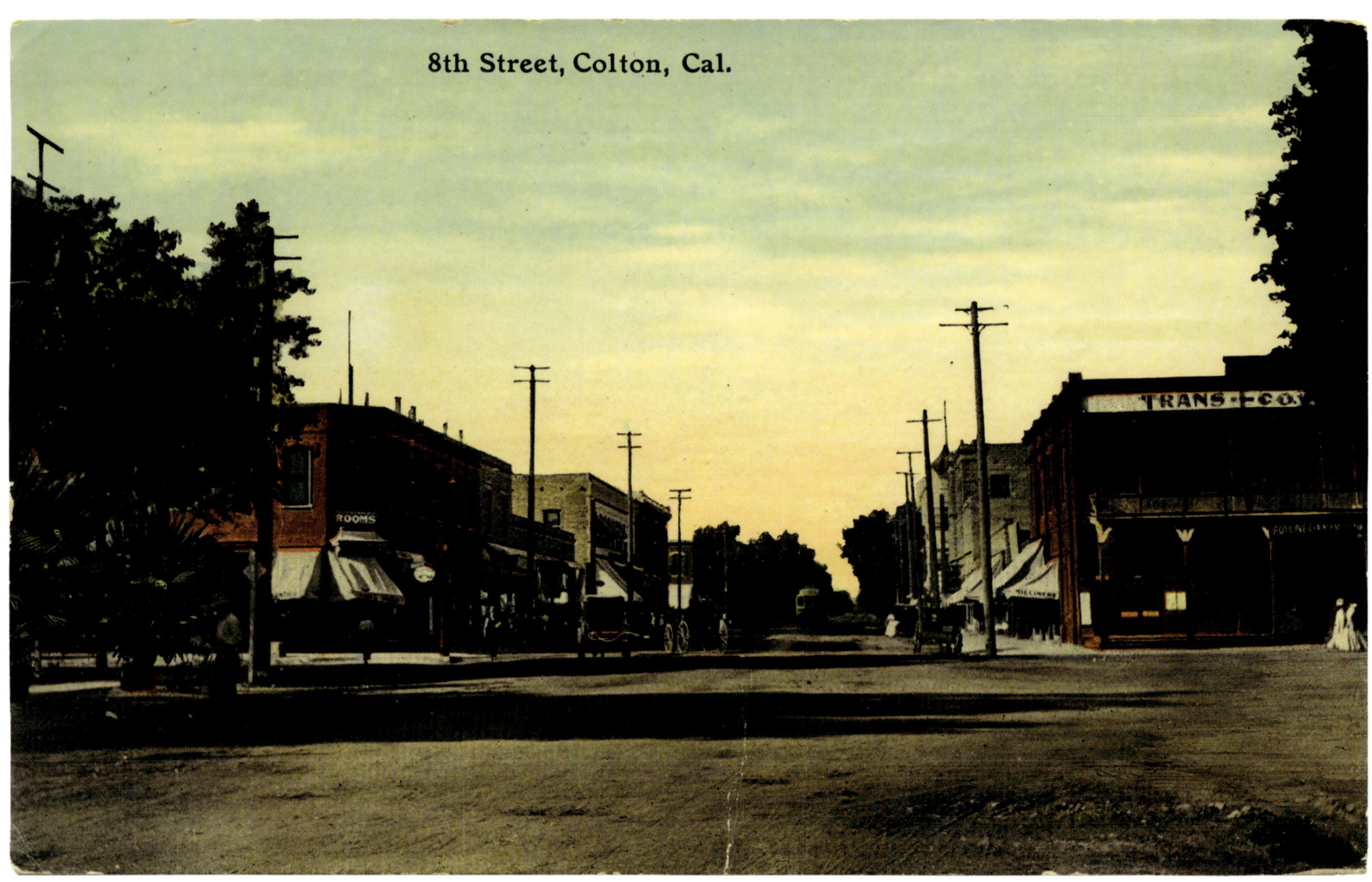

Postcard of Colton, California, mailed by Maud
to Dora Stevens in Clements, Kansas

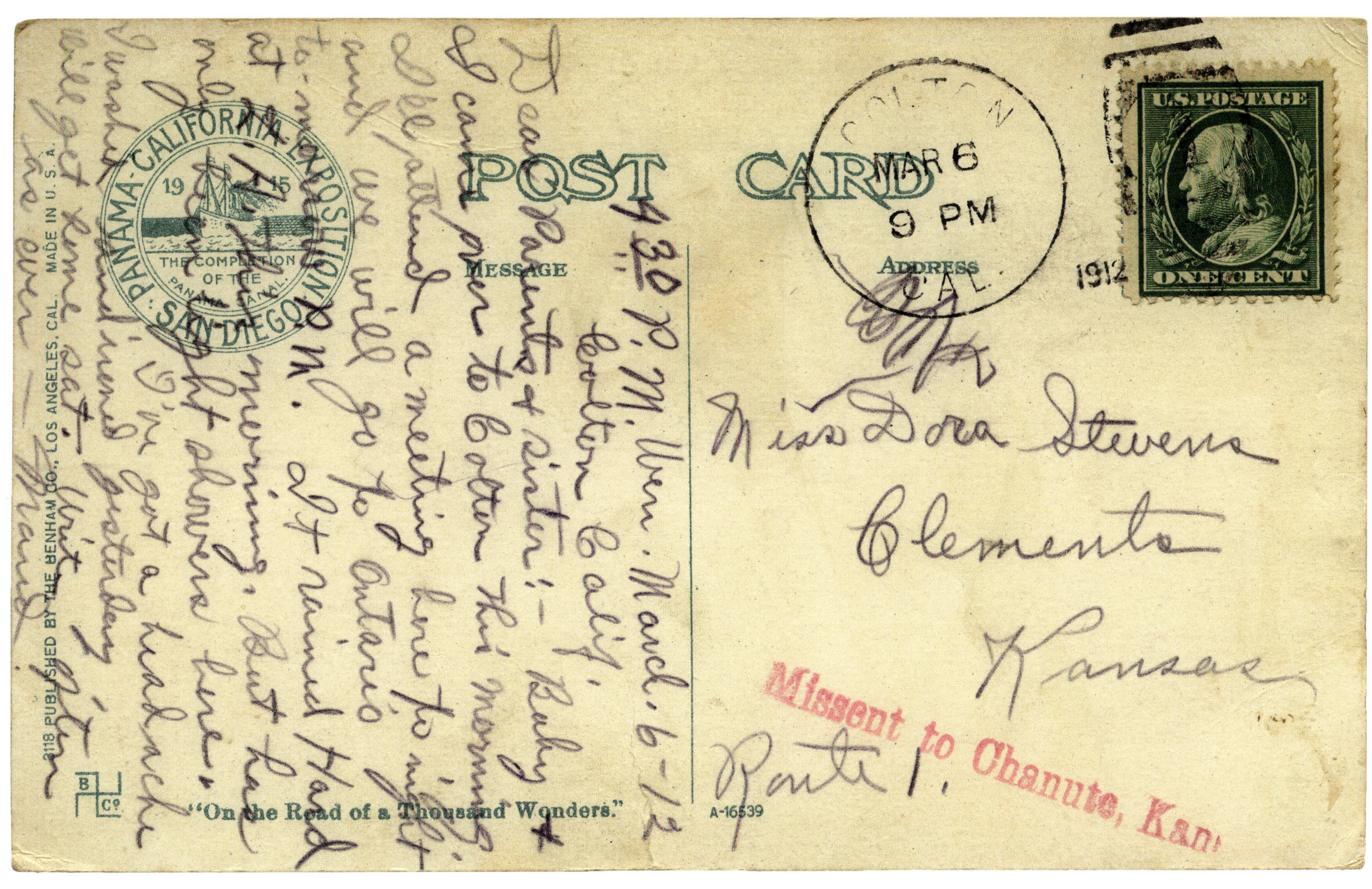

"Dear Parents + sister: Baby + I came over to Colton this morning. I'll attend a meeting here tonight and we will go to Ontario tomorrow P.M. It rained hard at L.A. this morning. But has only been light showers here. I've got a headache. I washed and ironed yesterday. Will get home Sat. Write often. As ever—Maud." Back of postcard, 1912.

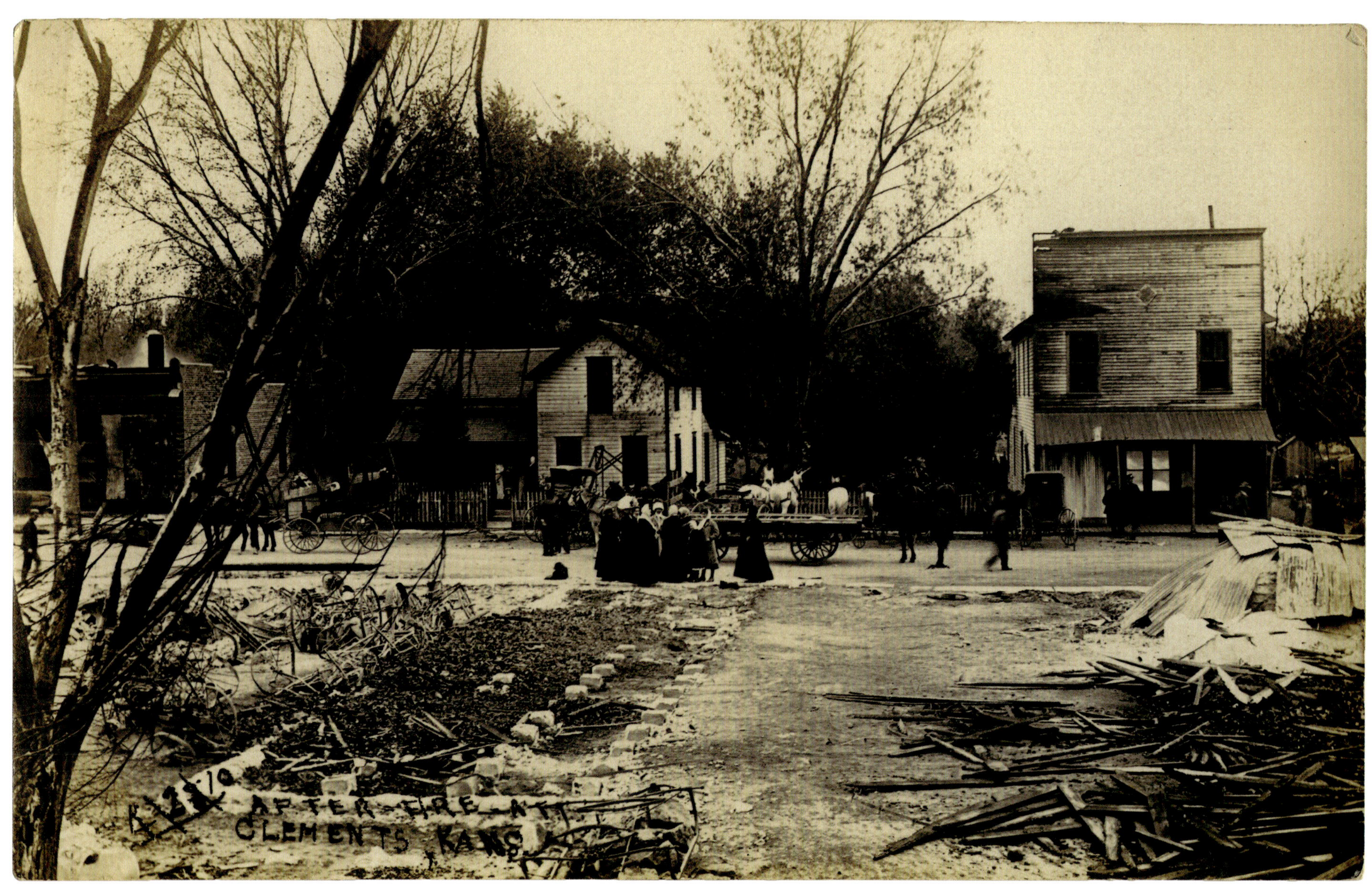

Real-photo postcard of Clements, Kansas, April 23, 1910

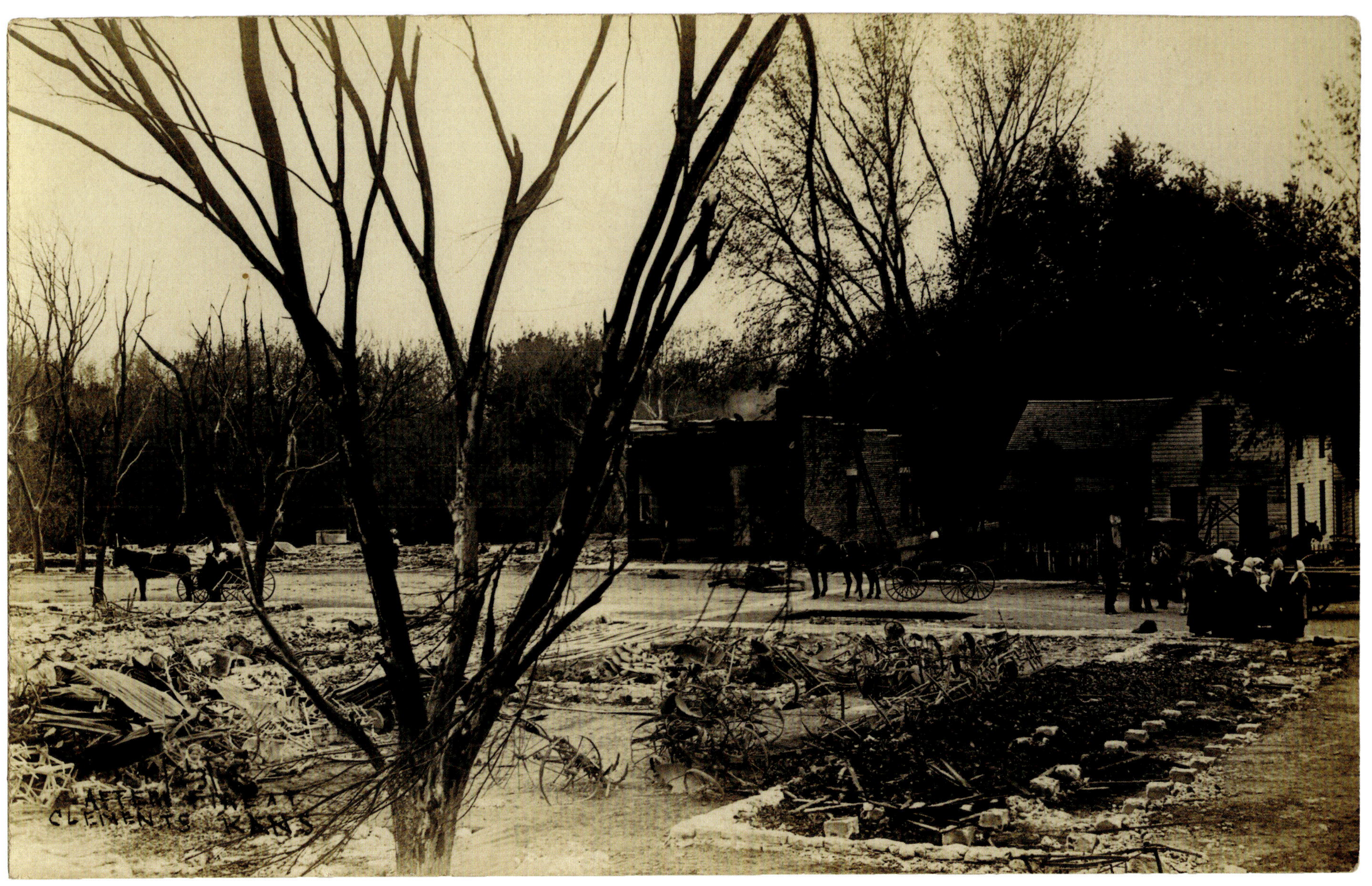

Real-photo postcard of Clements, Kansas, April 23, 1910

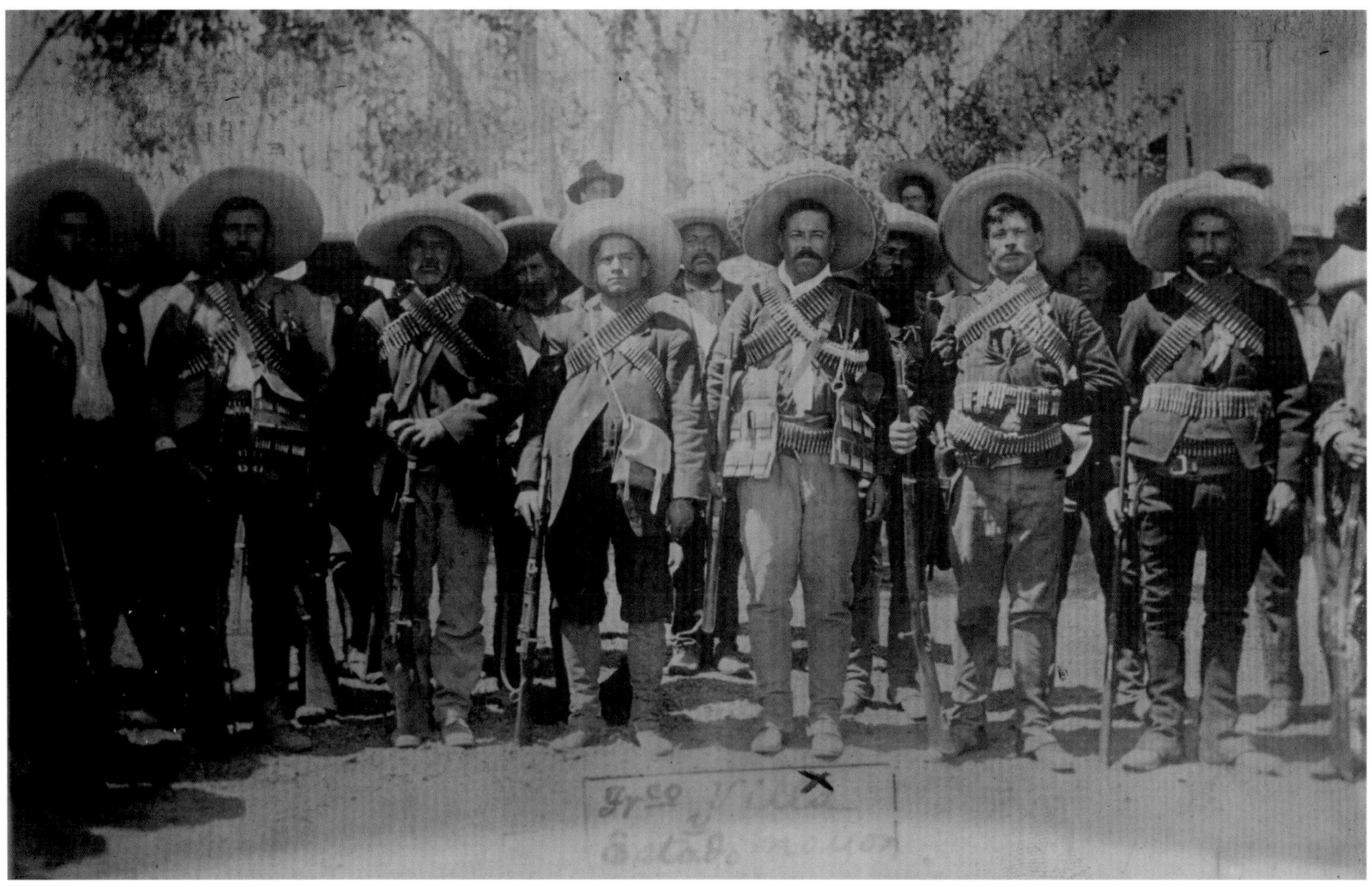

From Kansas, they traveled all over the states after that with various carnivals and circuses, tattooing. In front of the shows in them days, instead of having canvas banners or paneling like we do today, they had short picket fences, white picket fences. Rows and rows of white picket fences. And I remember very well when they started burning them.

Well, we went into Laredo, 1916. Pancho Villa and our men were skirmishing across the border. At night you'd hear bullets fly overhead. Zing! They'd whine. Never heard of casualties. Never heard a bullet go off in daytime. Nothing. That didn't bother us. We stayed on.

Opposite: Francisco "Pancho"
Villa (at the "X") at Hacienda de
Bustillos, Chihuahua, 1911

*Right: Detail from Gus Wagner's
scrapbook*

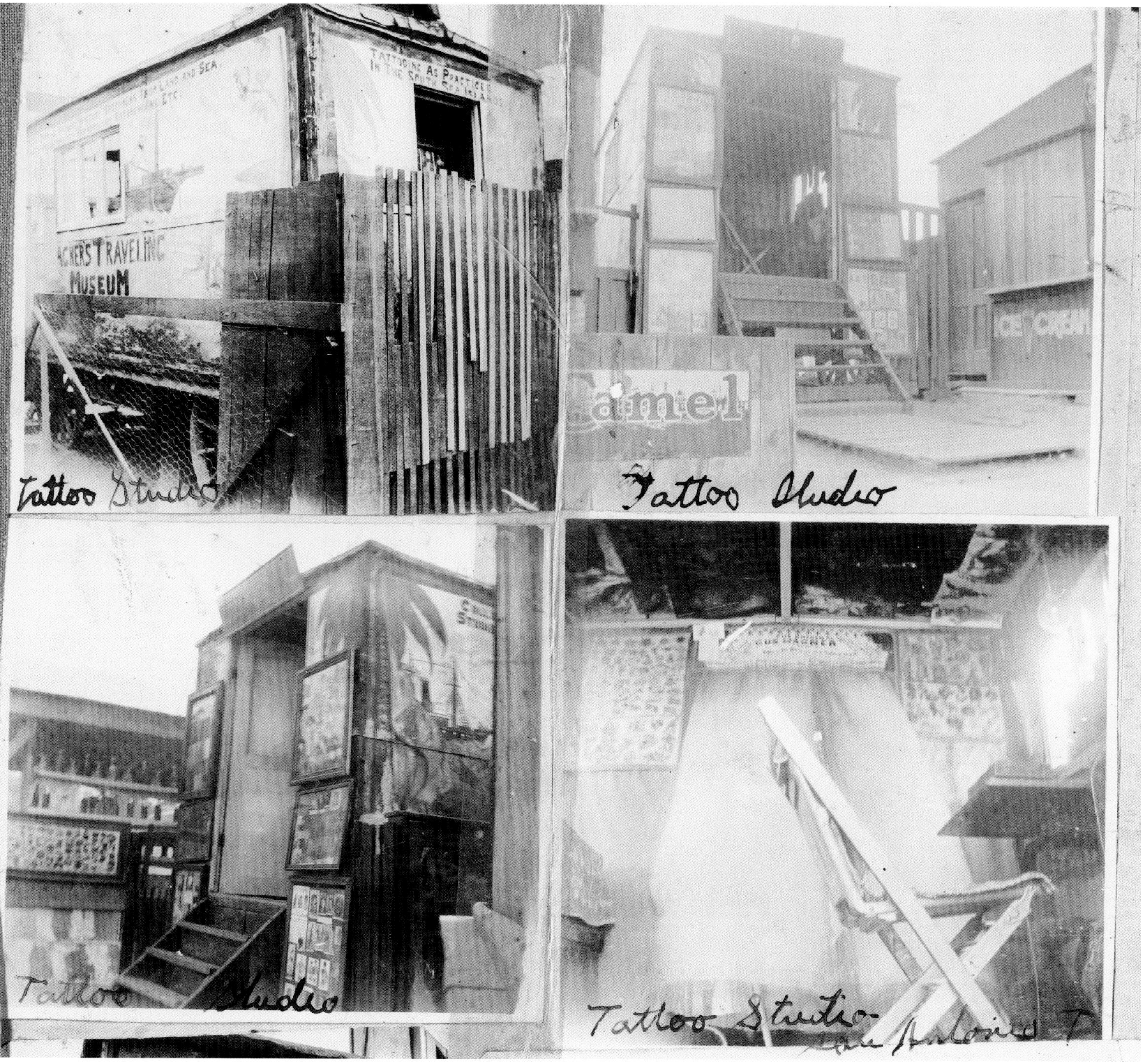

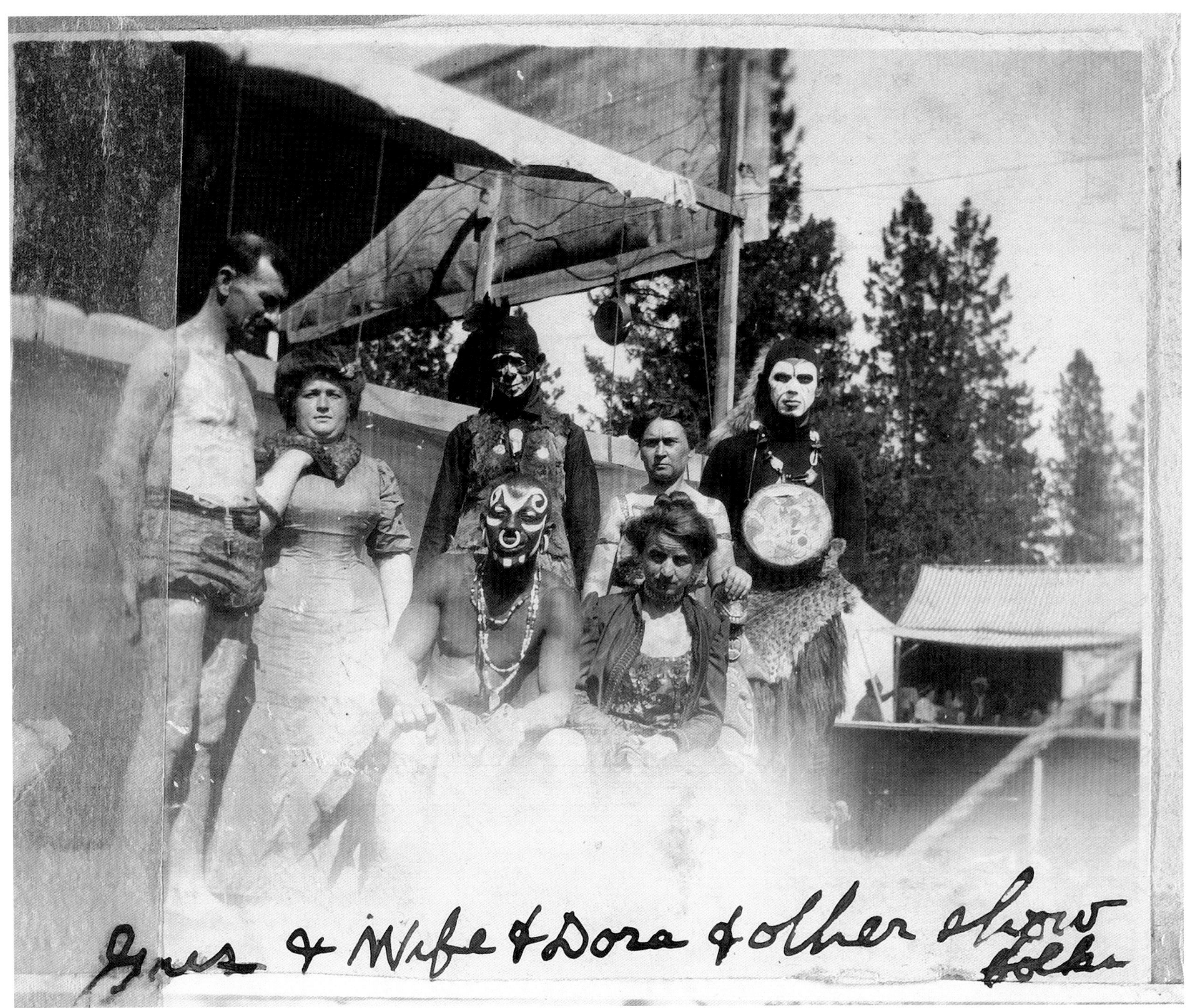

Gus & Wife & Dora & other show folks

*Opposite and right: Details from
Gus Wagner's scrapbook*

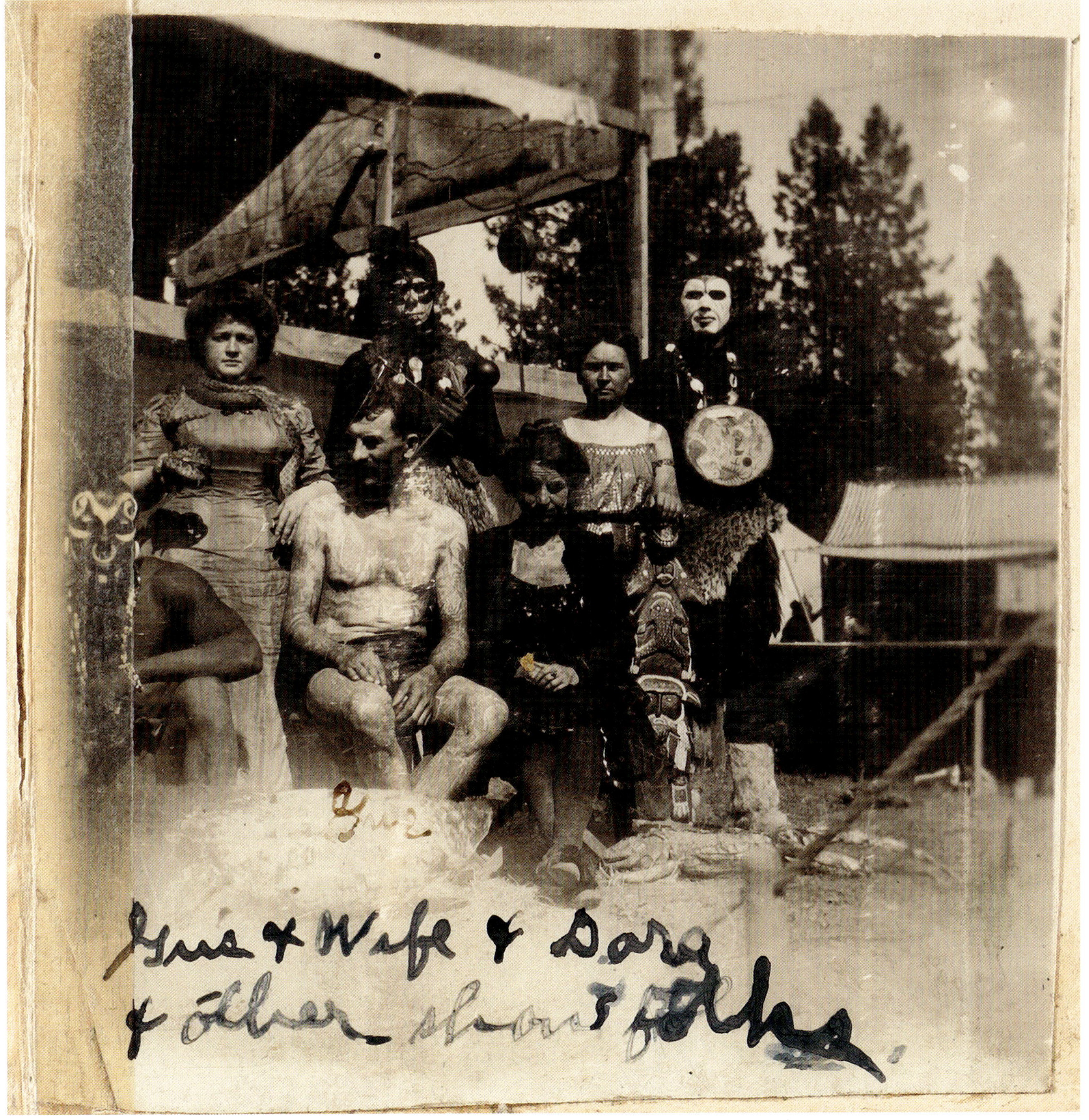

Then the smallpox broke out and we left. Went into San Antonio to the Gunter Hotel. And that night we met a man [named Dan] there from the Knaves and Ellis Circus. They had a one-ring circus and sideshow. Pulled little horses and wagons. That what we called the old mud show days. They had two pony teams, one mule team and three burro teams, and a trained burrow. Mama said, "No"; they both said "No"; they weren't going. They called again that night and they said, "I got a wagon and a team of horses for you. I want you to take the sideshow and go north with it." Mama said, "How far north you goin'?" He said, "To Wichita Falls." She said, "That's not too far from Wichita, Kansas." The ranch was 75 miles north of Wichita. She said, "OK." And when she went up to the room and told Papa, he said that's OK. Me, I knew what circus it was. I'd seen the big red wagons and I'd seen the gold carvings, and the fancy white horses with the big pawns on their heads. I was so glad we were going to have one of them wagons.

So, we got into Fredericksburg, and Dan met us at the train in his Ford. We went out to the circus lot, and I didn't see no big pretty rides. We went around back, and I still didn't see any big pretty rides. Dan drove up to a sheep herder's wagon, and said, "This here's your wagon." And he said, 'Here's your tent." One big old flea-bitten white horse. Looked like he was flea-bitten, but he was so old he had brown specks on him. And one very pregnant little bay and mustang mare. They were beautiful white horses. We spent seven months on the trip up to Wichita Falls. Went to Mexia during the oil boom, in Burkburnett, all through all of 'em.

My folks traveled around with several other shows for a few years. 1917 they went into San Antonio for the war. They put a tattoo shop in on West Houston Street, San Antonio. Tattooed through the war up there, in San Antone. After the war was over, they just traveled all over the United States, here, there, and yonder. And had tattoo shops in St. Louis one winter and Kansas City many winters. We went to Florida and all down through the East Coast. And all the time they were tattooing.

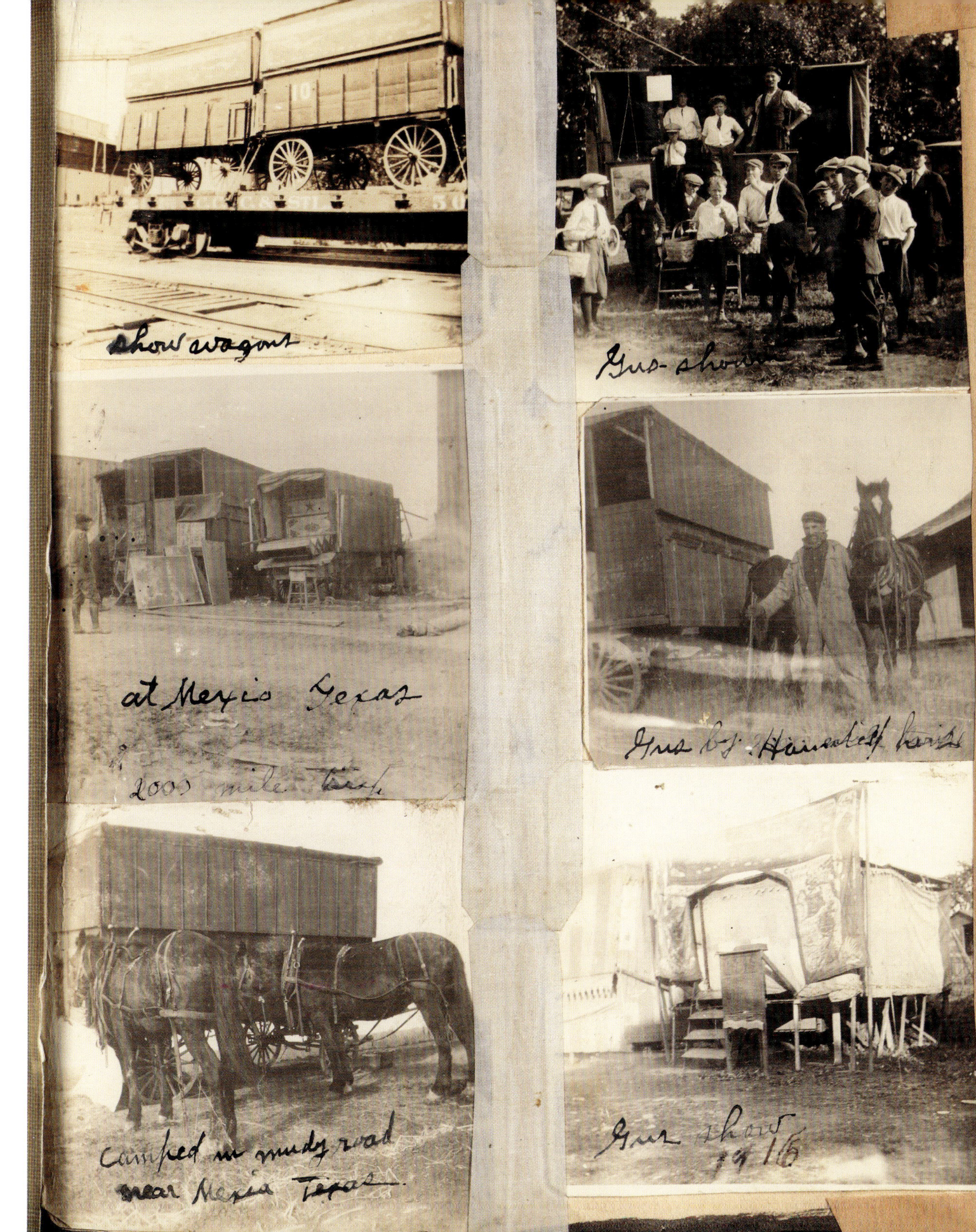

Page from Gus Wagner's scrapbook

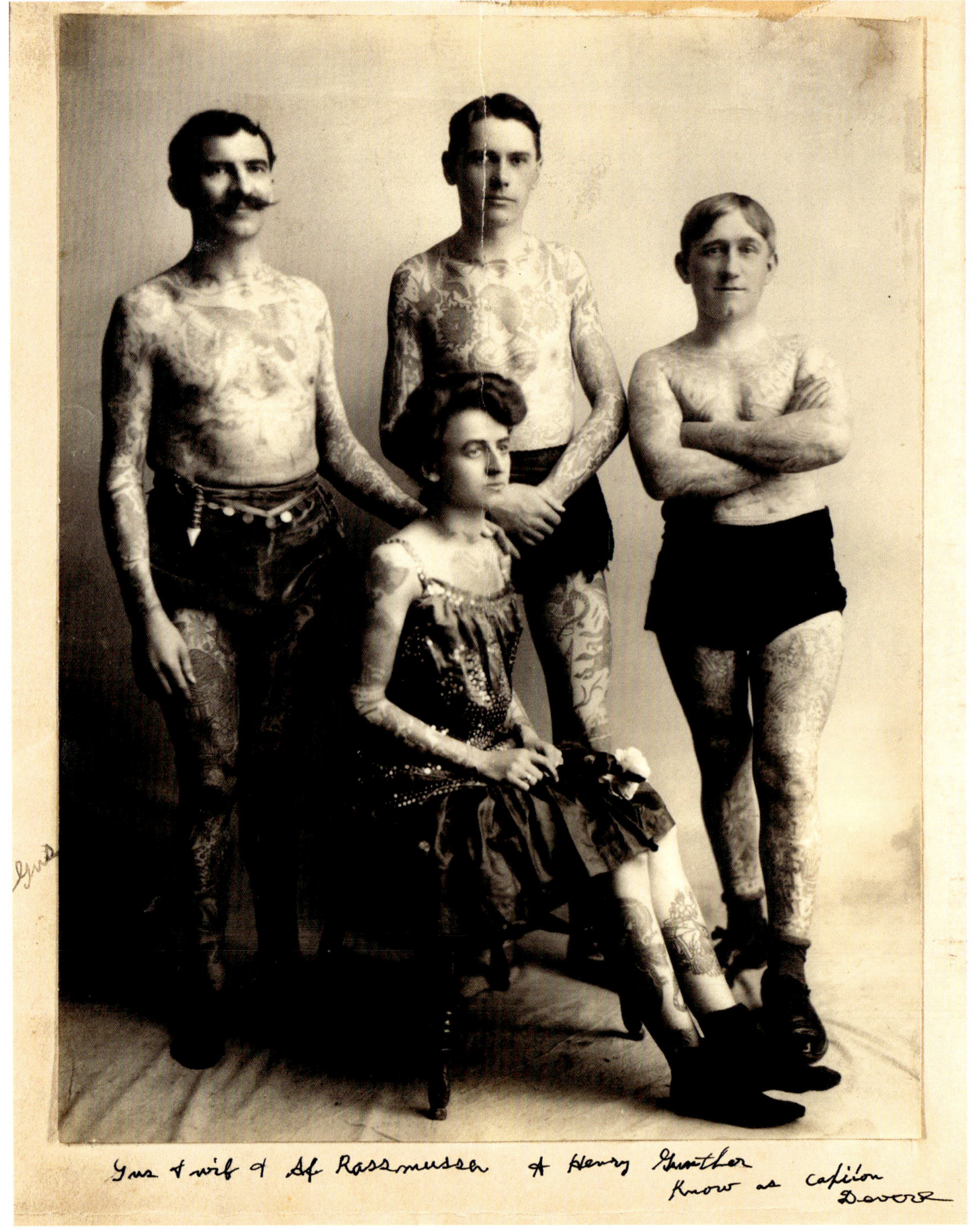

Left and opposite: Pages from Gus Wagner's scrapbook

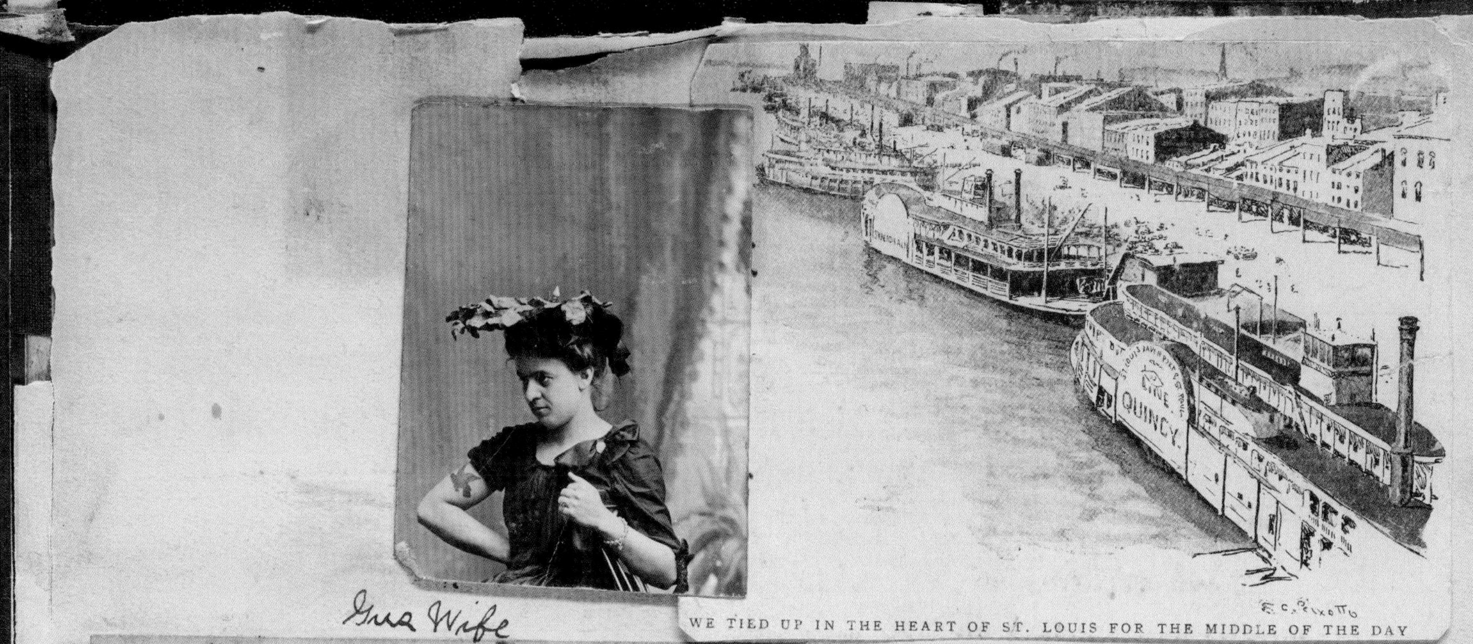

Gna Wife

WE TIED UP IN THE HEART OF ST. LOUIS FOR THE MIDDLE OF THE DAY

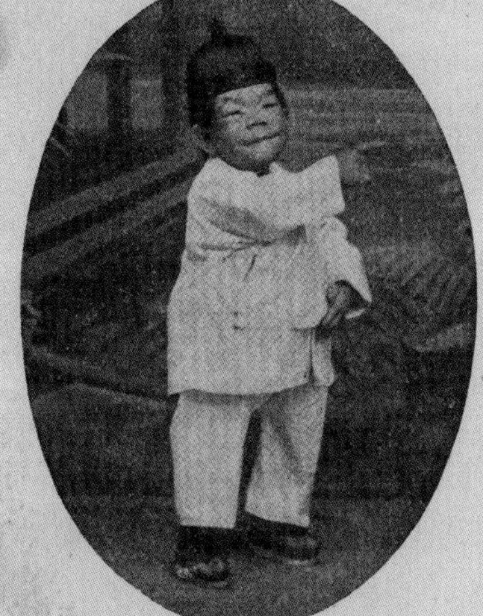

WAGNER & STEVENS SISTERS

—FEATURING—

"WU CHING MA"

Chinese Boxer Dwarf, and

"THE BABY MERMAID"

Found in the Polynesia Islands.

Two Separate Attractions in One Magnificent and Original Front.

CONTROLLING THE FOLLOWING :

"Australian Canon Illusion"   "Prince Charming's Barnyard"   "Horsemobile"
"Relics from Every Quarter of the Globe"   "Peter Kregster the Boer"

Age 44 years.   Height 27 inches.
Weight 48 pounds.

Our performances are continual.   We please the public.   We positively have nothing to offend the most fastidious.   Women and children can attend without escorts.

Here's to Mr.Wagner the one they call Gus,
    Globe trotter,Champion hand Tattoo artist,an independant cuss:
He is a man who never argues,for he has found it dosen't pay,
    So if you don't like his prices,his methods,or stile,be on your way.

For he always adheres to his methods in the strictist kind of form,
    He has never yet possoned,any one nor did them any harm.
His colors are pure,and the very best possible to obtain,
    Hseing antiseptic methods causeing little soreness,scabbing up,or pain.

And what ever Gus may tell you,may promise, or may say,
    He never falsefies,or misrepresents,therefore t'is bound to be that way.
By closely observeing this rule and method,Never cahngeing,always the same.
    Has placed him at the top of the ladder,of both success and fame.

He is well deserving of the title cahmpion for that is just what he is,
    And there is'nt a liveing person,who can beat him at his bis:
If ever you want tattooing done,just take this tip from me,
    Don't fail to look up old GUS WAGNER where ere he may chance to be.

He has now built himself a house upon awagon,so where ever he may roam
    He shall always have along with him his cosy little home.
For the present you may find him in his wagon home so neat
    At No.________ __Huston Street.

                        By Prof. W.O.Read.
                        Written especially for Gus
                        in san Antonio Texas June 8th/17.

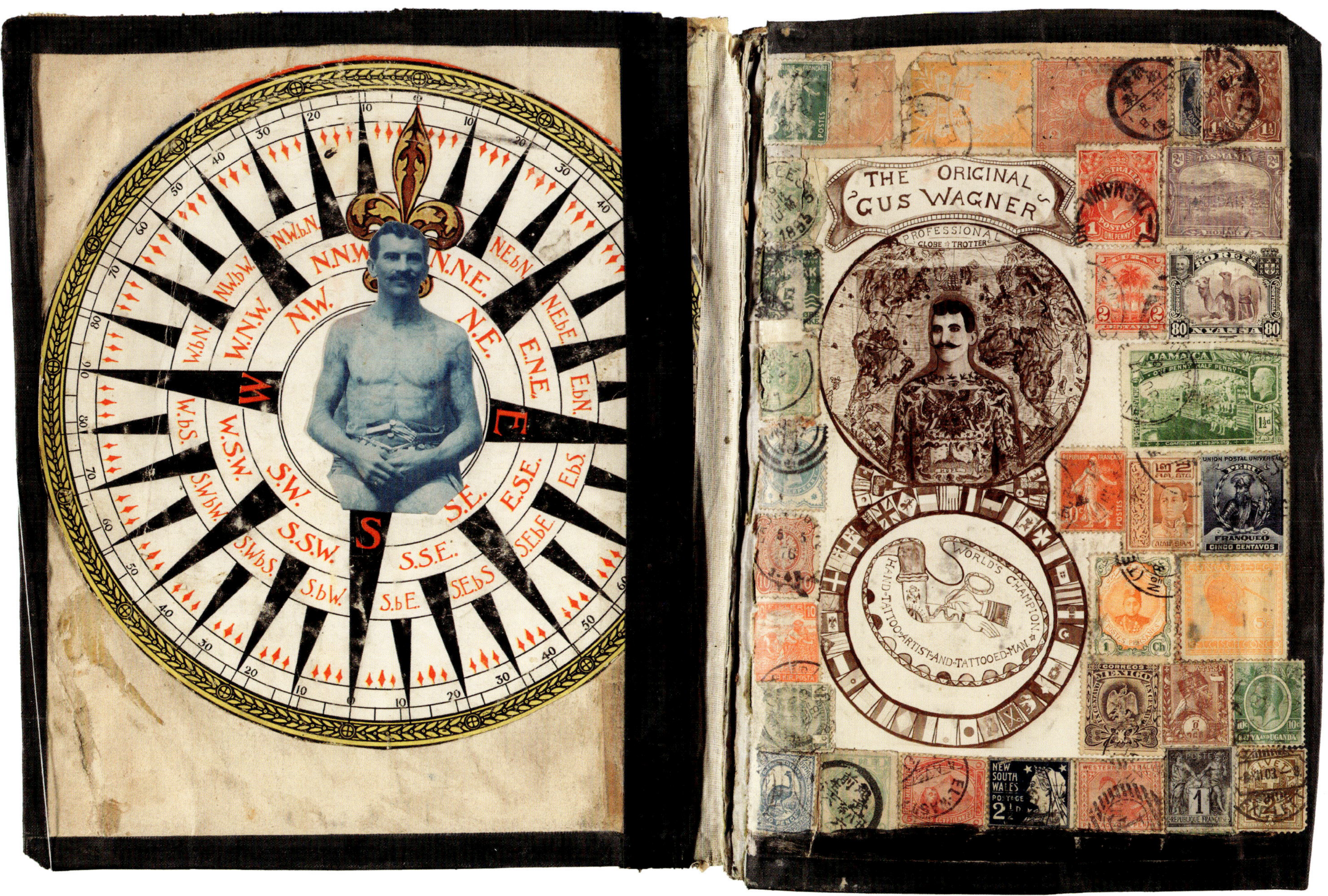

Opposite: Poem about Gus Wagner.
Page from Gus Wagner's scrapbook

Above: Pages from Gus Wagner's scrapbook

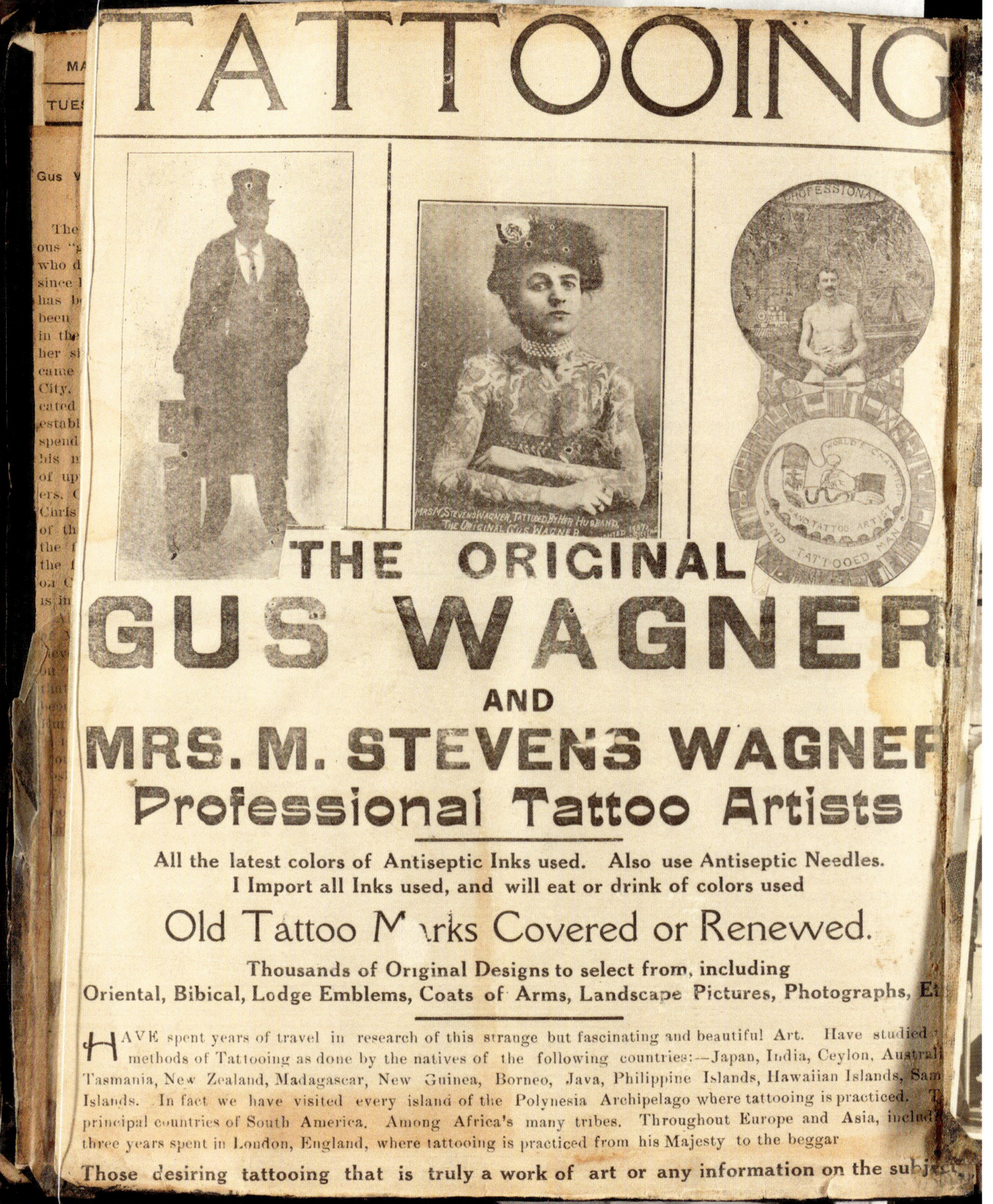

Left: Page from Gus Wagner's scrapbook

Opposite: Detail from Gus Wagner's scrapbook

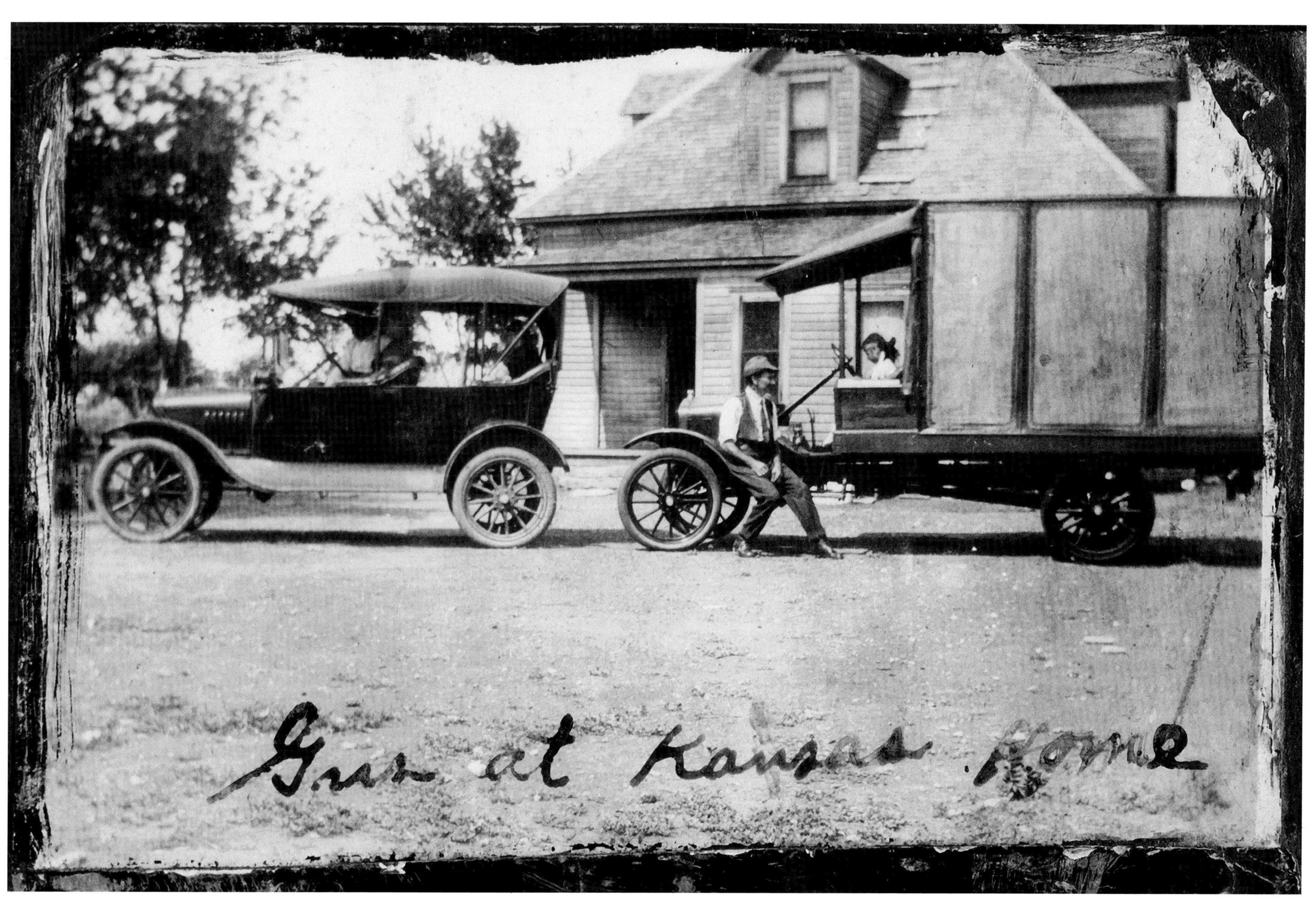

Grss at Kansas Home

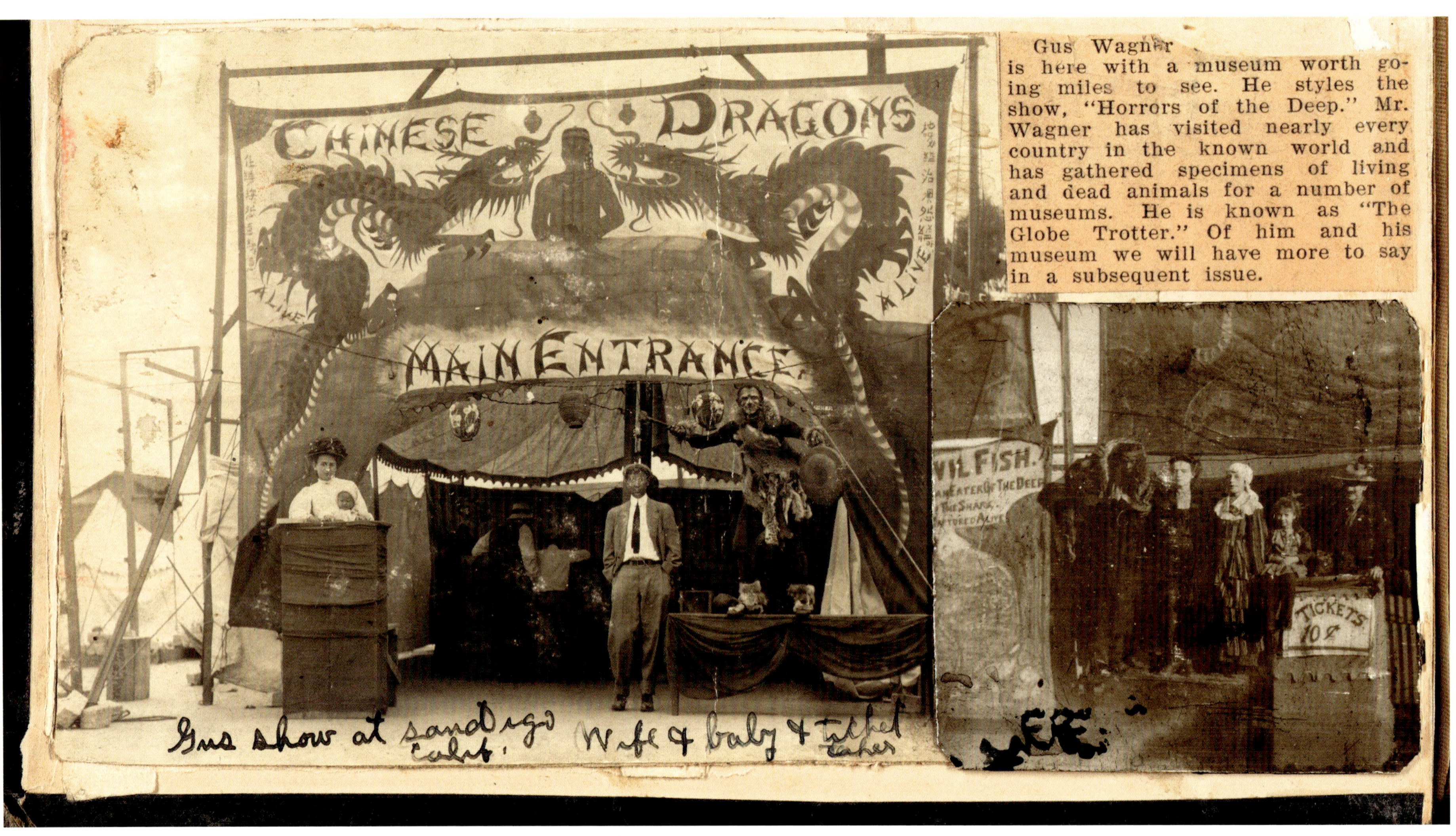

Above: Detail from Gus Wagner's scrapbook

Opposite: Pages from Gus Wagner's scrapbook

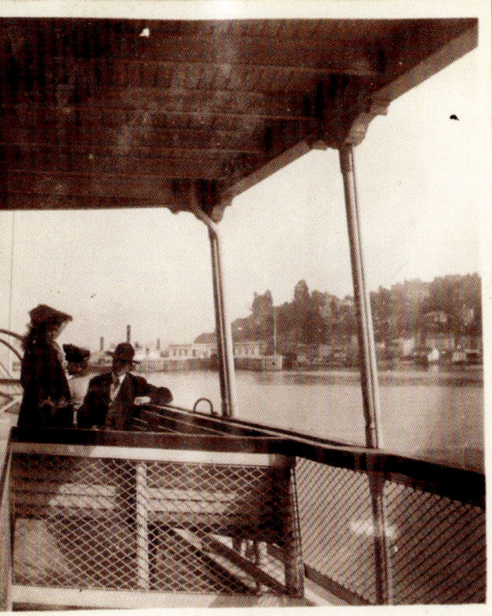

Wife and friend san Francisco boat 1906

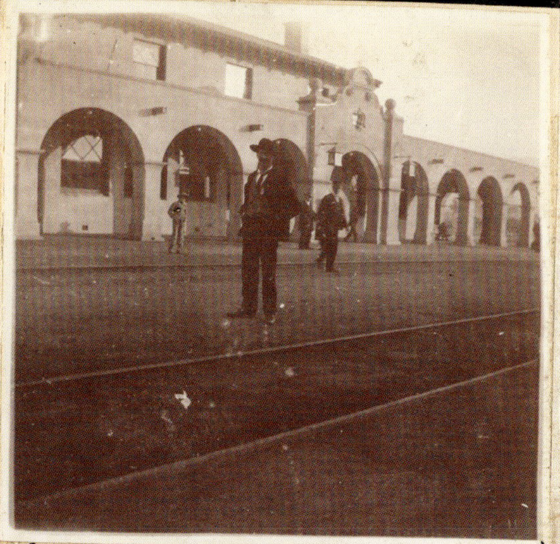

Gus santa Barbara 1909

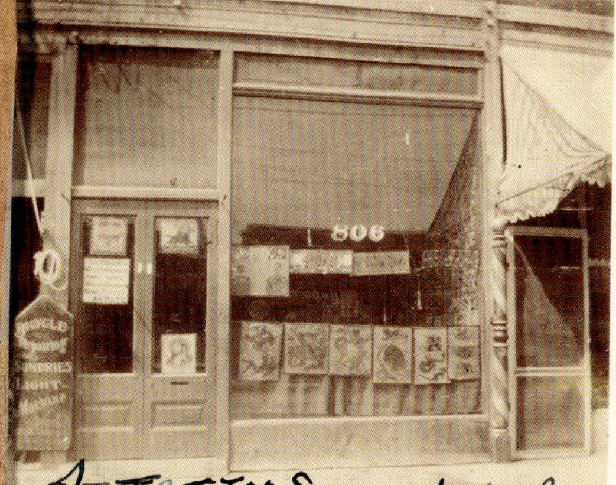

At Tattoo Studio Los Angeles Cal.

GUS WAGNER

THE ORIGINAL AND OLD RELIABLE
HAND TATTOO ARTIST

❦

PROFESSIONAL GLOBE TROTTER

❦

COLLECTOR IN INDIAN ARROWHEADS, ANTIQUES,
GEM ROCKS, MOSS AGATES, ETC.

TRADE TATTOOING WORK AND
TATTOO DESIGNS FOR SAME

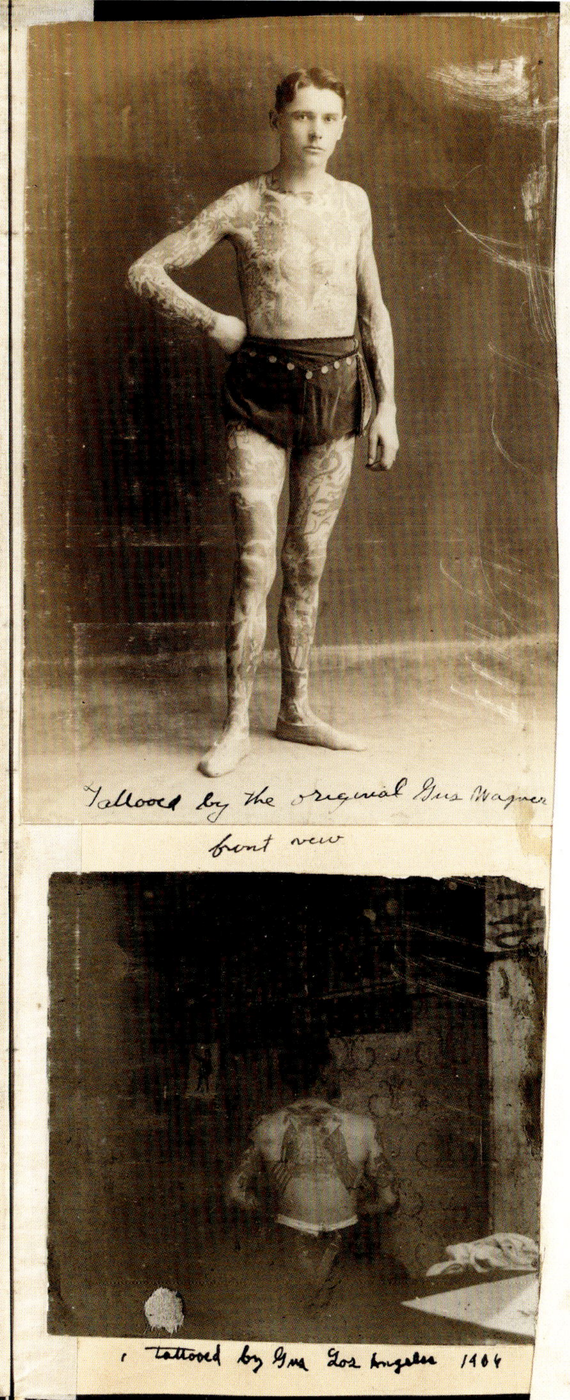

Tattooed by the original Gus Wagner

front view

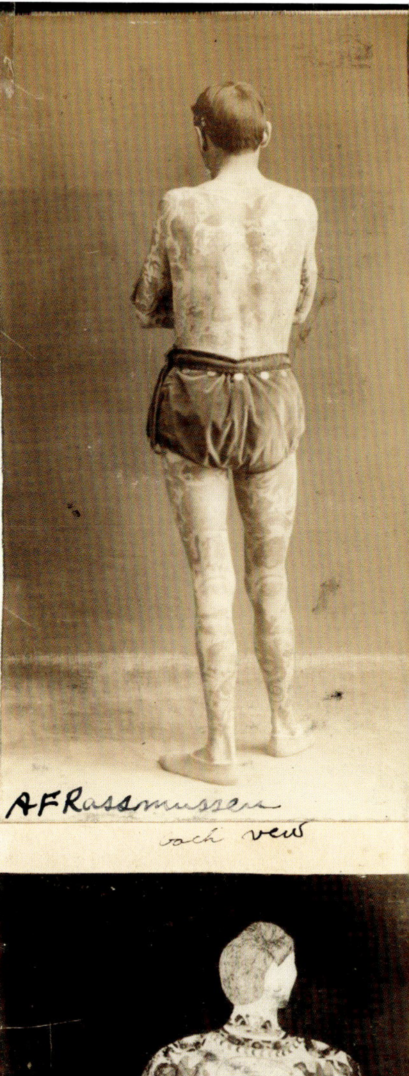

A F Rassmussen

back view

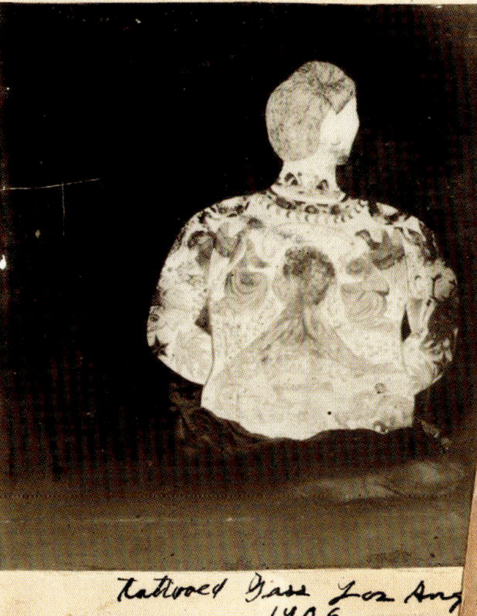

tattooed by Gus Los Angeles 1904

Tattooed Gus Los Ang 1906

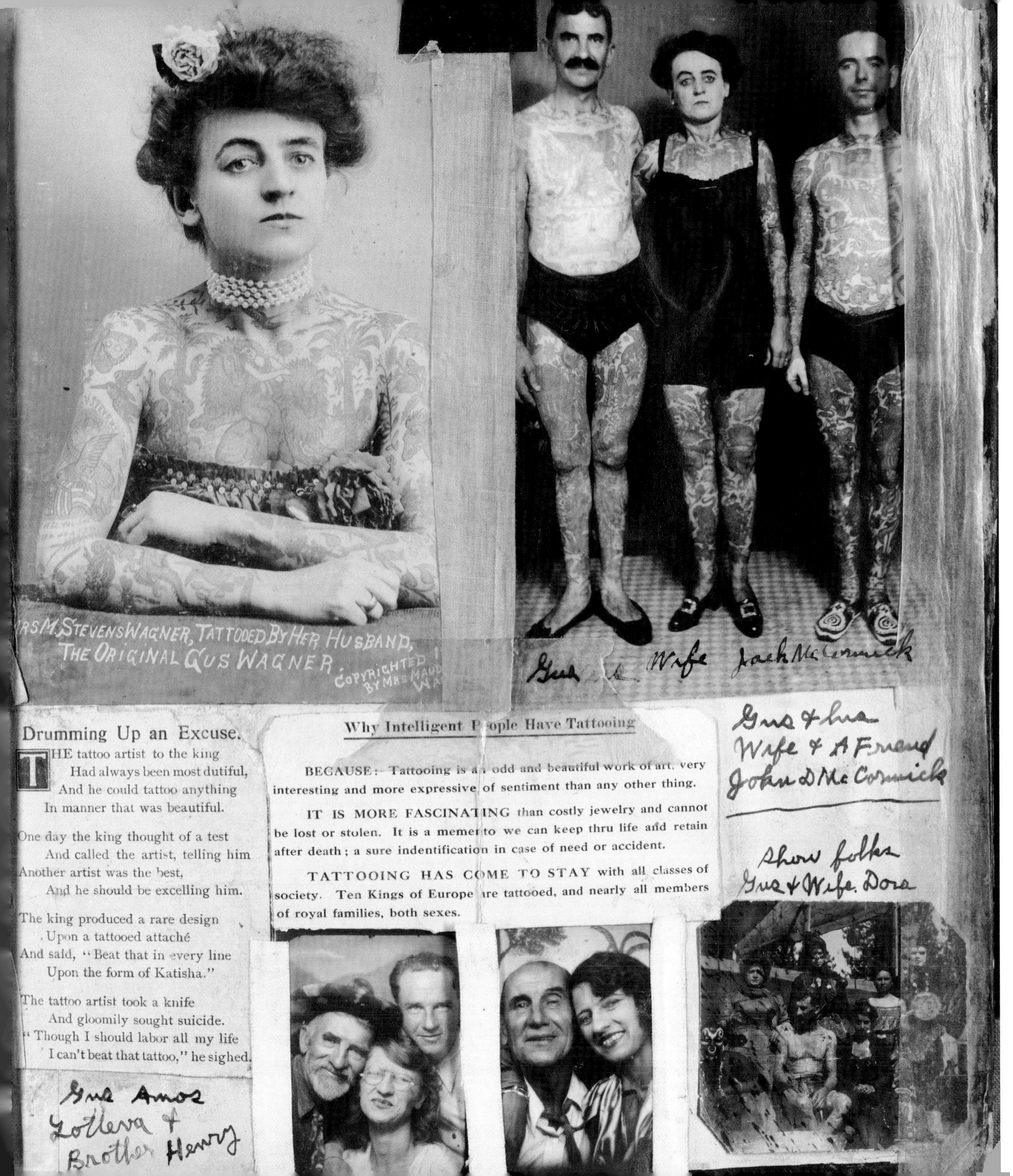

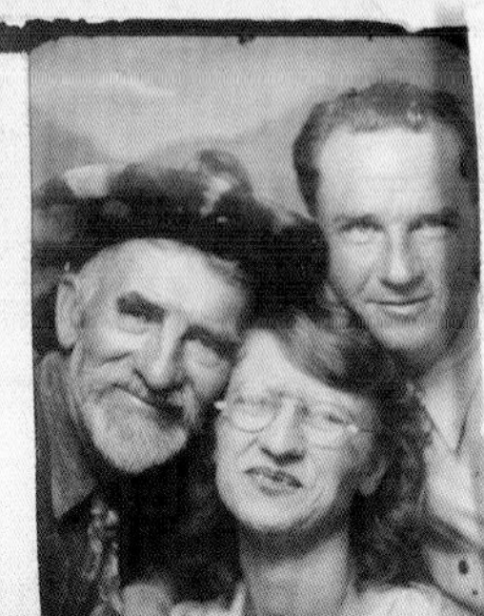
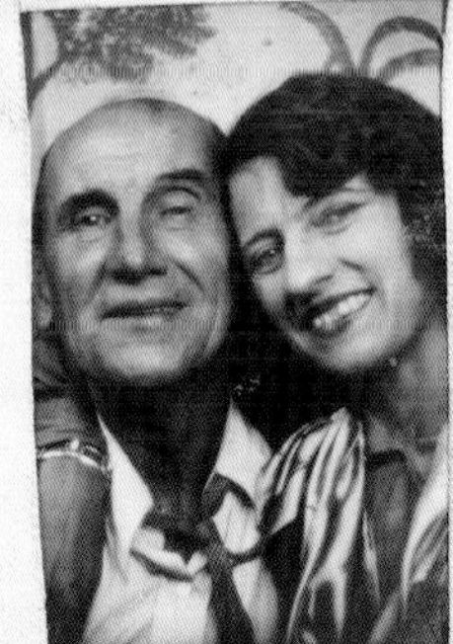
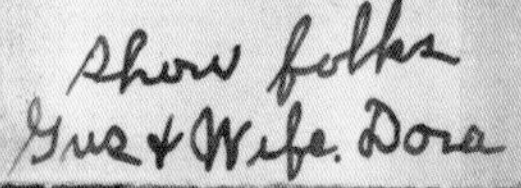
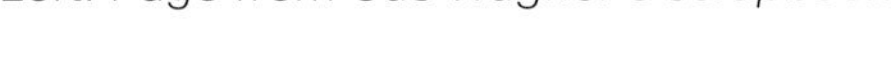

Left: Page from Gus Wagner's scrapbook

Opposite: Gus Wagner with wood carvings, ca. 1930–41

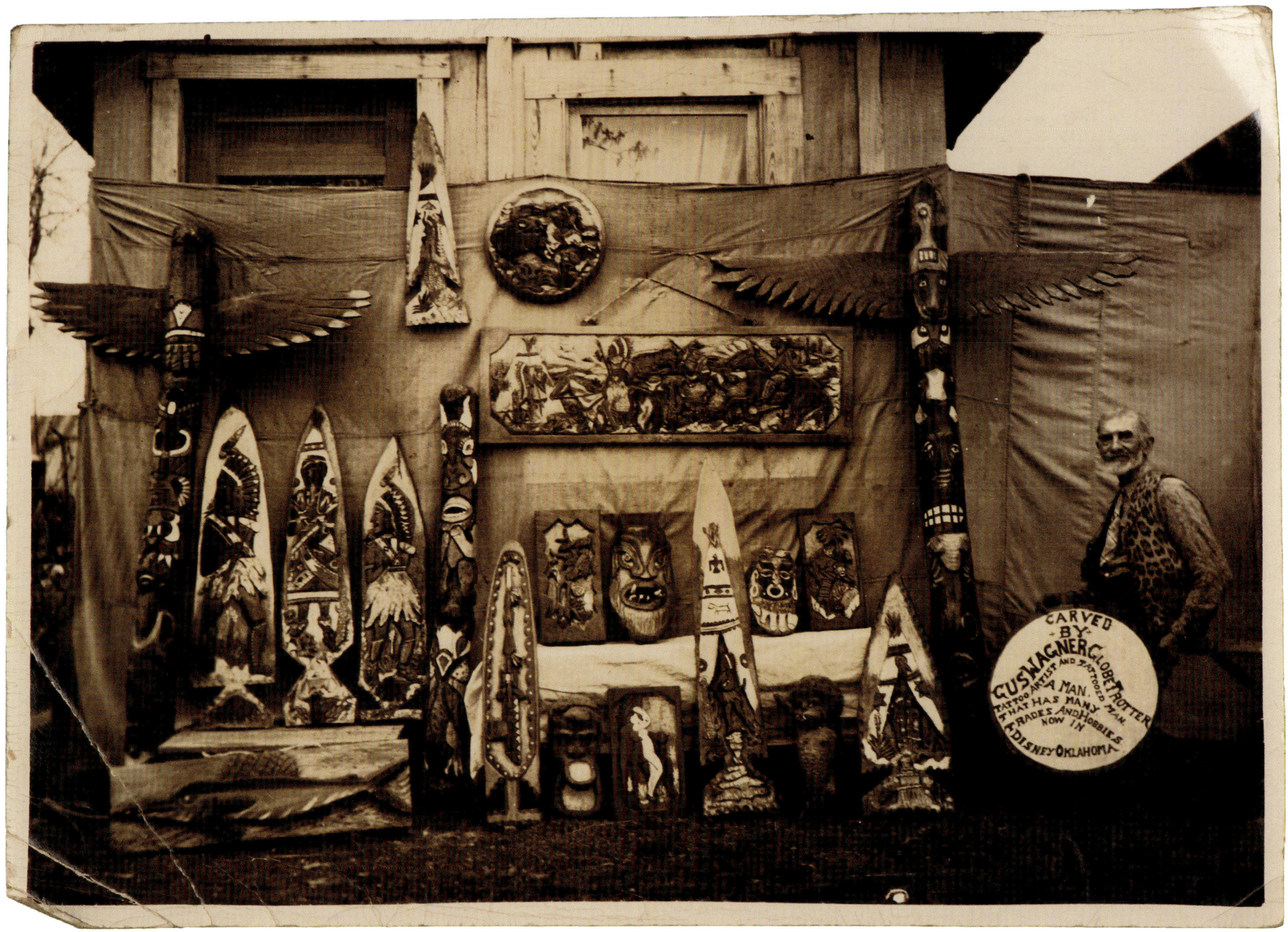
CARVED
BY
GUS WAGNER GLOBE TROTTER
TATTOO ARTIST AND TATTOOED MAN
A MAN
THAT HAS MANY
TRADES AND HOBBIES
NOW IN
DISNEY OKLAHOMA

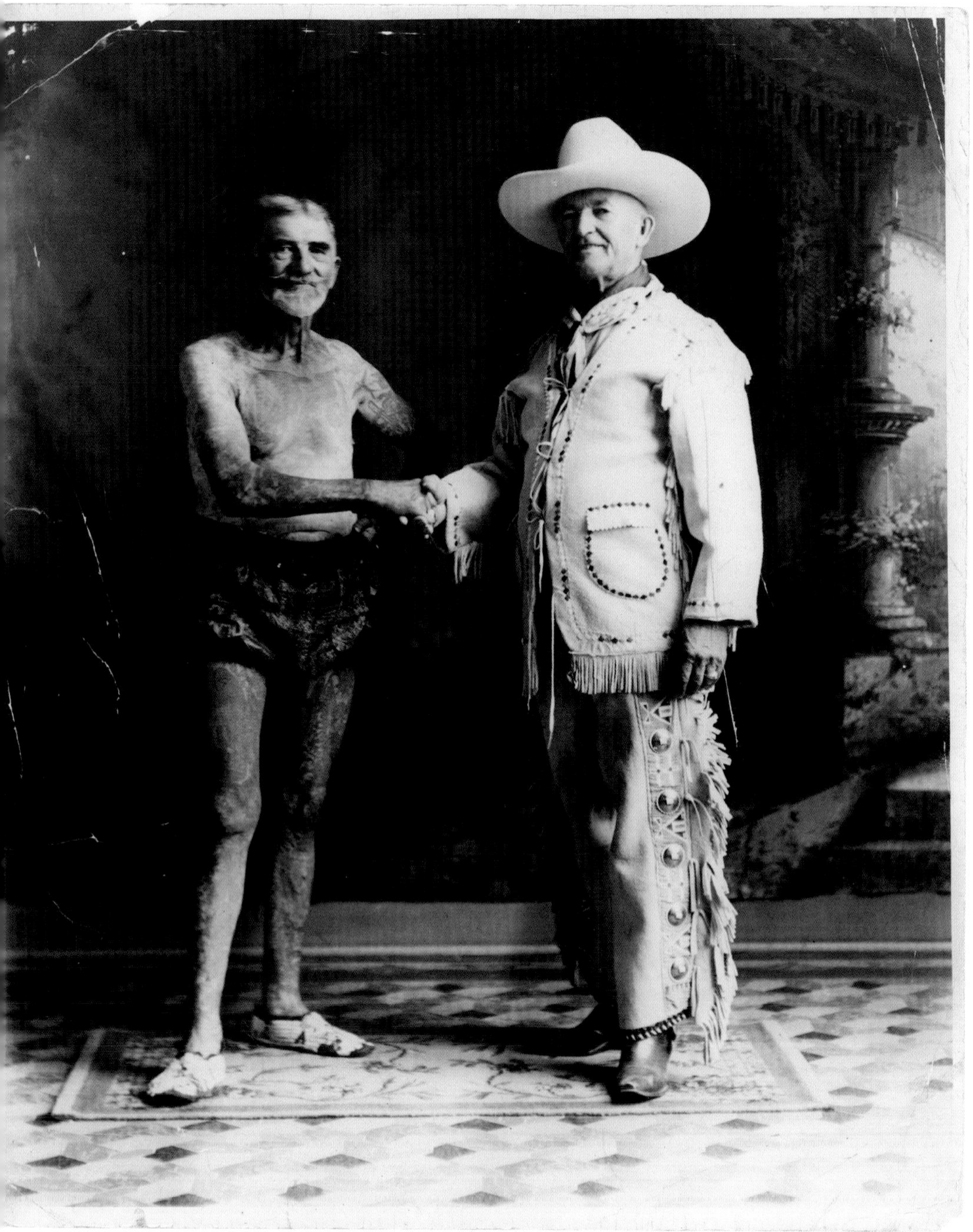

Gus Wagner and Mr. Neff, December 1940

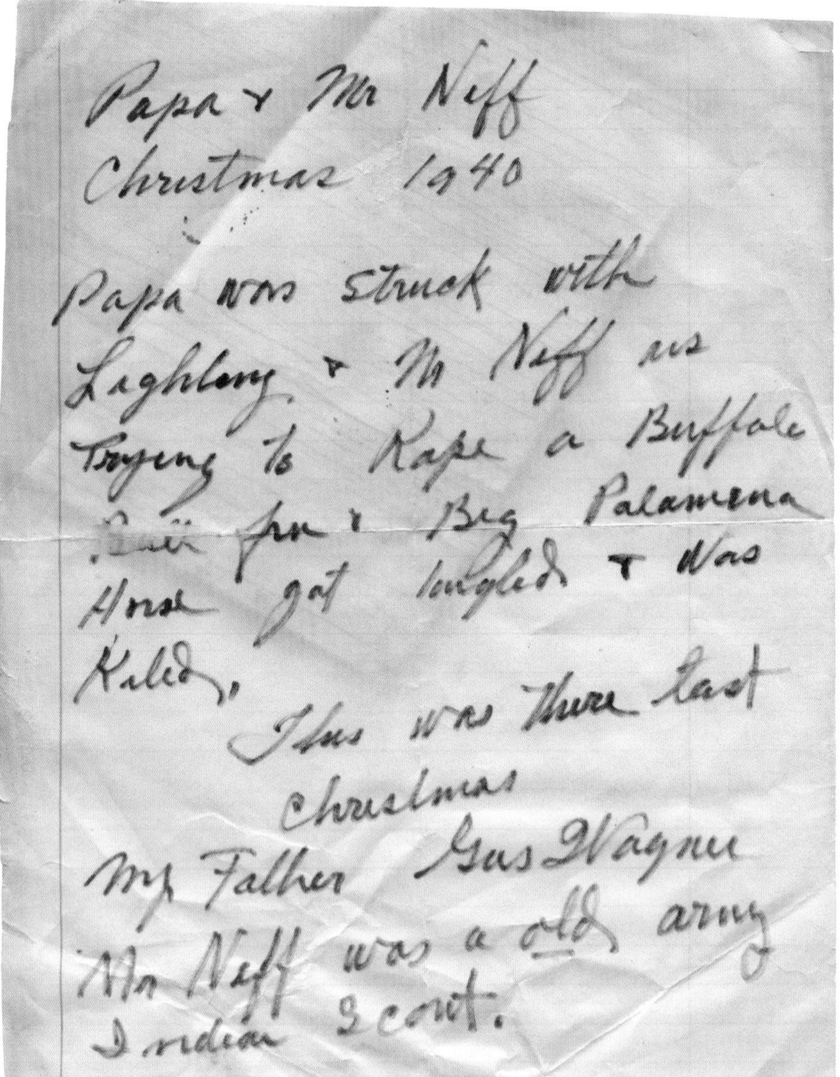

"Papa + Mr. Neff
Christmas 1940
Papa was struck with lightning + Mr. Neff was trying to rope a buffalo bull from a big Palamena [*sic*] horse got tangled + was killed. This was there [*sic*] last Christmas. My father Gus Wagner. Mr. Neff was a old army Indian scout."

Note from Lotteva about these photos

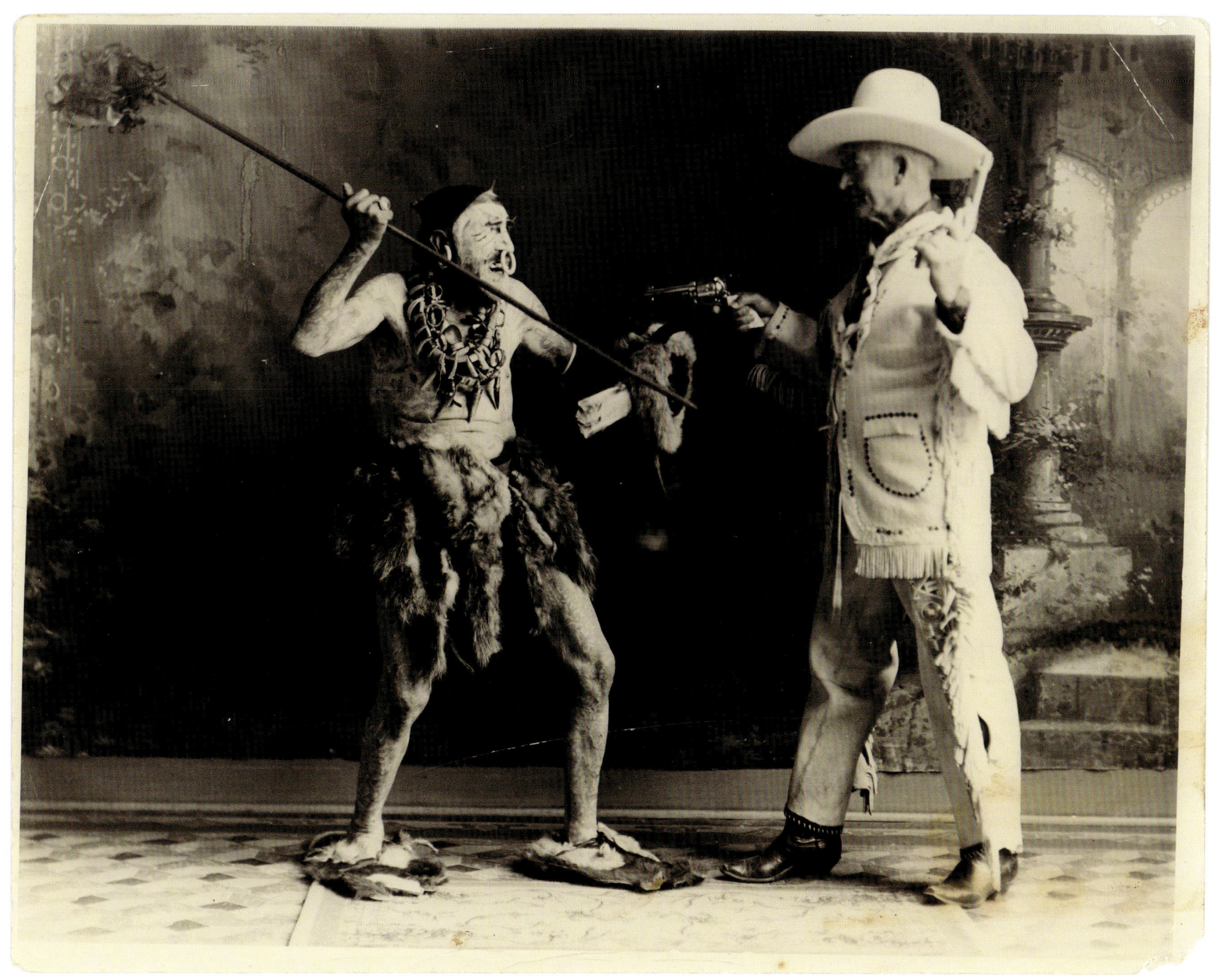

Gus Wagner and Mr. Neff, December 1940

OBITUARIES AND NEWSPAPER CLIPPINGS

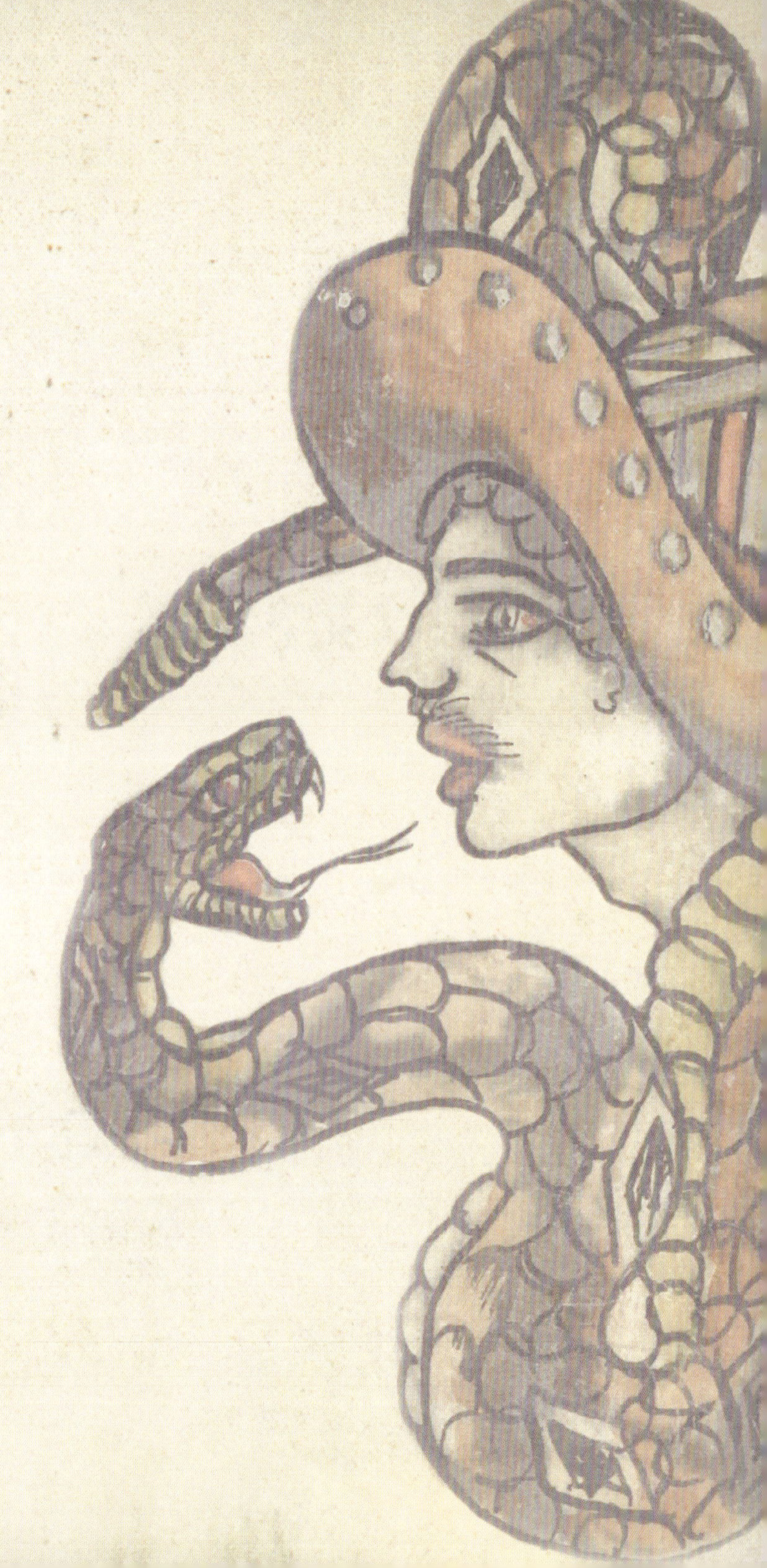

DEATH OF GUS WAGNER

Gus Wagner died at his home at Homestead Tuesday afternoon, June 10. The funeral services will be held Sunday afternoon at 2:00 o'clock at the Stevens home where Mr. Wagner lived. The services will be conducted by Rev. Ray Twining and internment will be in the Homestead cemetery.

Mr. Wagner was 68 years of age. He had been in the show business much of his life and had traveled widely. It was said he had been around the world several times and had visited many foreign countries.

Besides his wife he leaves one daughter and many other relatives.

Obituary (source unknown), courtesy Ron Dolecek and the Wagner family

Wagner Services Are Held Sunday

Homestead Resident Had Traveled Widely With Shows During His Lifetime.

Funeral services for Gus Wagner, Homestead resident for many years, were held Sunday afternoon at the Homestead church and burial was in the cemetery there. Rev. Ray Twining conducted the services.

Mr. Wagner died Tuesday of last week after a year's illness. He was stunned by lightning about a year ago while in Oklahoma and never fully recovered from the shock.

Mr. Wagner was perhaps Chase County's widest traveler. He said he had been around the world twice with show troupes and had been over the greater part of the United States in the show business.

Mr. Wagner lacked six days of reaching his 69th birthday. He was born June 16, 1872.

A daughter of Mr. Wagner has become quite well known around Strong.City and Cottonwood Falls through the cowboy sketches she has put on windows before the Flint Hills rodeos.

GUS WAGNER'S HISTORY MADE UP OF MANY TRAVELS

The life of Gus Wagner who died June 10 at Homestead was an interesting one. He was born June 16, 1872 at Marietta, Ohio. His father was born near Berlin, Germany and his mother at Alsace-Lorraine, France. In early childhood his father came to America with his parents. They were united with the German Lutheran church.

Mr. Wagner married Miss Maud Stevens in the fall of 1903 at Chillicothe, Ohio, while she was touring the east lecturing. Miss Stevens was a native of Kansas residing at the home in Homestead community at that time.

Mr. Wagner spent many years in travel throughout the world. His travels began December 15, 1896 when he left Marietta for a trip to California and the Pacific coast. In the summer of 1897 he visited the Klondike gold fields in Alaska. He returned in the fall to Portland, Oregon, then crossed the United States via the Great Lakes to New York City. Then his career as a globe trotter really began.

He sailed from New York for Europe where he visited Rotterdam, Holland; Aberdeen, Scotland; and Sheldon, England. The next three years he made his headquarters in London, England, though he saw little of England during that time. The same year, 1897, he visited Christiania, Norway; Stockholm, Sweden; Copenhagen, Denmark; St. Petersburg, then the capitol of Russia; and Hamburg, Germany.

In June 1898 he went aboard the British ship "The Indian Prince" and sailed to the West Indies. During his stay with the "Indian Prince" he also visited the Caribbean Sea and the principal Atlantic ports of South and North America.

In the spring of 1899 he left London aboard the "Harleigh Castle" enroute [*sic*] to Odessa, Russia. On this trip he visited Havre, France; Seville, Spain; Marseille, France; Rome and Naples, Italy; Palermo, Sicily; Athens, Greece; and Constantinople. At Odessa he transferred to the steamer "Orient" bound for Eastern Siberia, via the Suez Canal, Red Sea, Indian Ocean, Malacca Straits and the six seas bordering the Eastern coast.

Leaving the "Orient" at Osaka, Japan, Mr. Wagner spent six months on the Island of Nippon in connection with an English plantation. Leaving Japan in the fall of 1899 he visited the Chinese coast and the Philippines. In Feb. 1901, he left Manila for Borneo where he was taken sick with fever and was in a native hospital for many weeks. When able to travel he went to Ceylon, an island south of India, famous for its tea gardens and healthful climate.

A few months on this island and his health was fully regained then he left Ceylon for Bombay, India. Later he visited the Himalaya mountains and crossed the desert of Thurr where an Indian sand storm was encountered.

Leaving India from Calcutta months later, he sailed for Madagascar and Africa. In South Africa he traveled inland 6 weeks with Sanker Bros. circus. From Africa Mr. Wagner went to Australia where he again established headquarters in a foreign country for some time. During this period of time he spent much time around Tasmania, north and south New Zealand and the islands of the Polynesian chain.

During the winter of 1902 he sailed from Honolulu for San Francisco and returned to his beloved home, Marietta, Ohio, having spent 6 years on every sea open to commerce, visited every country that had a flag and many savage lands that knew no flag. His travels and ventures in foreign lands (of which not half have been mentioned) were colorful events that he loved to talk about. After returning from foreign lands, Mr. Wagner then traveled extensively throughout the States, Mexico, Canada and South America.

His chief occupation in life was art and Mr. Wagner had studios in many of the larger cities of the West and midwest. The last seven years he devoted nearly his entire life to wood carving, specializing in Western life and Alaskan Indian totem poles.

Between the years 1909 and 1930, Mr. and Mrs. Wagner spent parts of many summers traveling with shows over much of the western hemisphere.

There were only a few of the ships and places visited by Mr. Wagner but these tell much about his life.

Chase County Leader-News, 1941

FUNERAL SERVICES FOR MISS DORA STEVENS

Miss Dora Stevens was born January 17, 1869, near Toledo, Ohio [Iowa,] and passed away June 30, 1949, at the St. Mary's hospital, Emporia, Kansas, age 80 years, 5 months and 13 days.

When she was 4 months old, her parents, Mr. and Mrs. David V. Stevens started the long trek to Kansas in a covered wagon. When they arrived in Emporia her grandfather Stevens [Roswell W. Stevens] met them. They spent the next year at construction work on the Santa Fe Railroad. In 1870 her father homesteaded 11 miles south of Emporia in what is now known as The Section Community. It was here where she spent her girlhood days, herding cattle on the open range, riding a mustang of the early day type. Her second saddle horse was a white Arabian which died at the age of 26 years at her home in Chase County.

The family moved from Lyon County to Chase County February 1906 [1896,] settling in the Homestead community which is their present home.

In the early 1900s she spent some time in Oklahoma when it was sparsely settled and many cities of today had only a depot and general store.

During her 80 years she traveled over the greater portion of the U.S. but was always happy to return to the plains of Kansas. She wished to rest through Eternity here besides her pioneer parents.

Survivors include, her sister, Mrs. Maud Stevens Wagner, a niece L. [Lotteva] Wagner Doris [Davis], an uncle I. N. McGee of Ponca City, Oklahoma and a host of cousins and friends.

HOLD RITES AT HOMESTEAD FOR MRS. MAUDE WAGNER

Graveside funeral services for Mrs. Maude S. Wagner, who died Saturday at her home in Lawton, Okla., were held at 3:30 p.m. Tuesday at the Homestead cemetery. Mrs. Belle Bond officiated. The pallbearers were David Mercer, Alfred Mercer, Lee Gurney, John Gurney, Cecil Yoakem and Albert Odle.

Maude Stevens was born February 12, 1877, in Emporia a daughter of David and Sarah Stevens. She was married to Gus Wagner in St. Louis, Mo., on October 3, 1904. Mr. Wagner died in 1941. The Wagners lived for many years in the Homestead vicinity. For the last 12 years Mrs. Wagner had made her home with a daughter, Mrs. Lotteva Davis in Lawton, who is her only immediate survivor. Besides her parents and husband, she was preceded in death by an infant daughter, Sarah J. and a sister, Dora.

Those attending from Lawton, Okla., were R. E. Davis, Mrs. C. A. Elkins, G. P. Horton, Lee Sever, and C. B. Falley. The group was at the Alfred Mercer home for lunch following the services.

Chase County Leader-News, February 1, 1941

FLASH IN GUS WAGNER'S COLLECTION

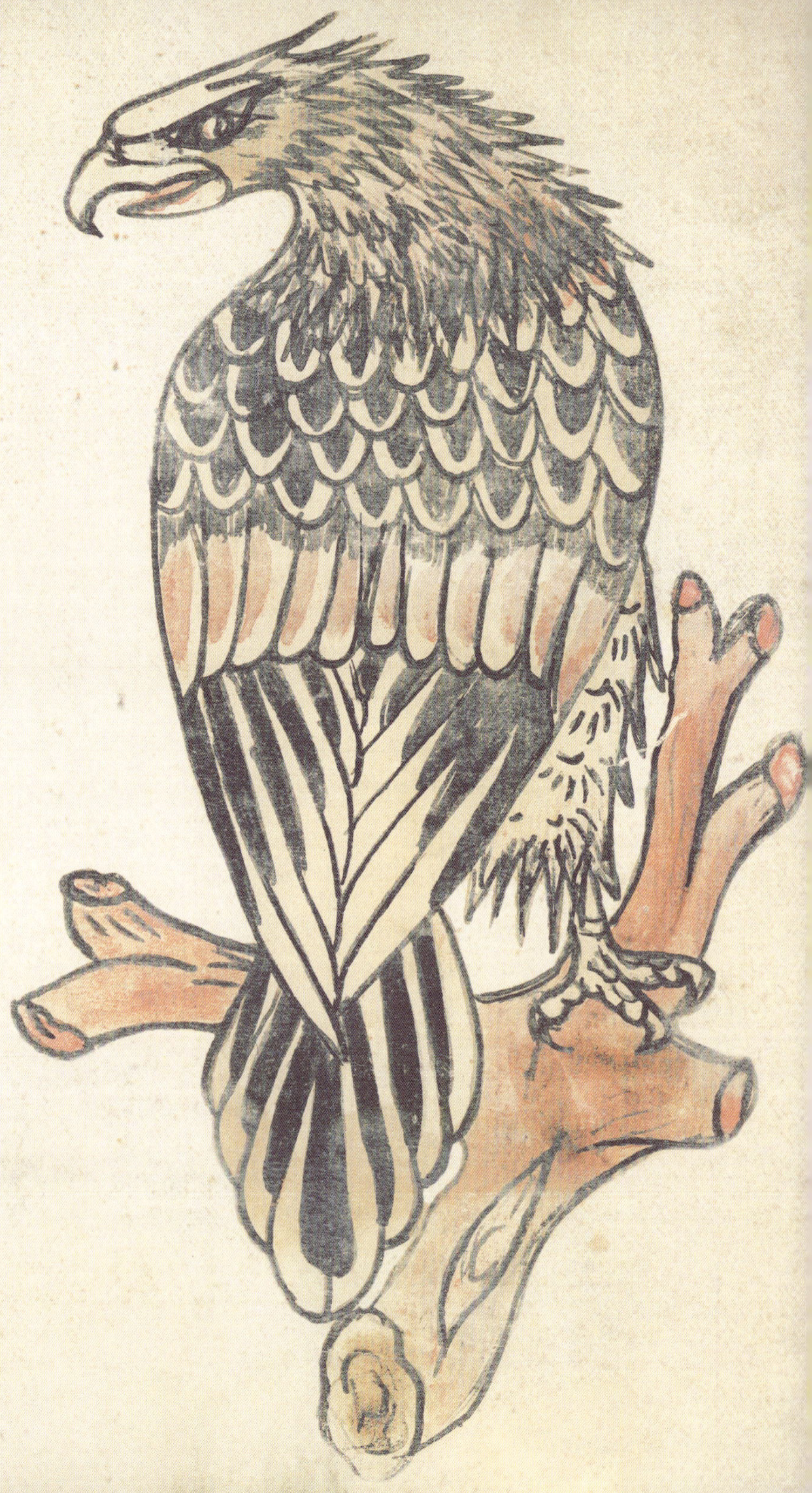

While Gus Wagner rarely signed his flash, it's clear that most of the pieces in his collection were likely made by him. Some are signed by others, and there are additional unsigned pieces where the artist is unclear.

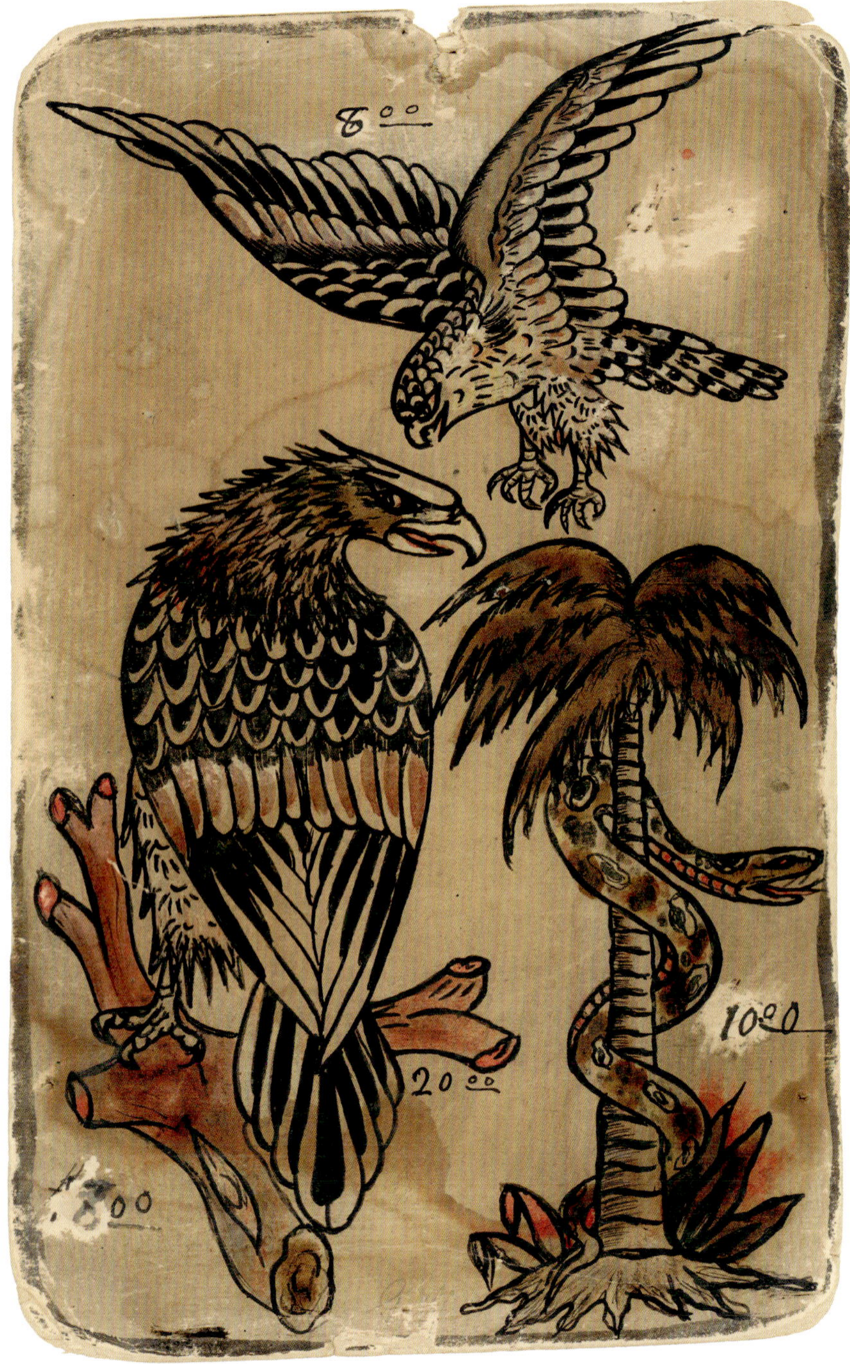

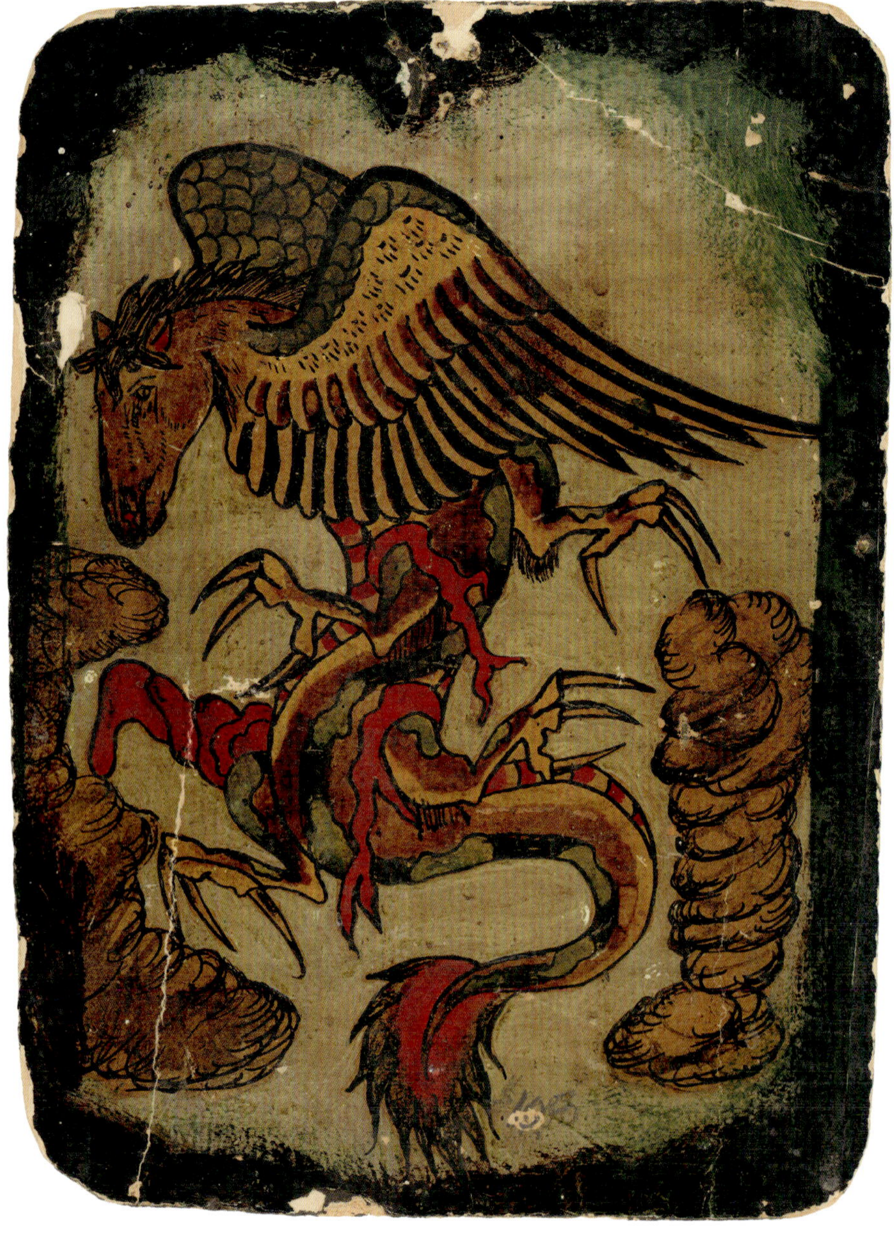

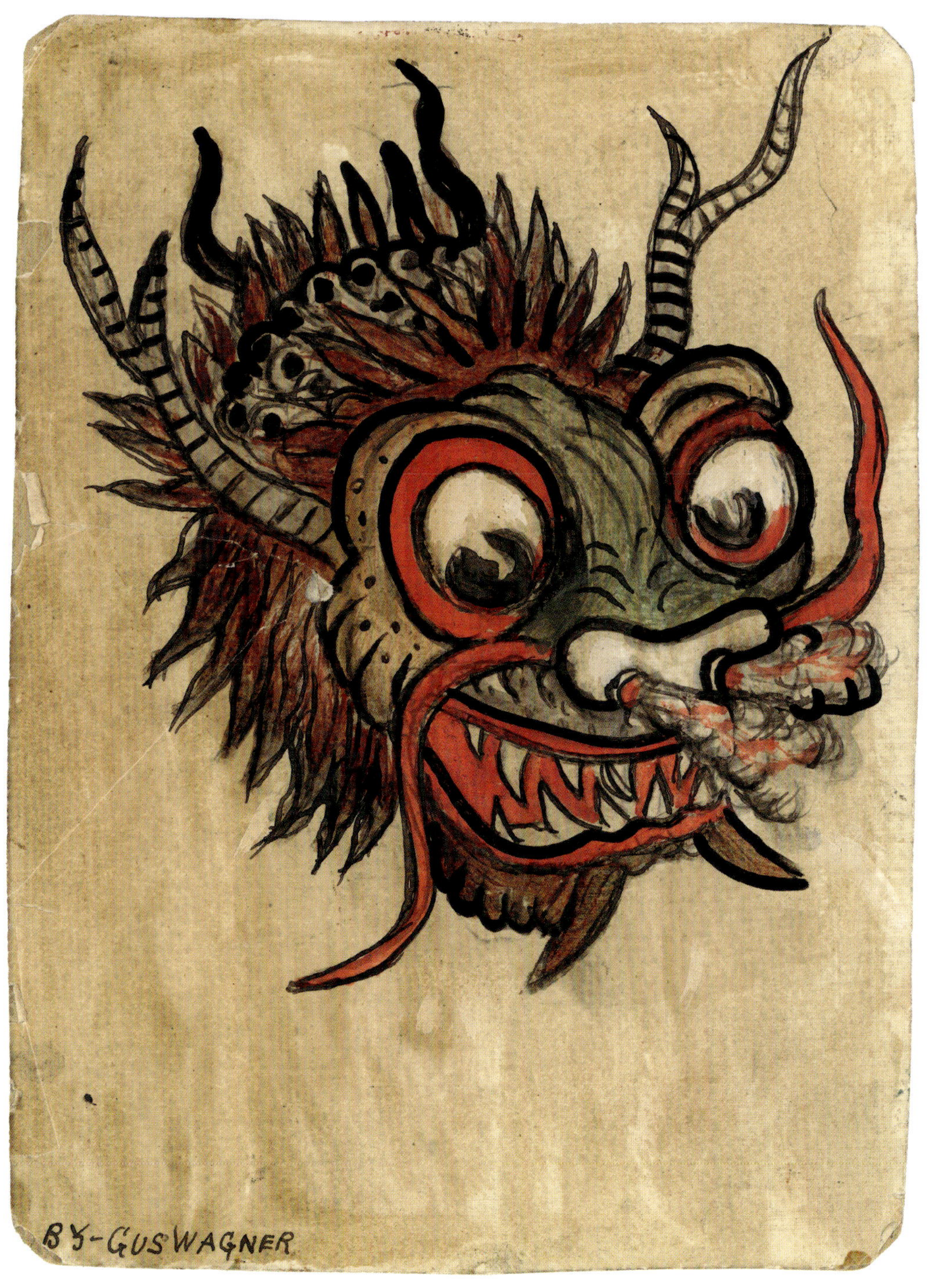
BY-GUS WAGNER

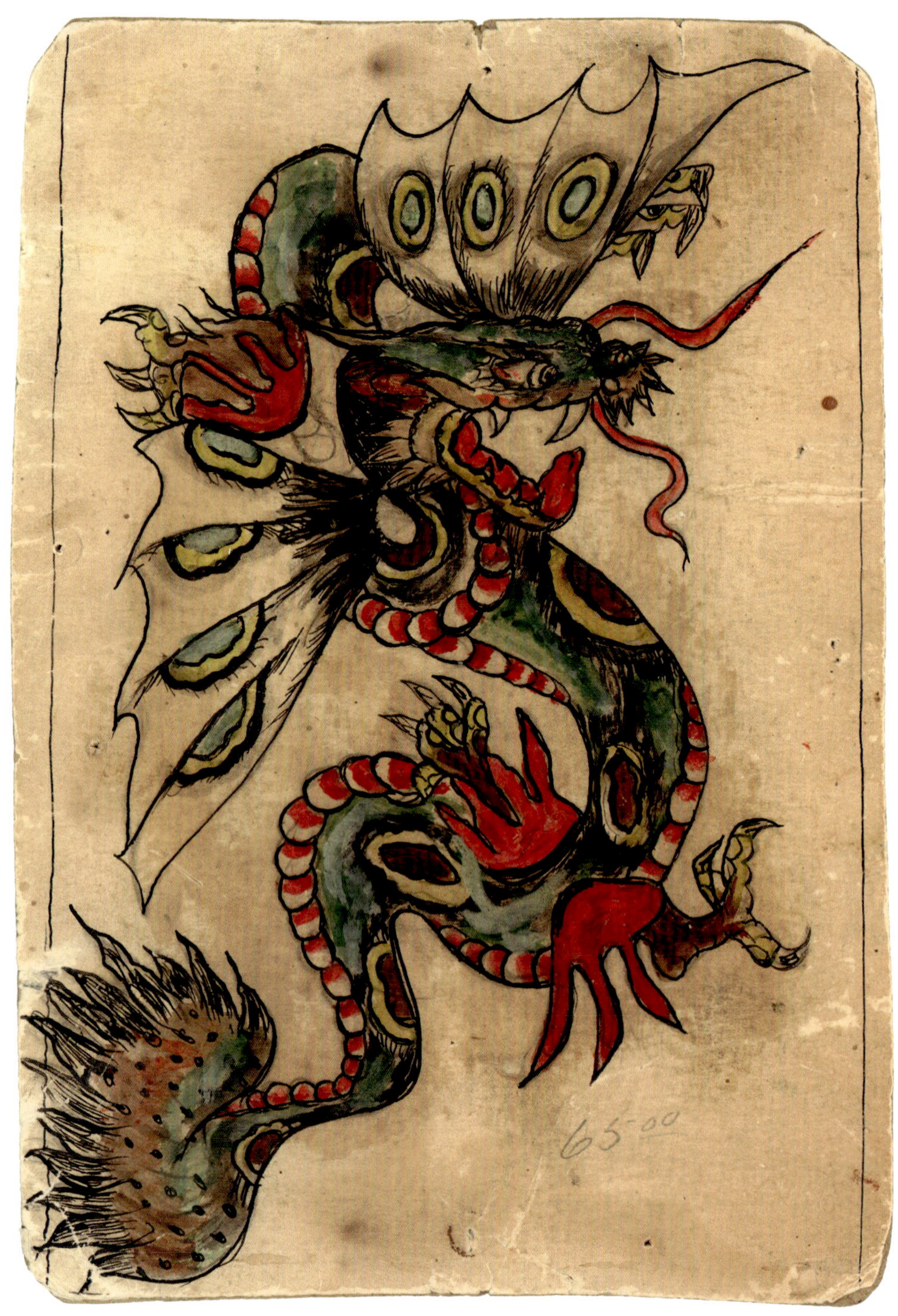

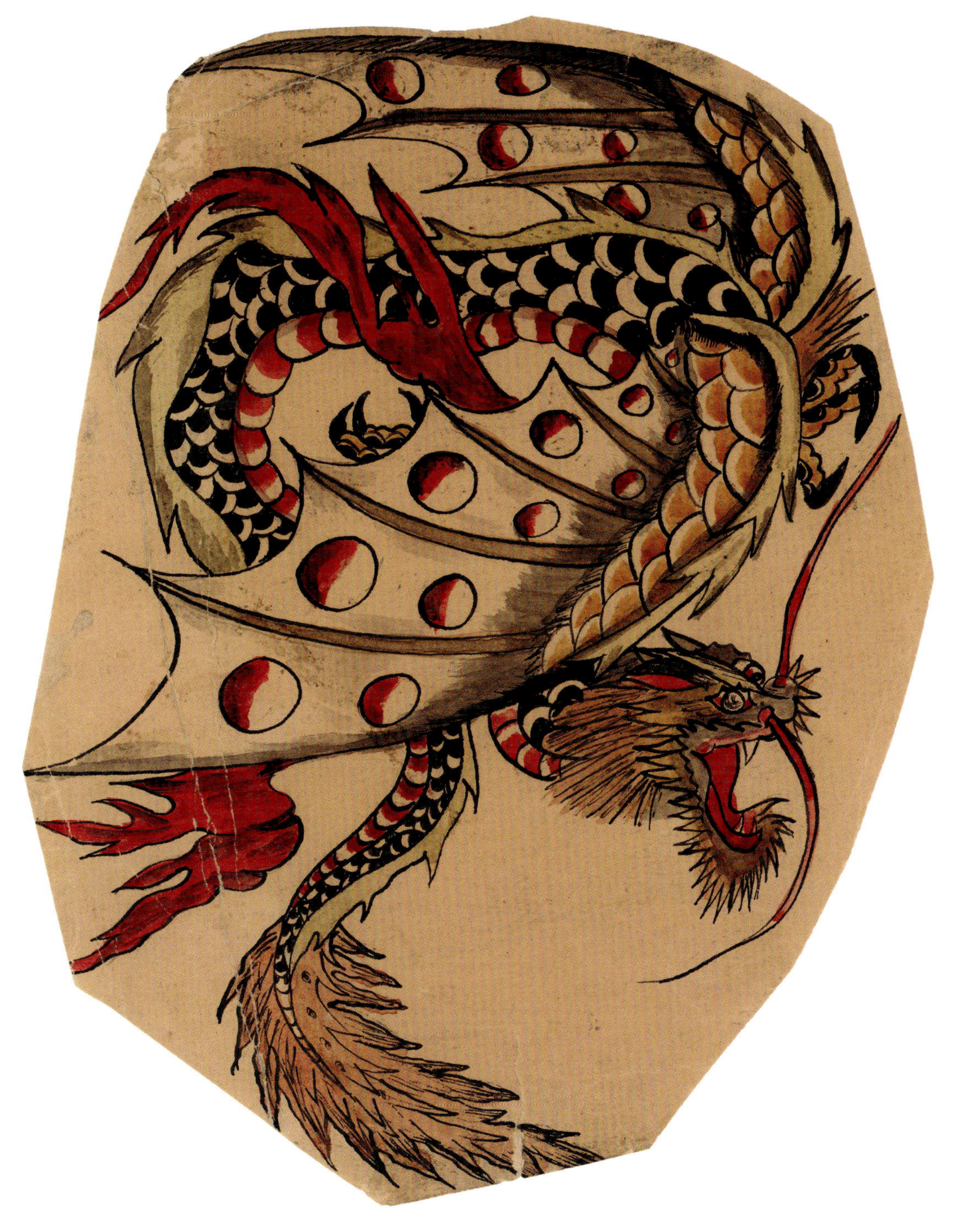

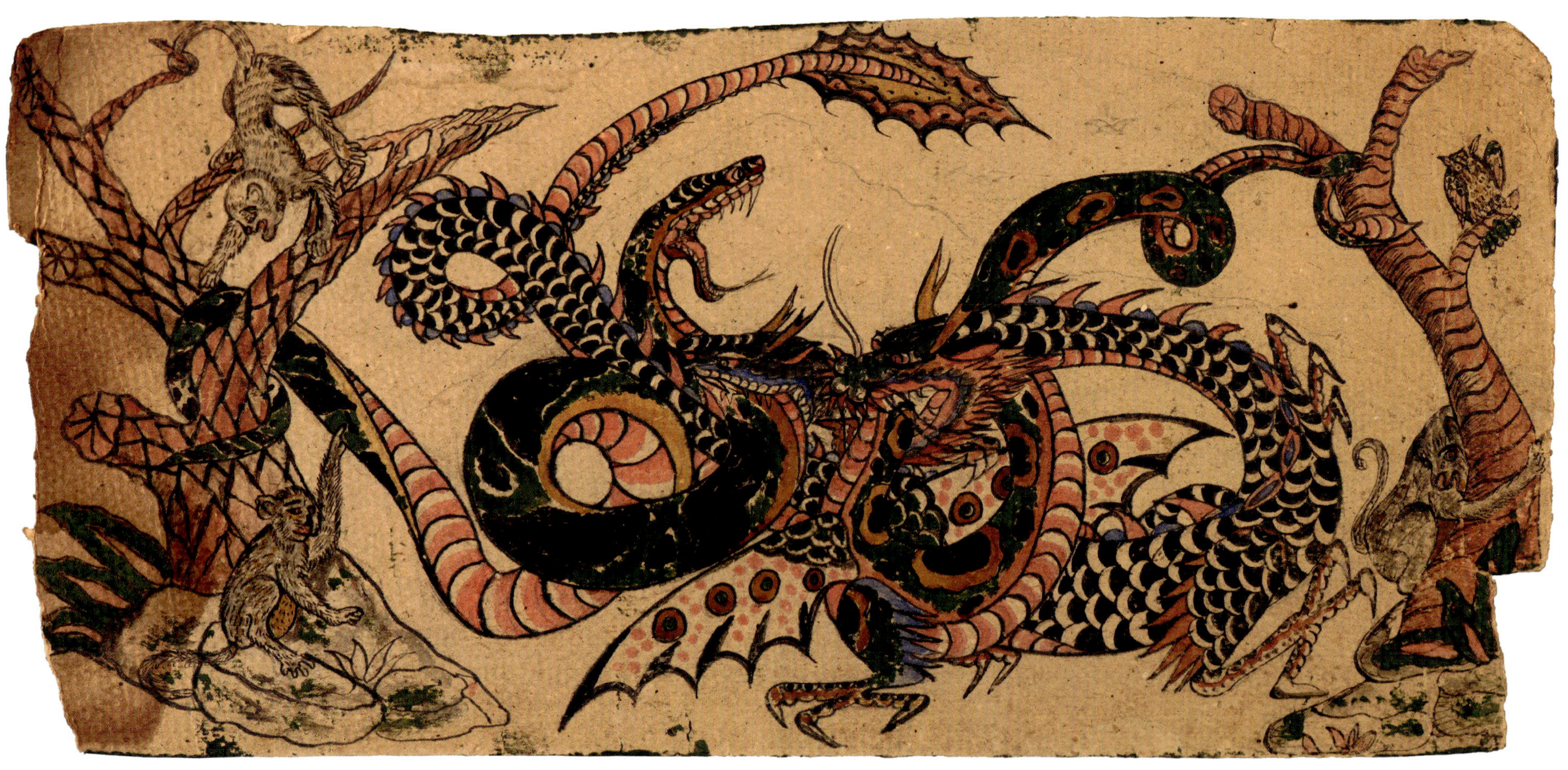

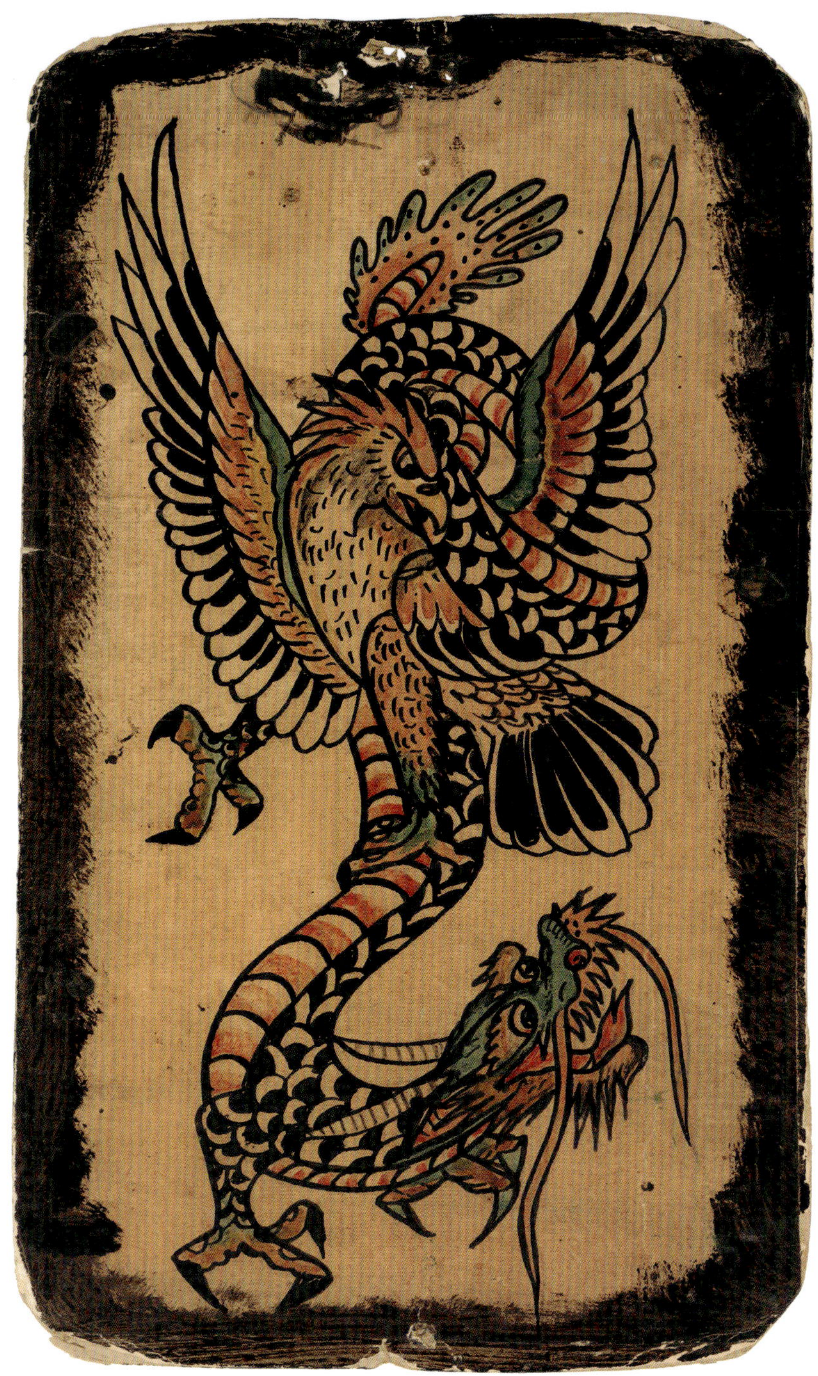

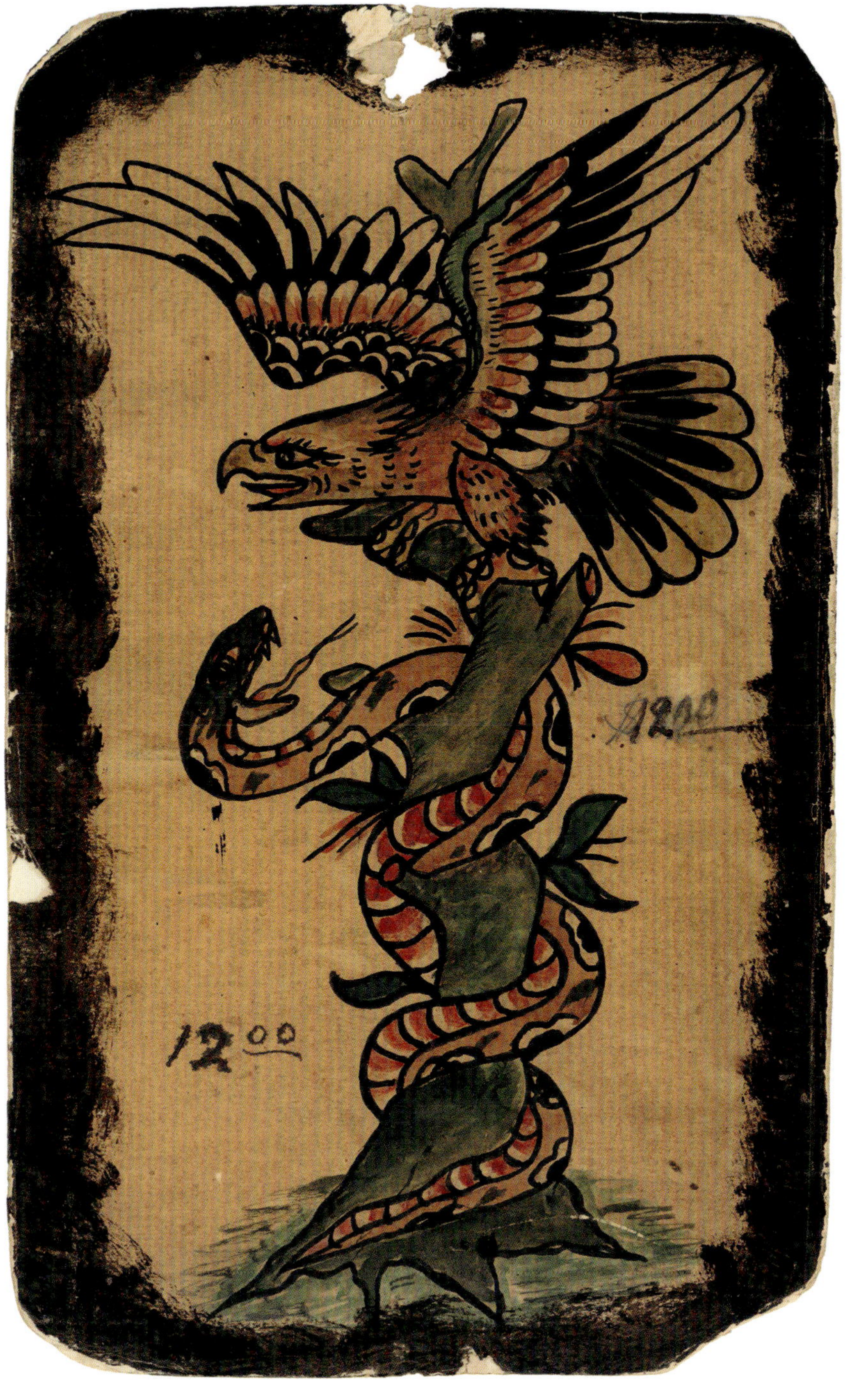

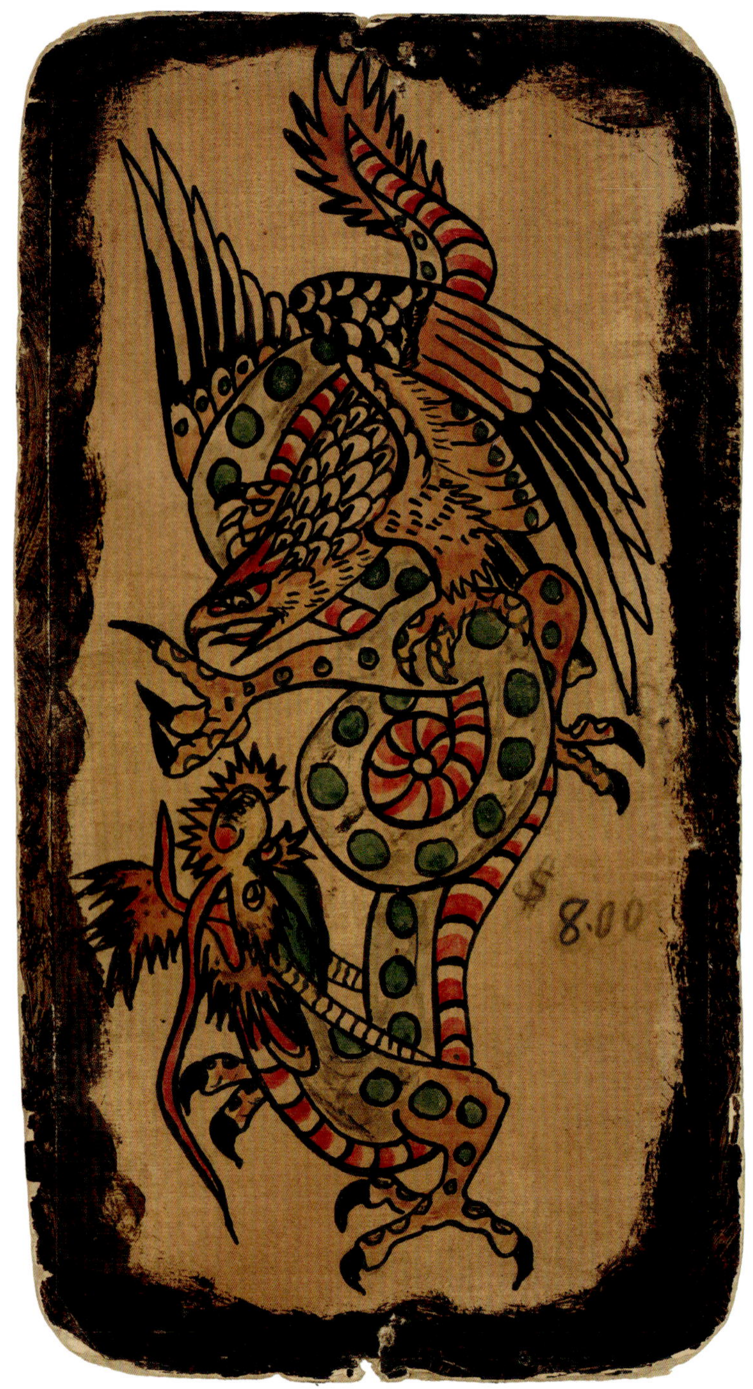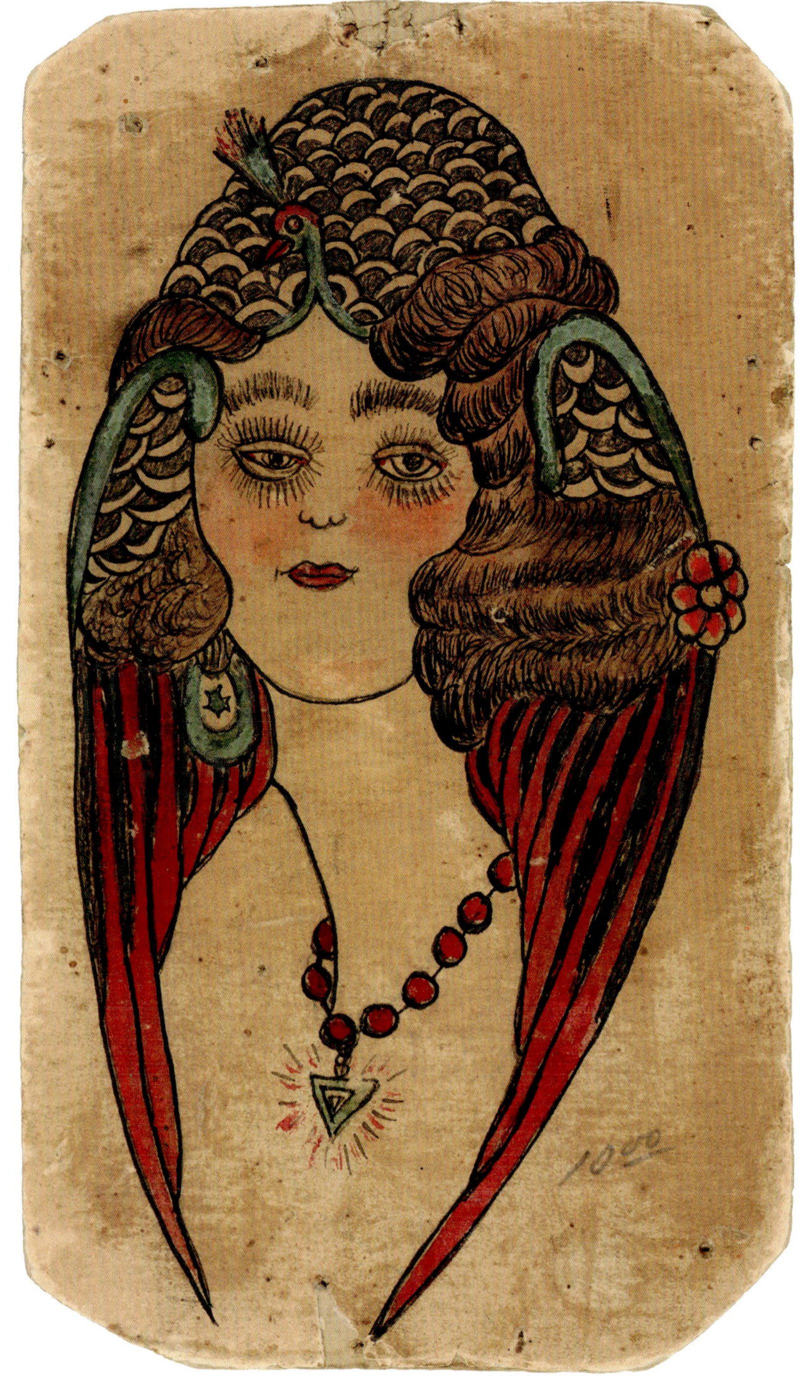

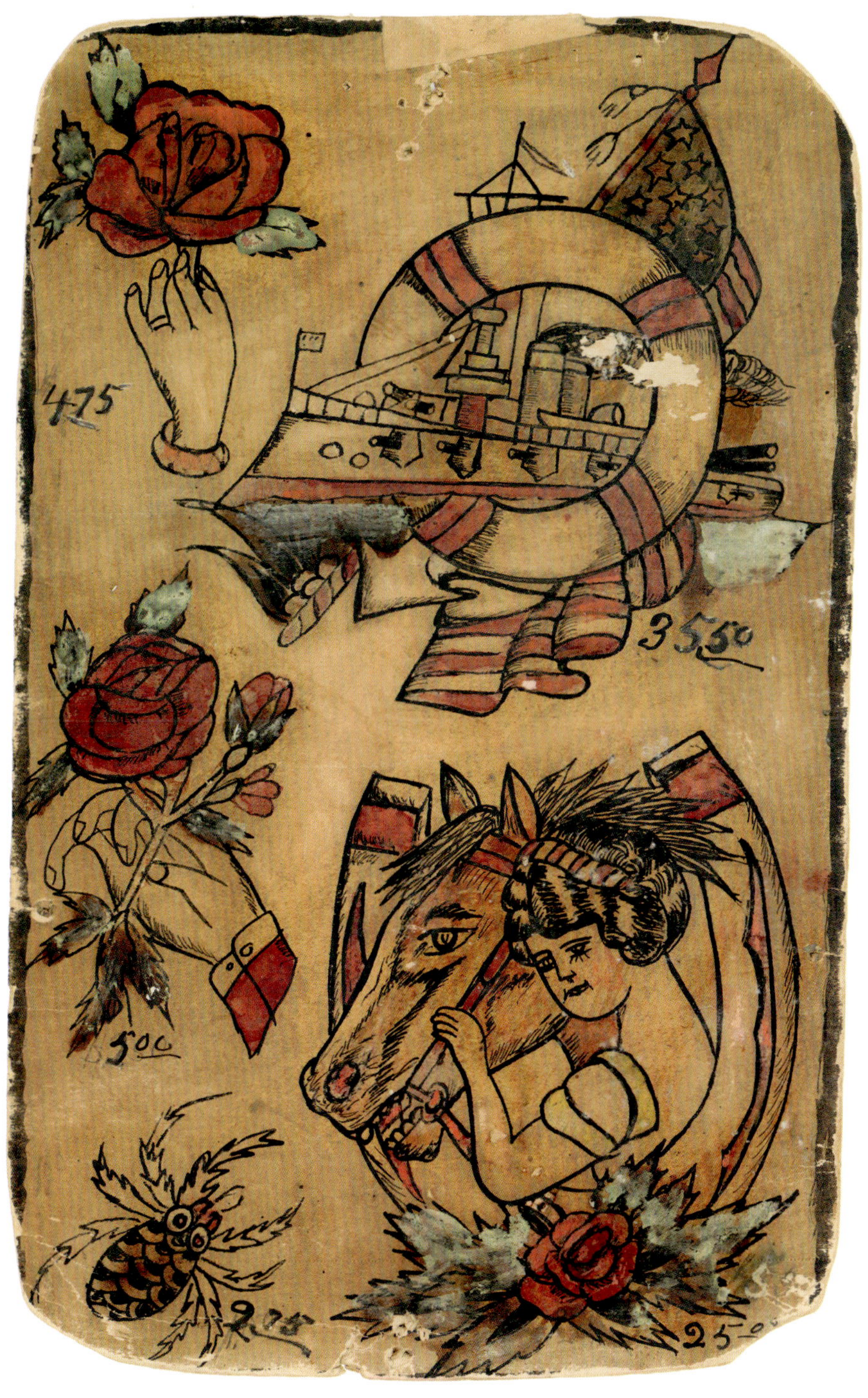

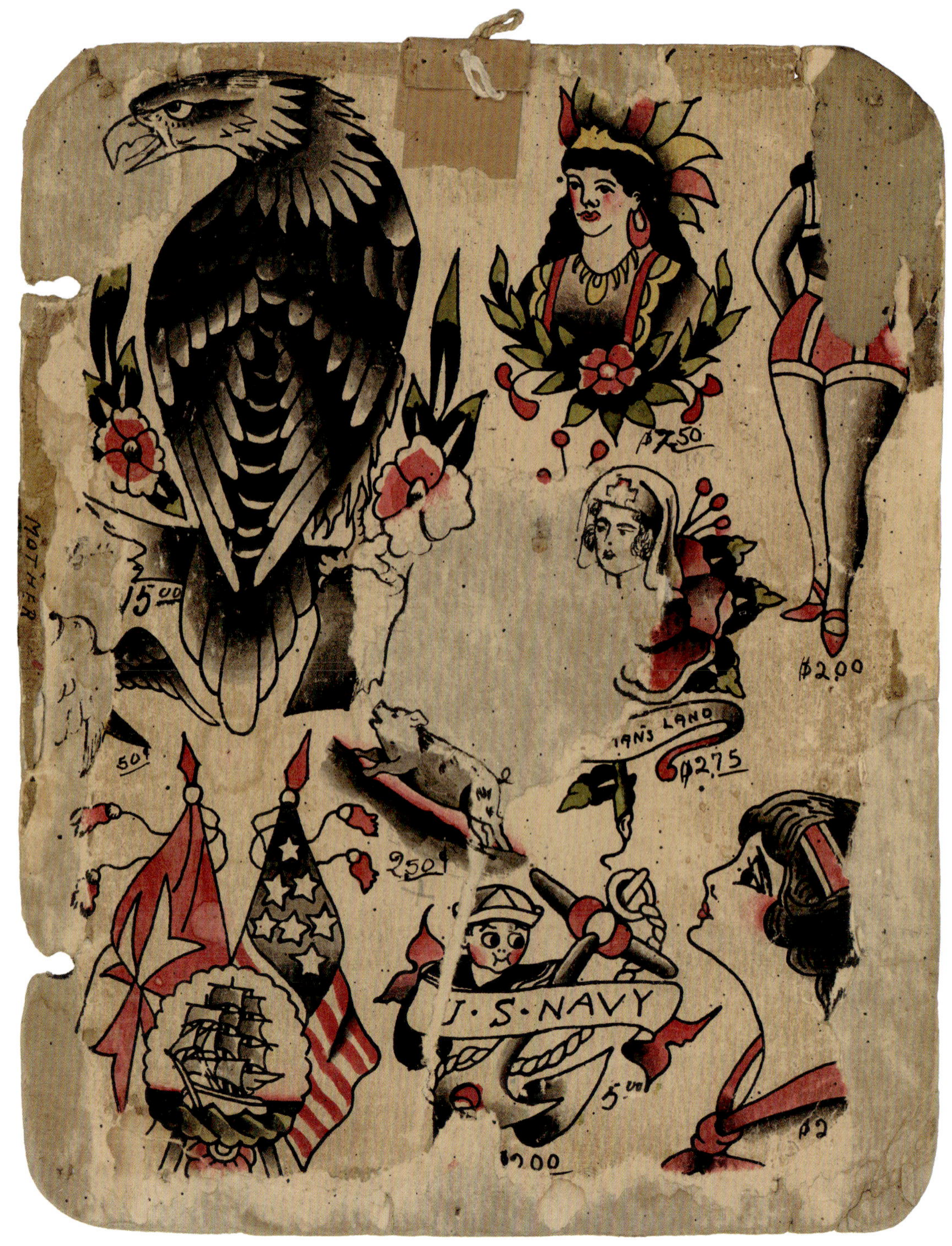
$7.50
$2.00
19ns LAND
$2.75
J·S·NAVY

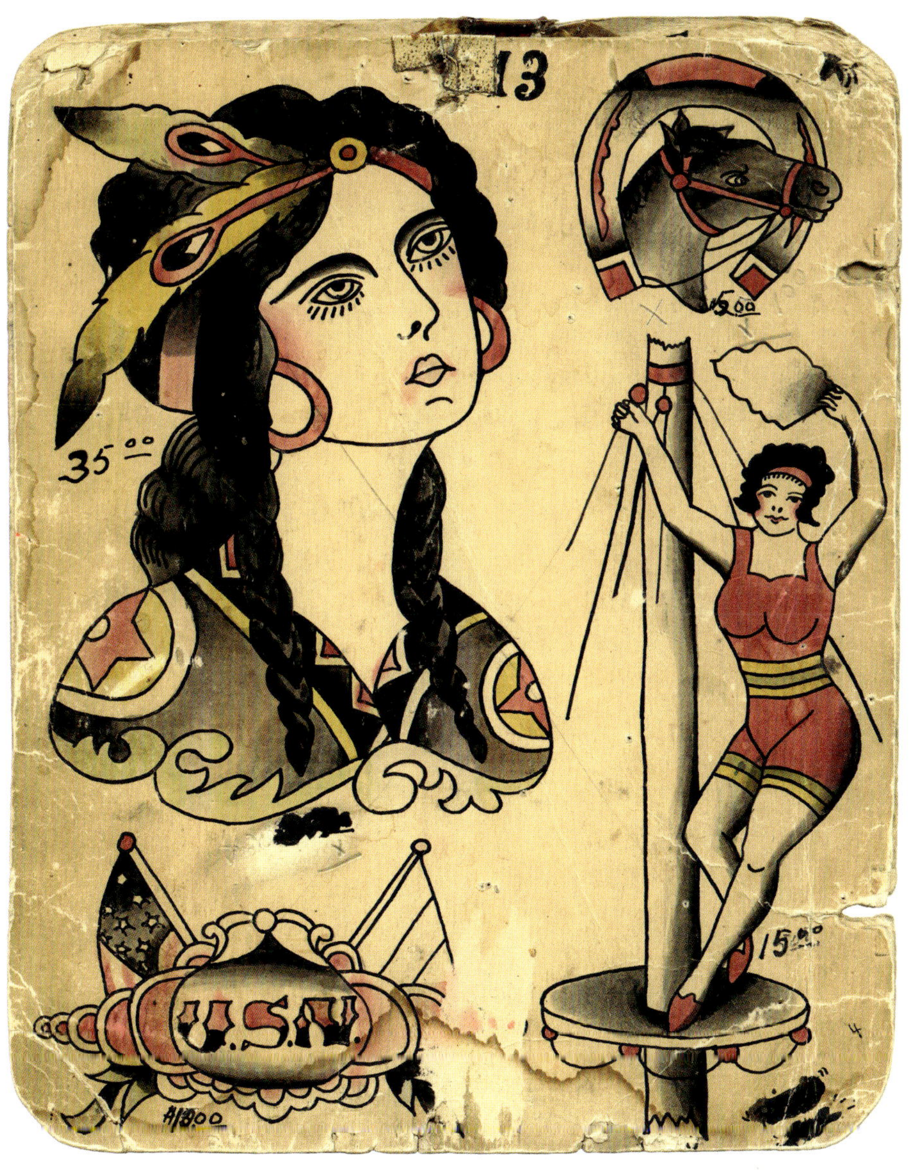

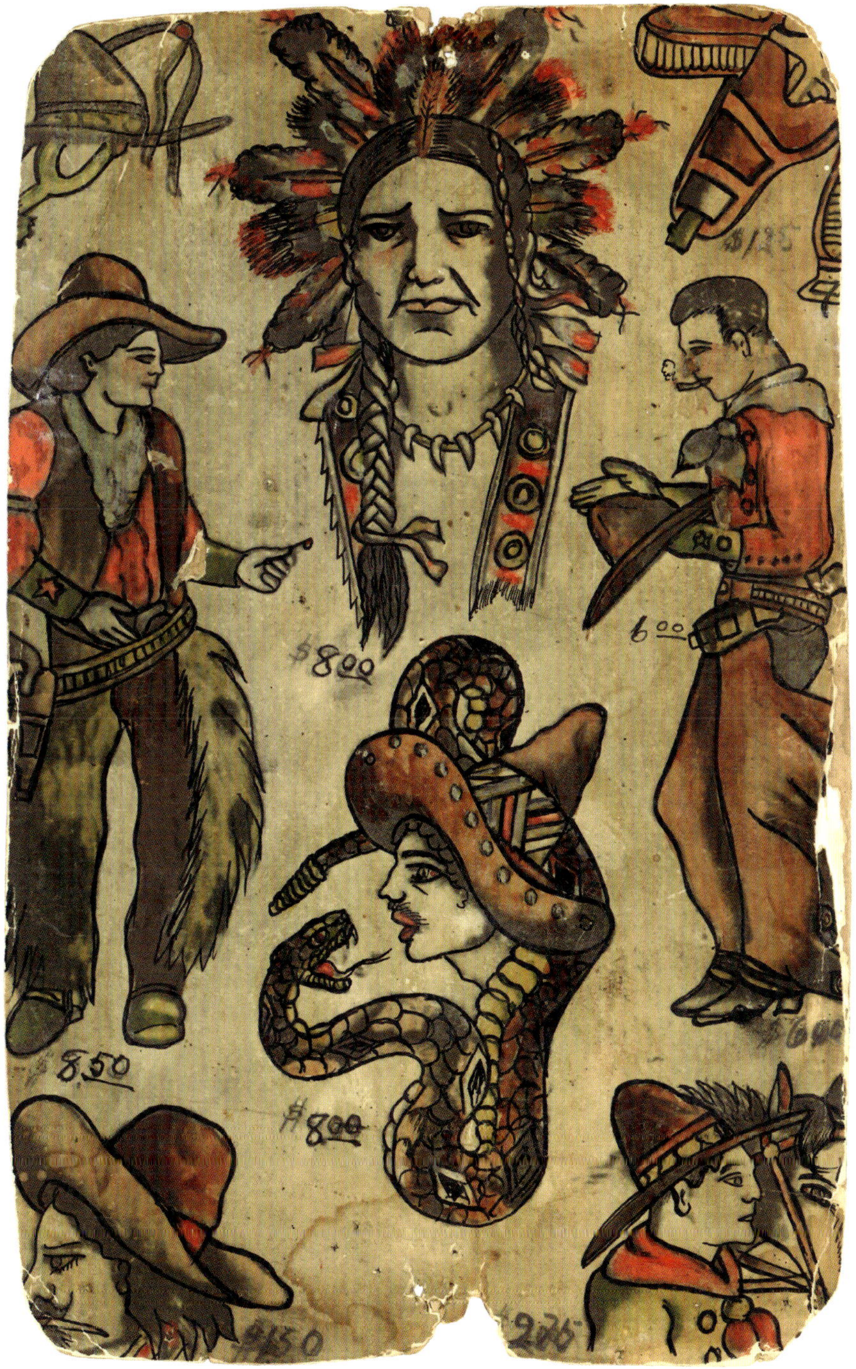

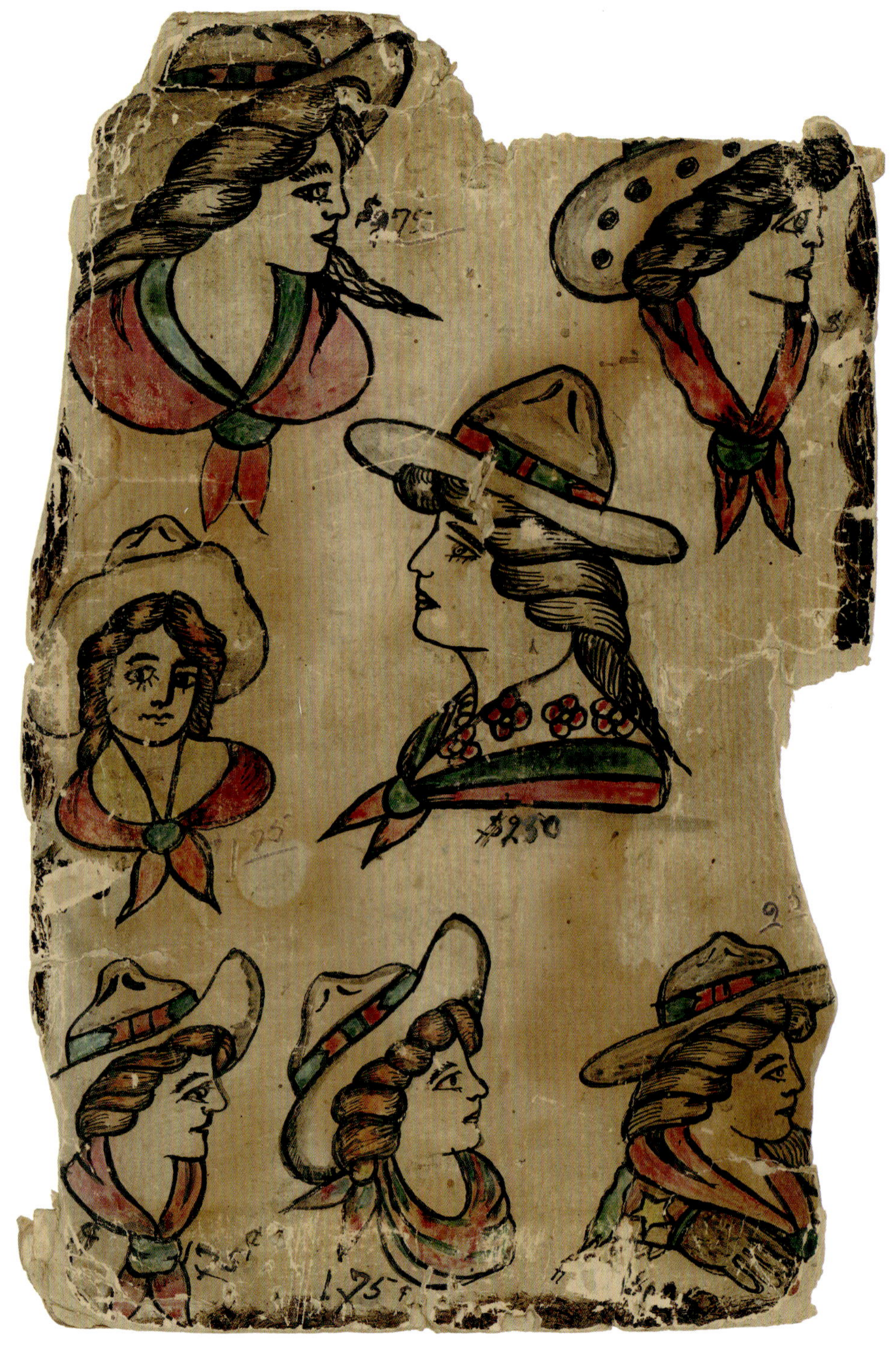

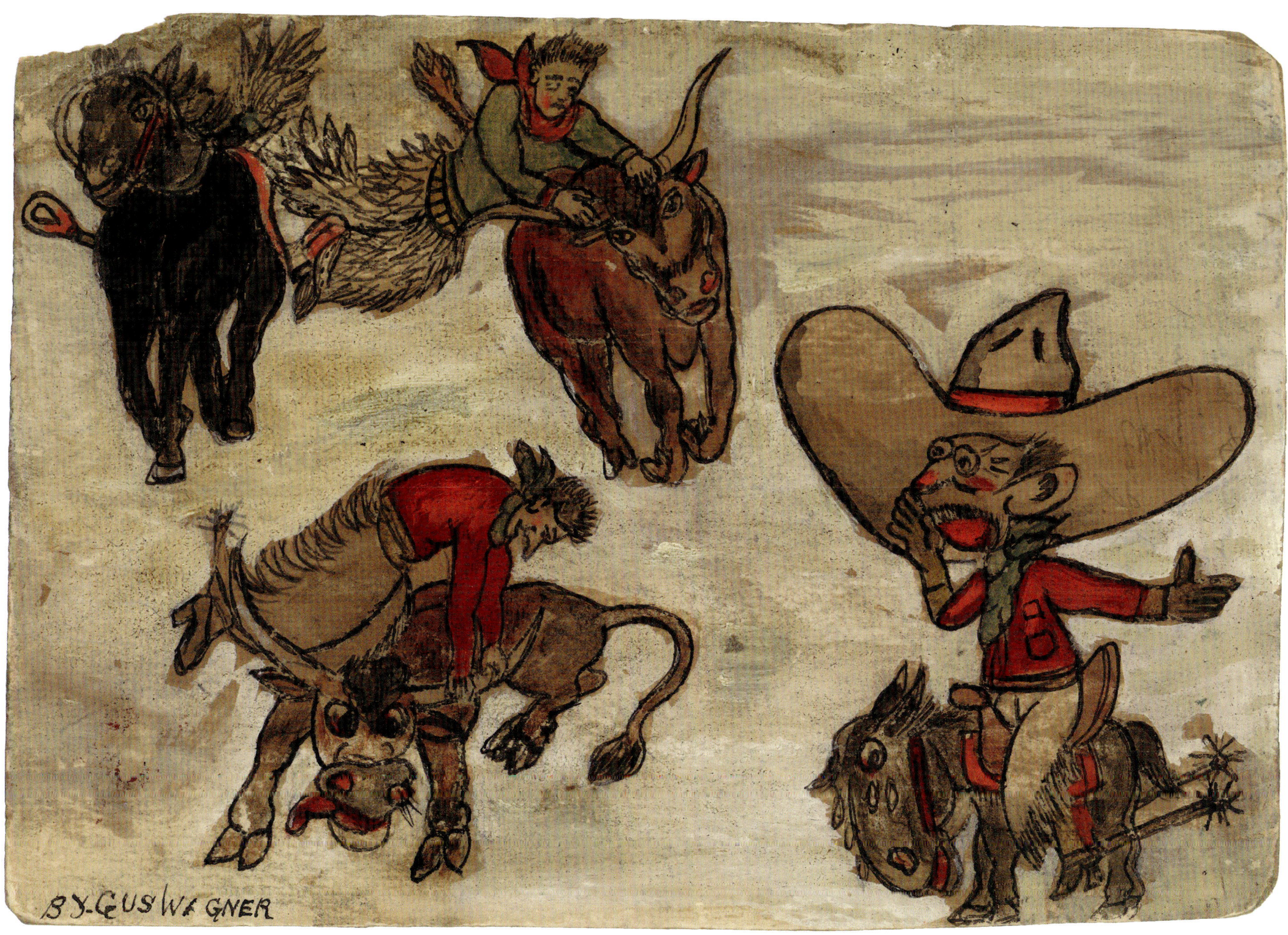
BY GUS WAGNER

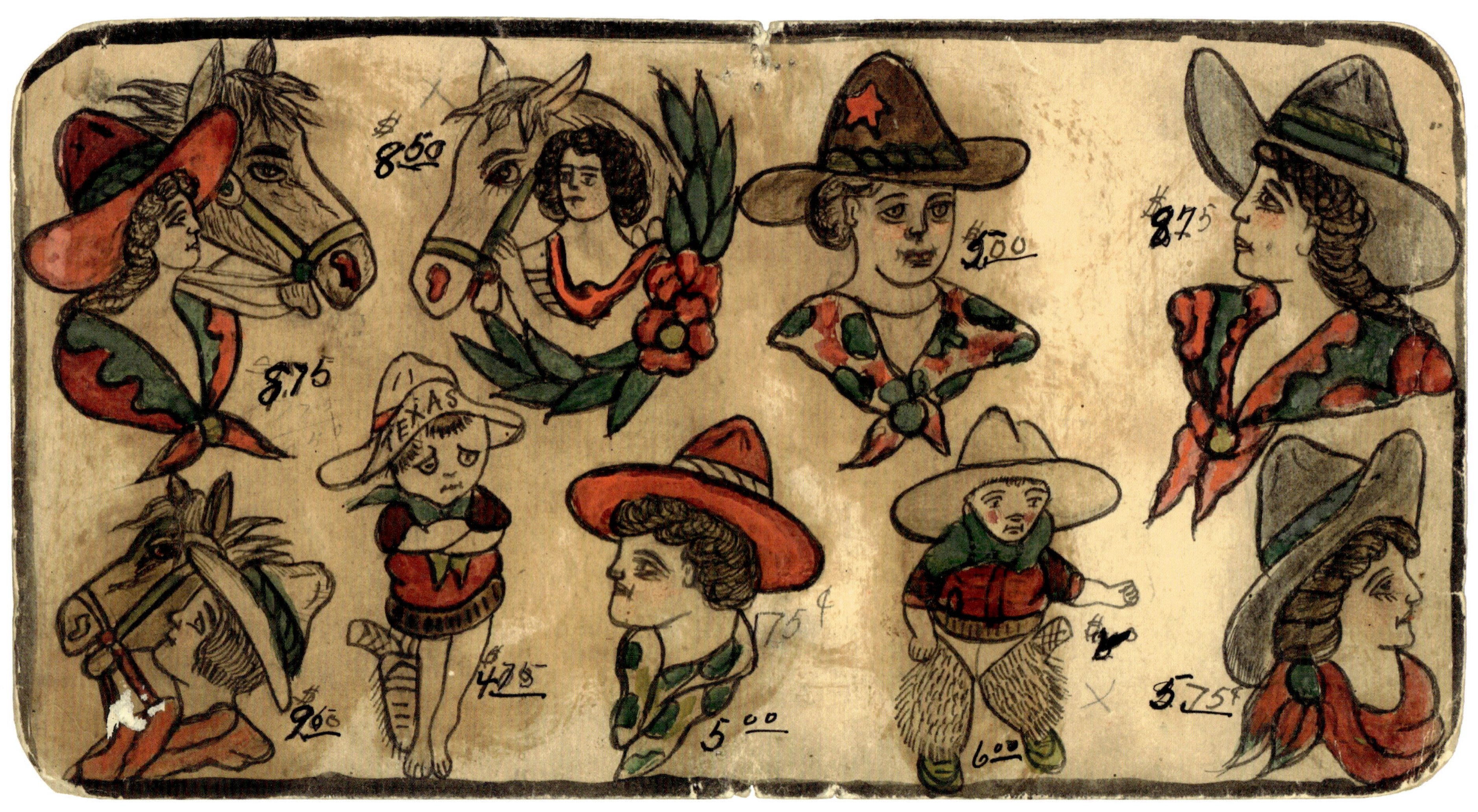

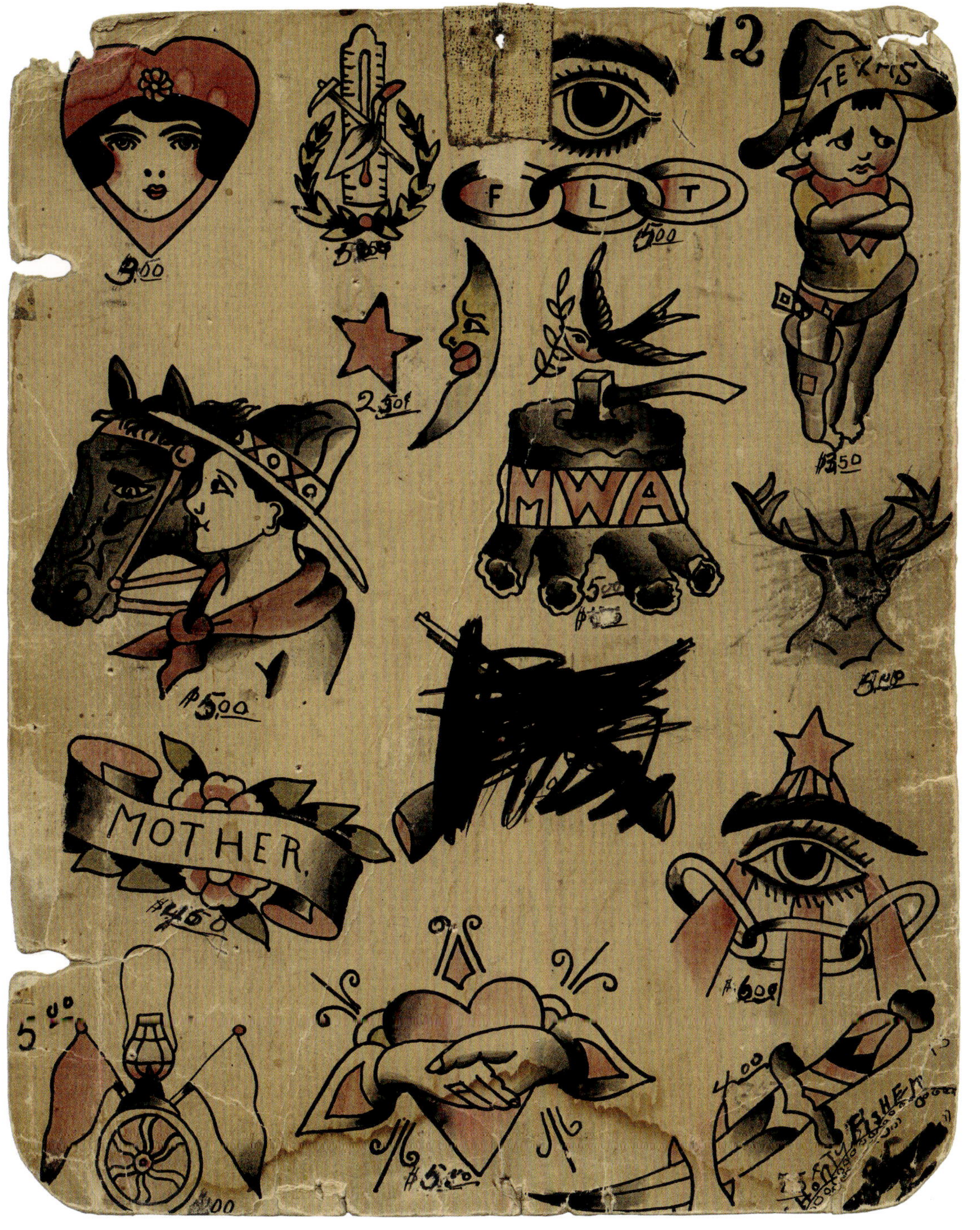

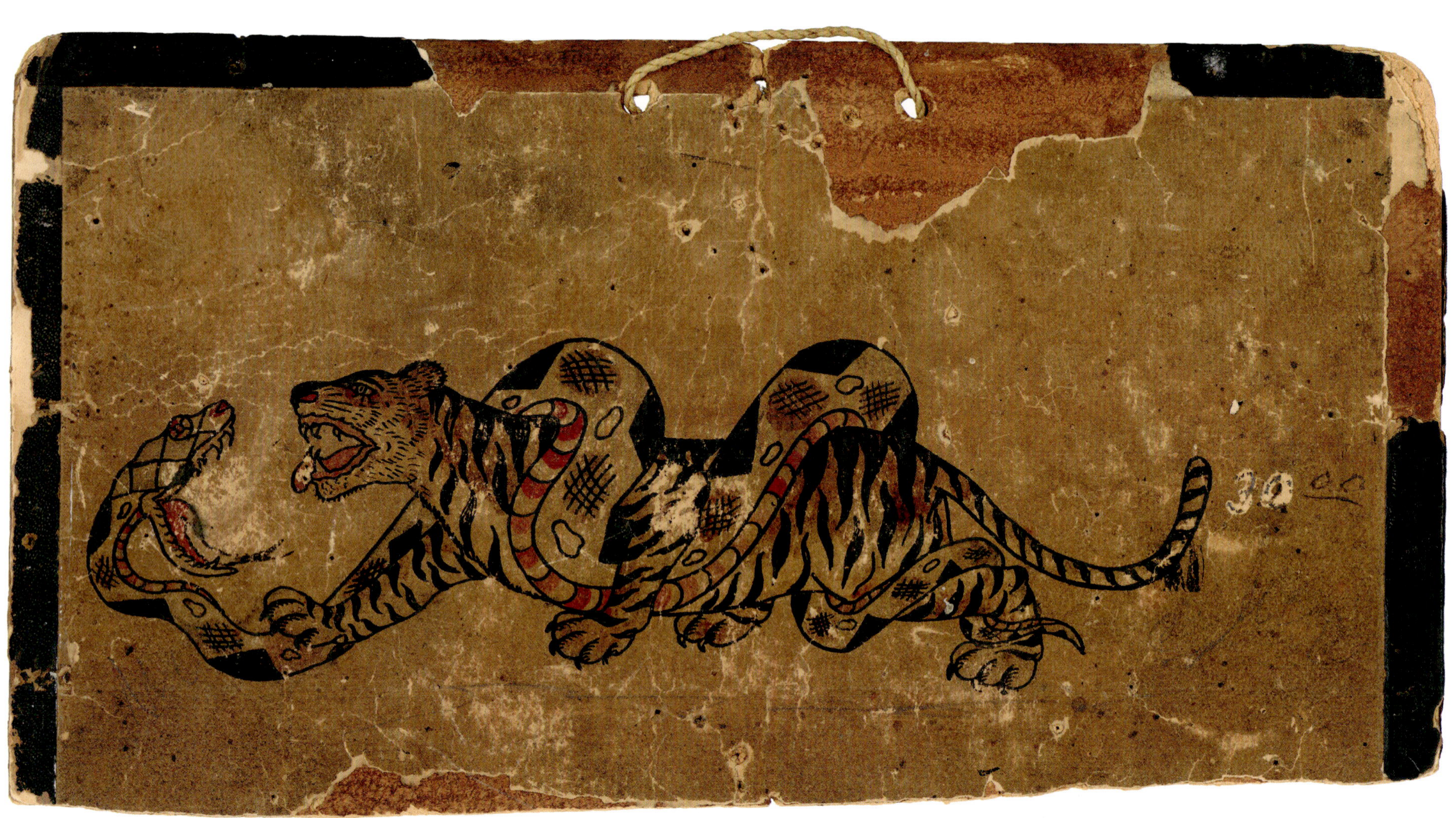

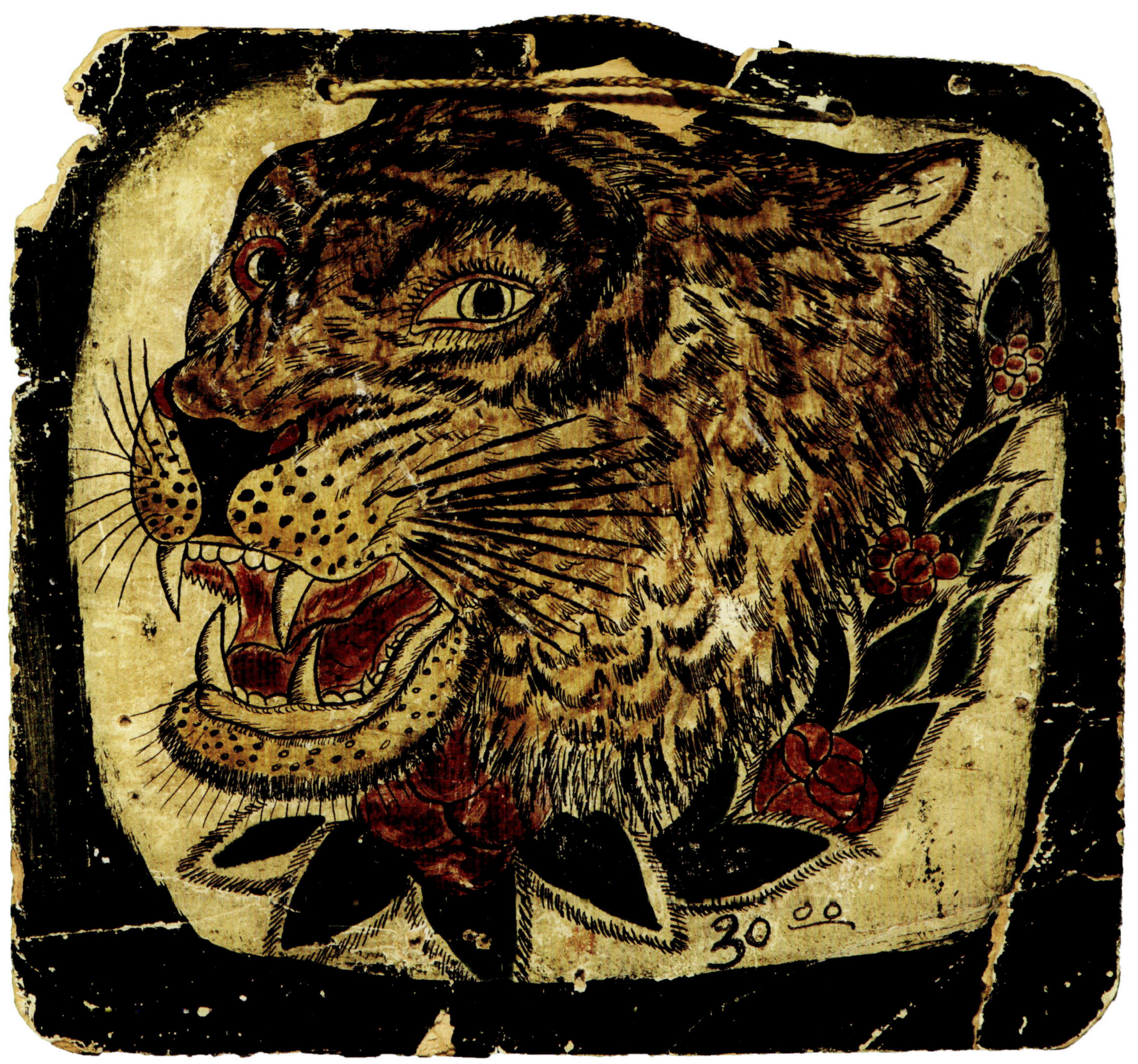

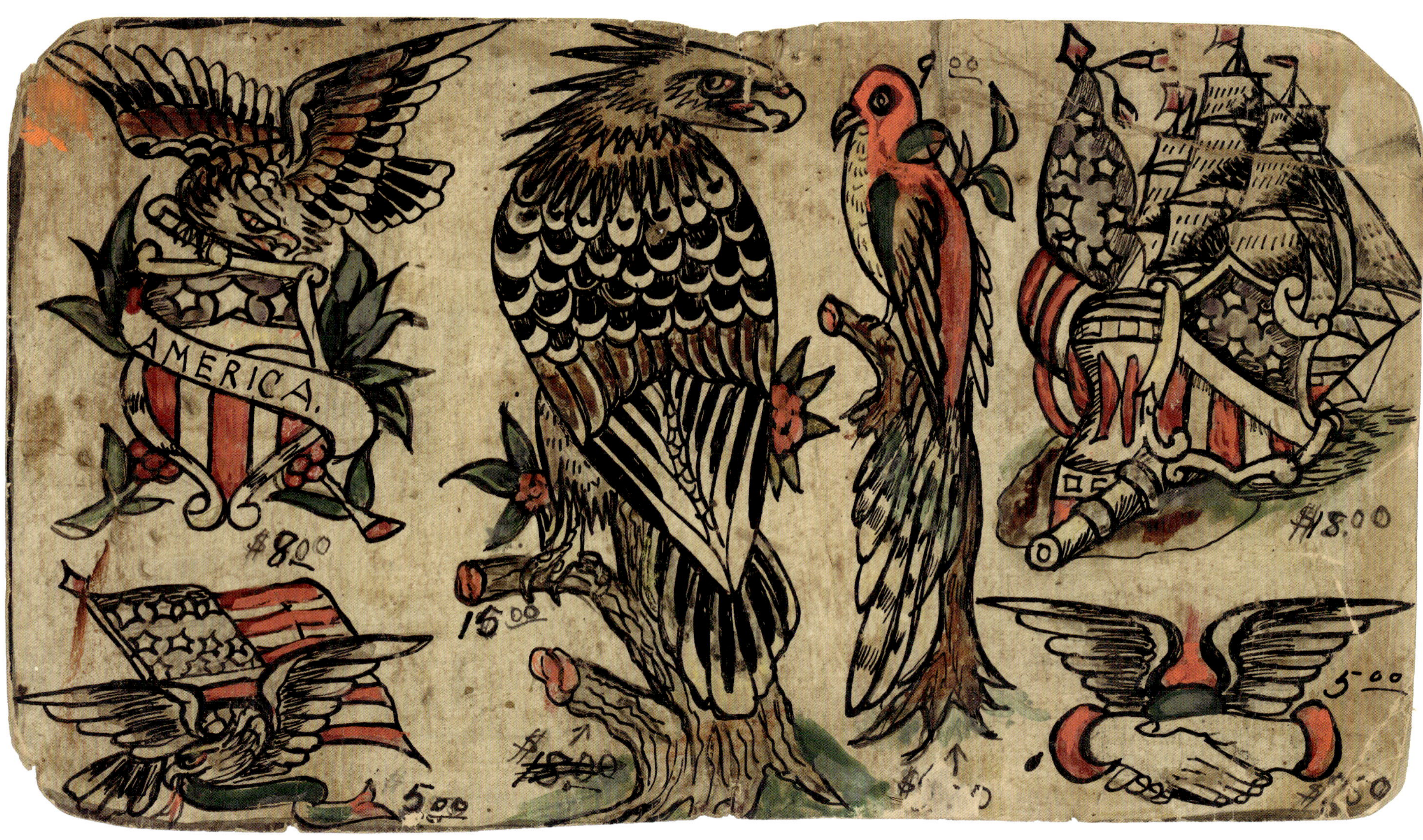

AMERICA.

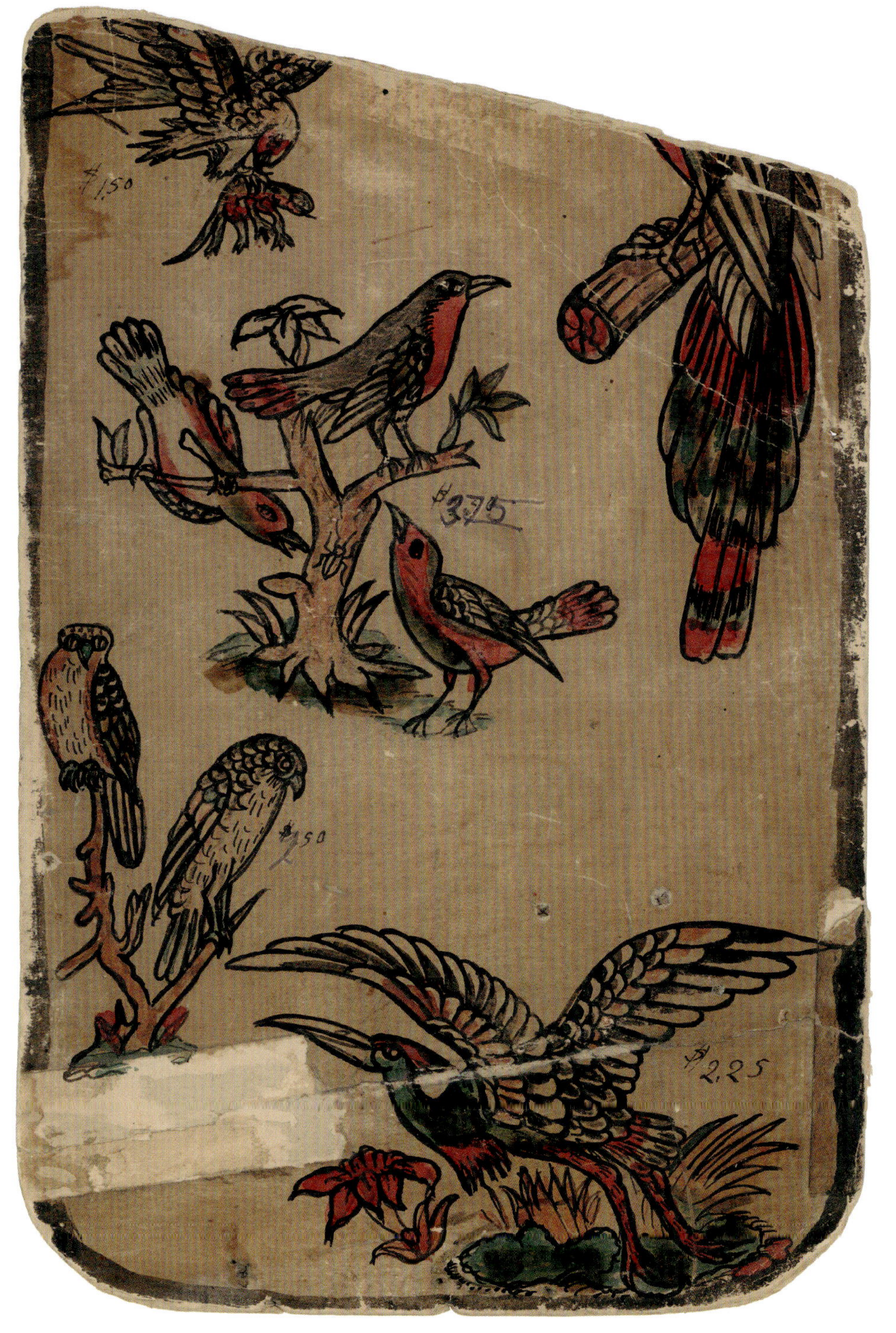

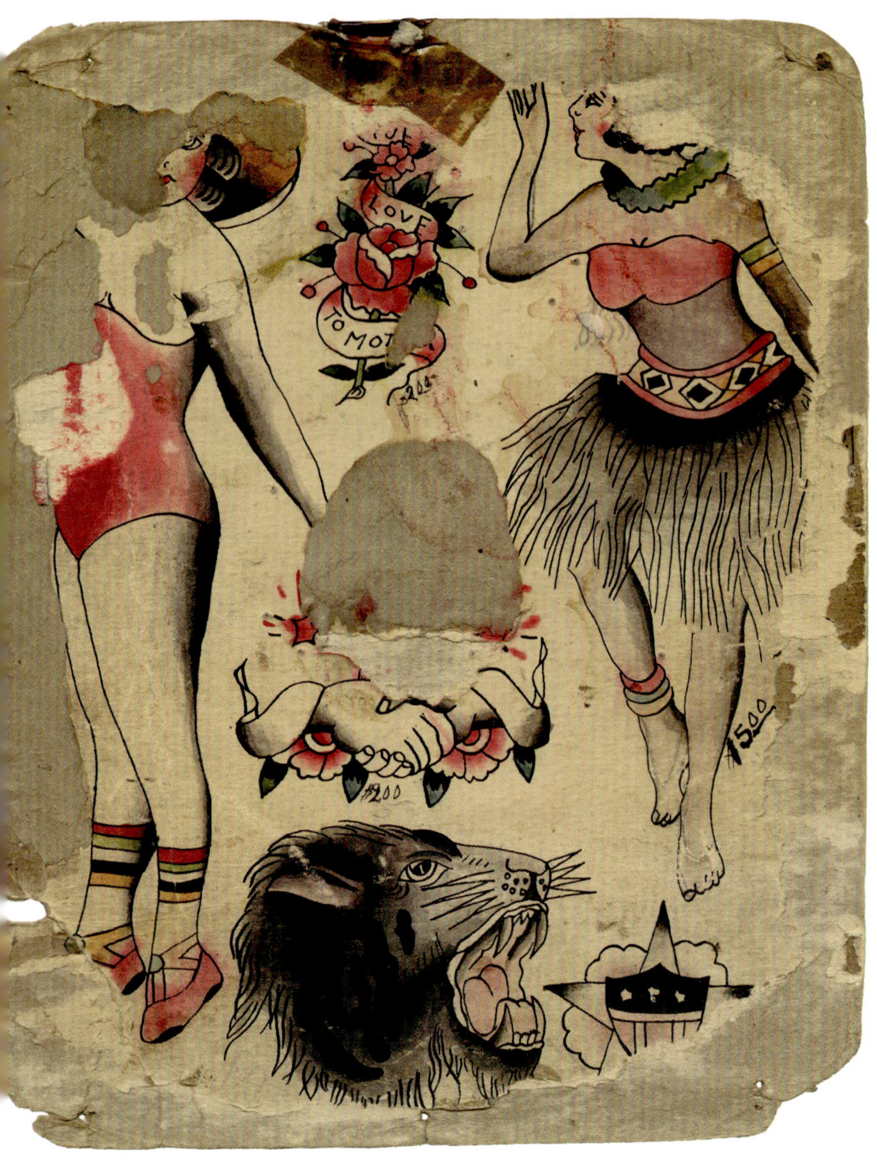

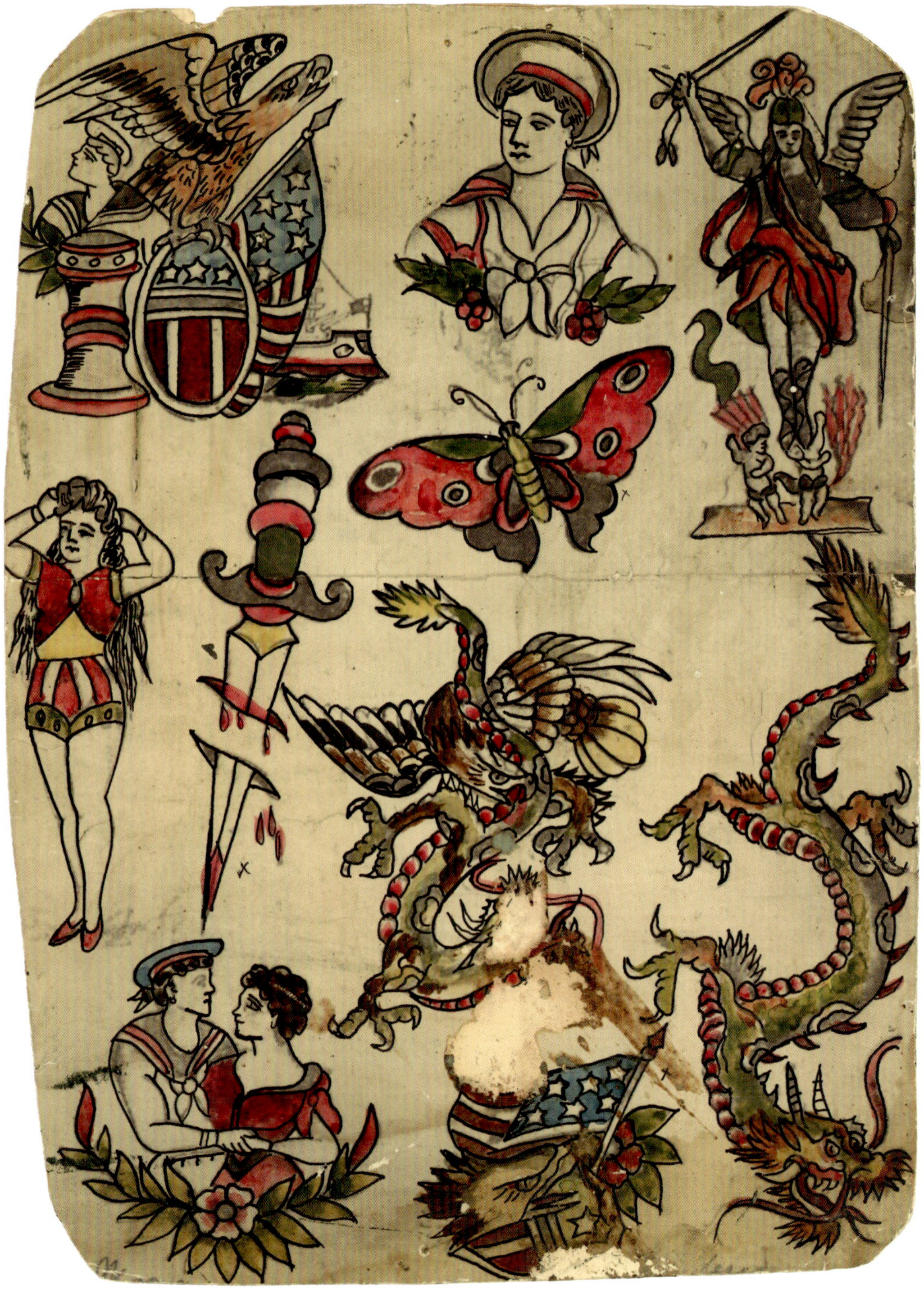

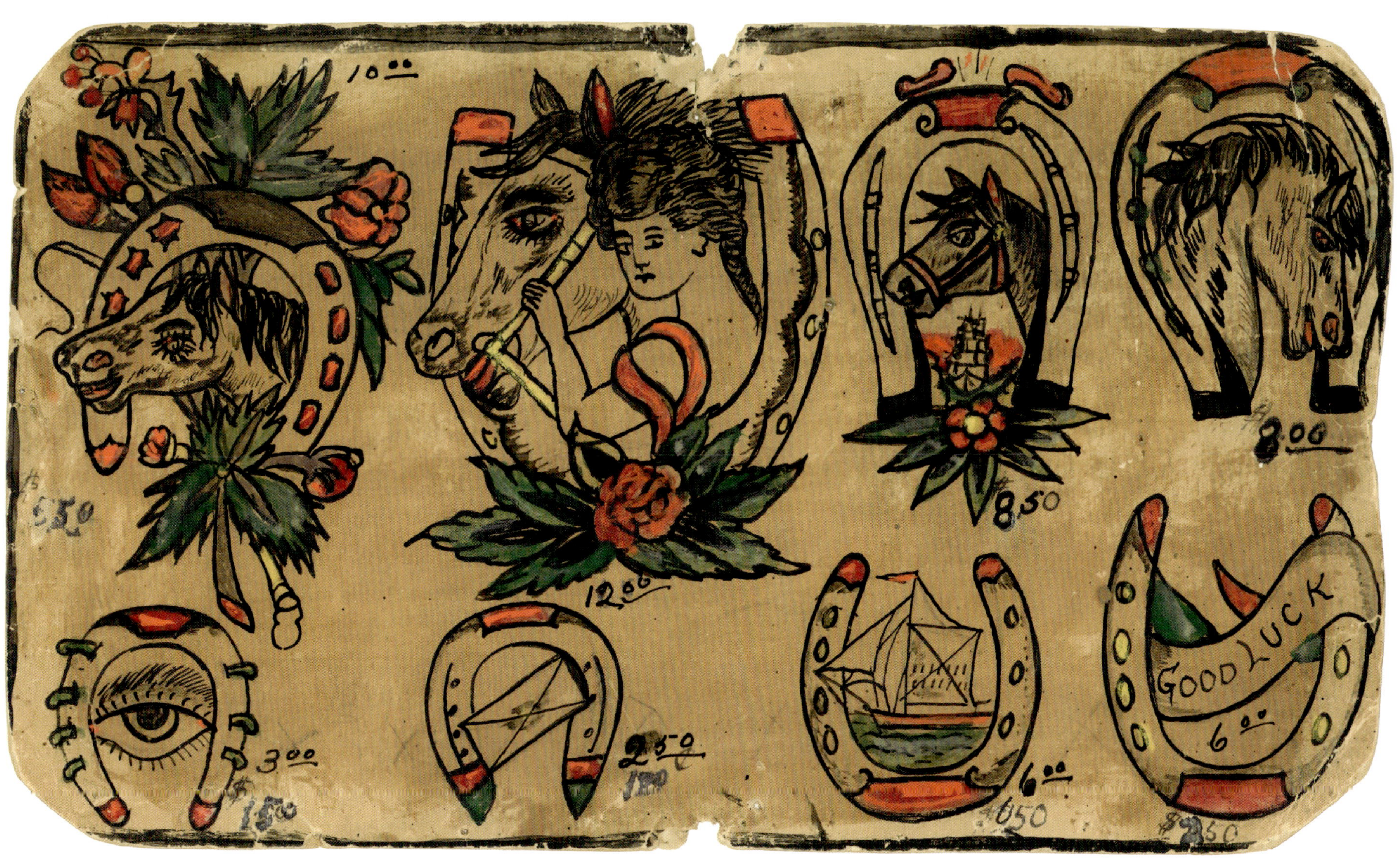

GOOD LUCK

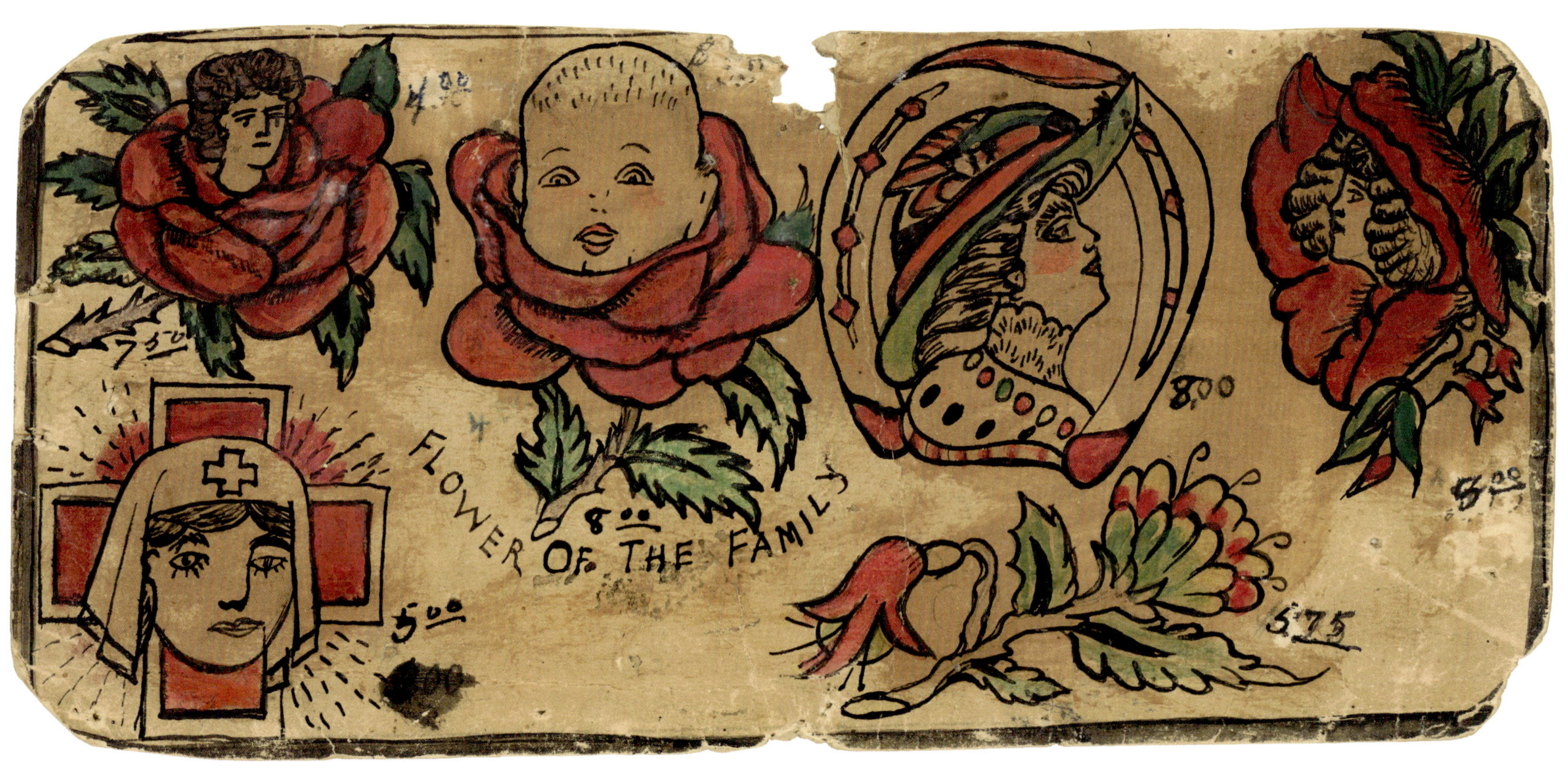

FLOWER OF THE FAMILY

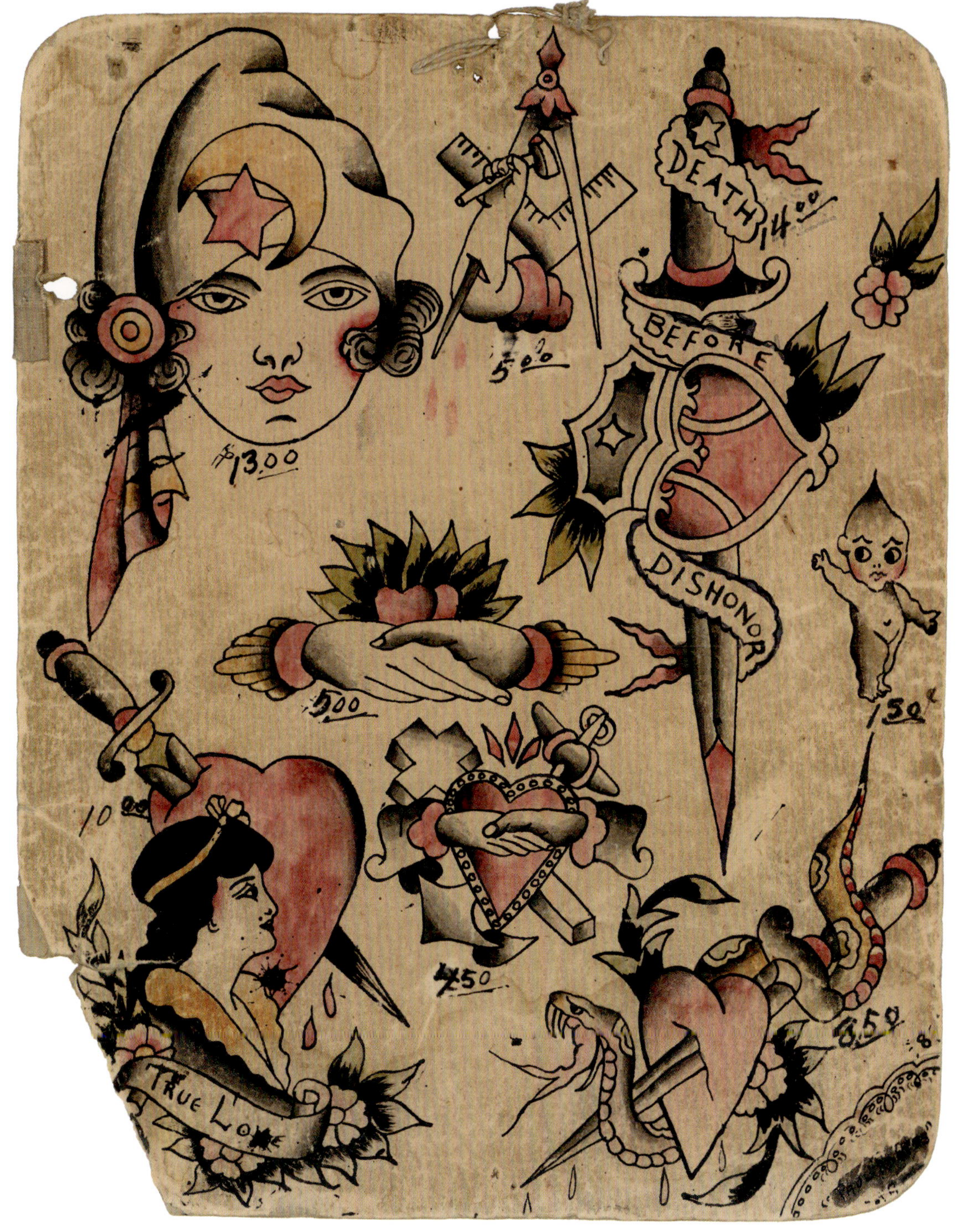

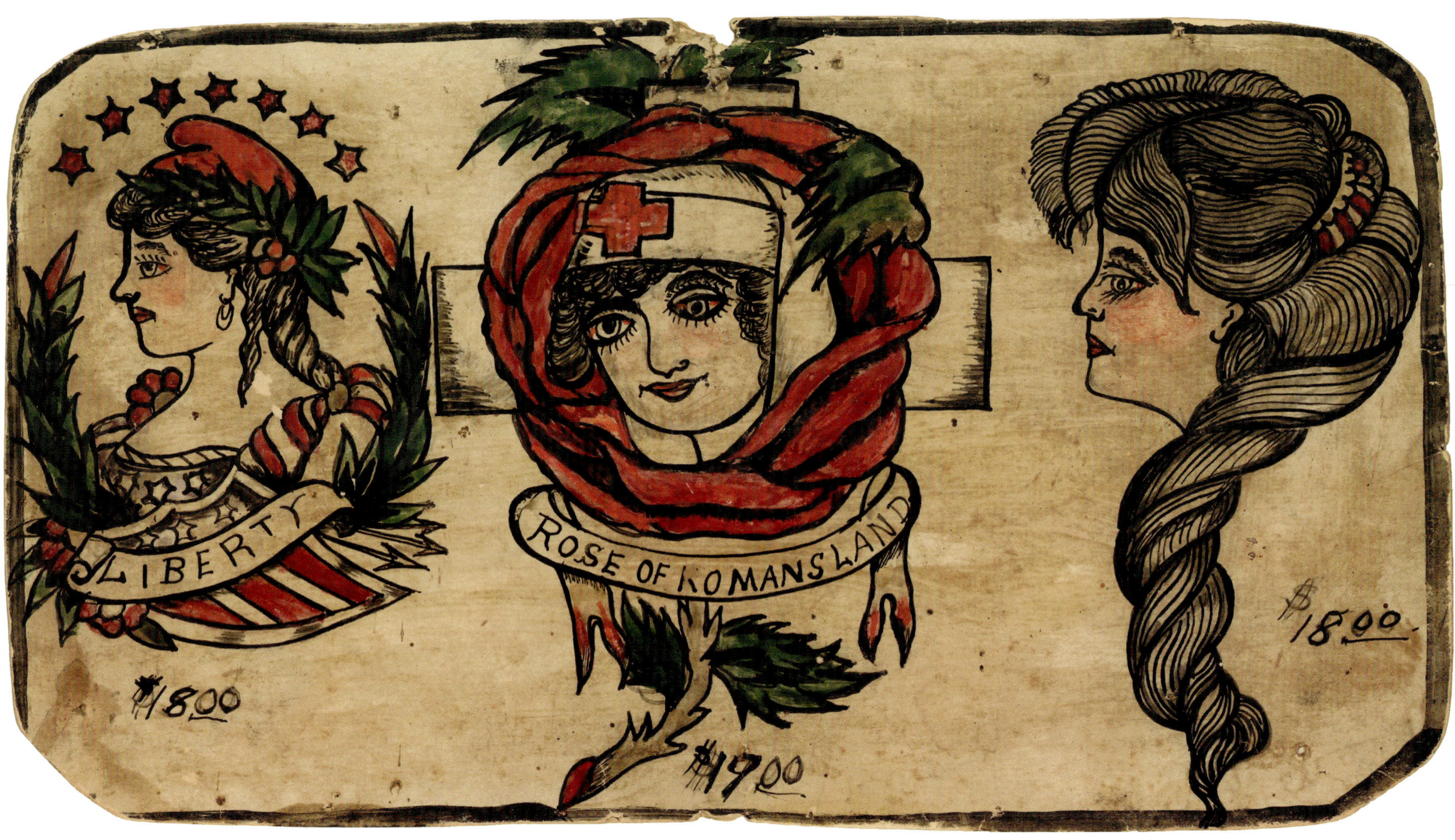

LIBERTY
$1800
ROSE OF ROMANSLAND
$1700
$1800

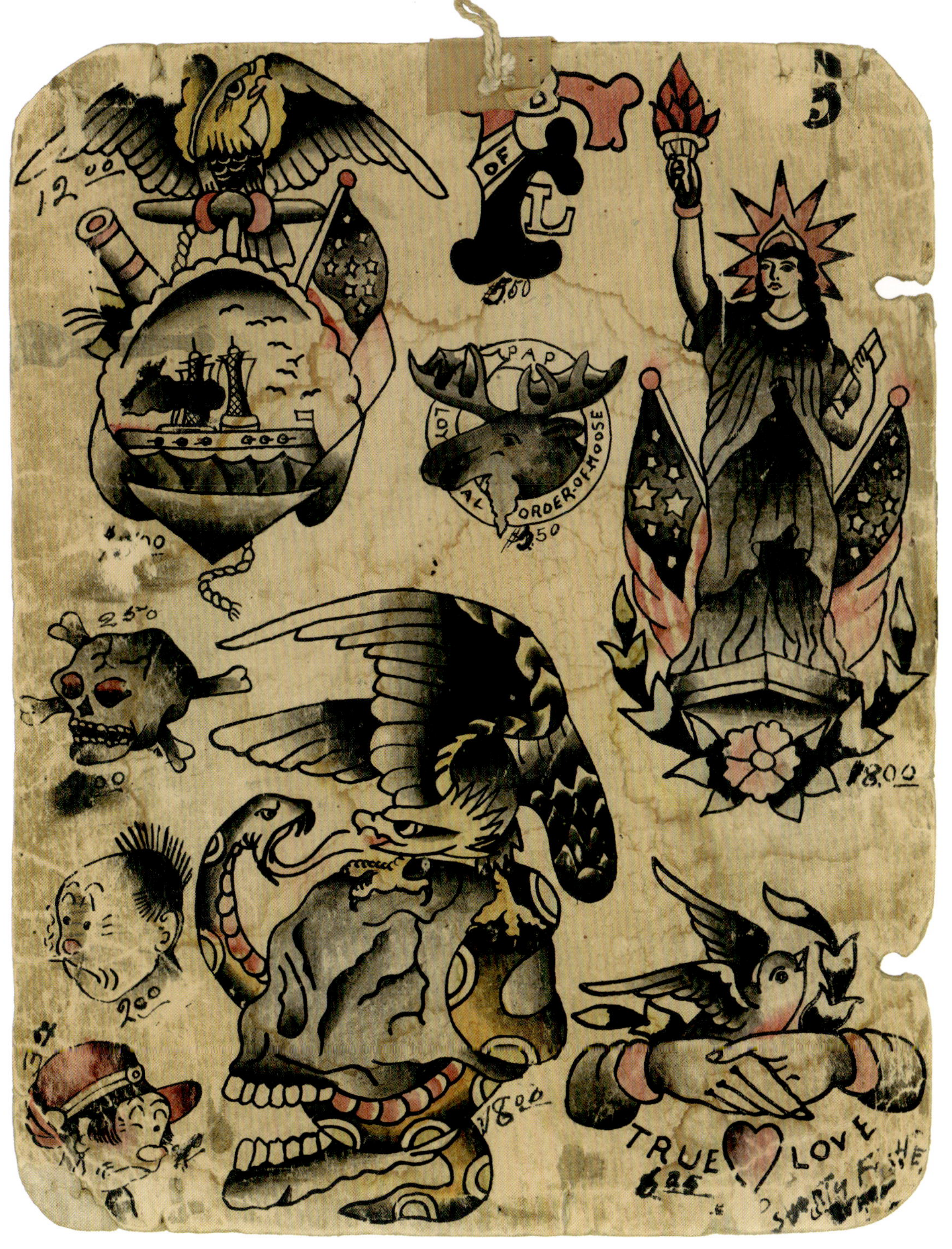

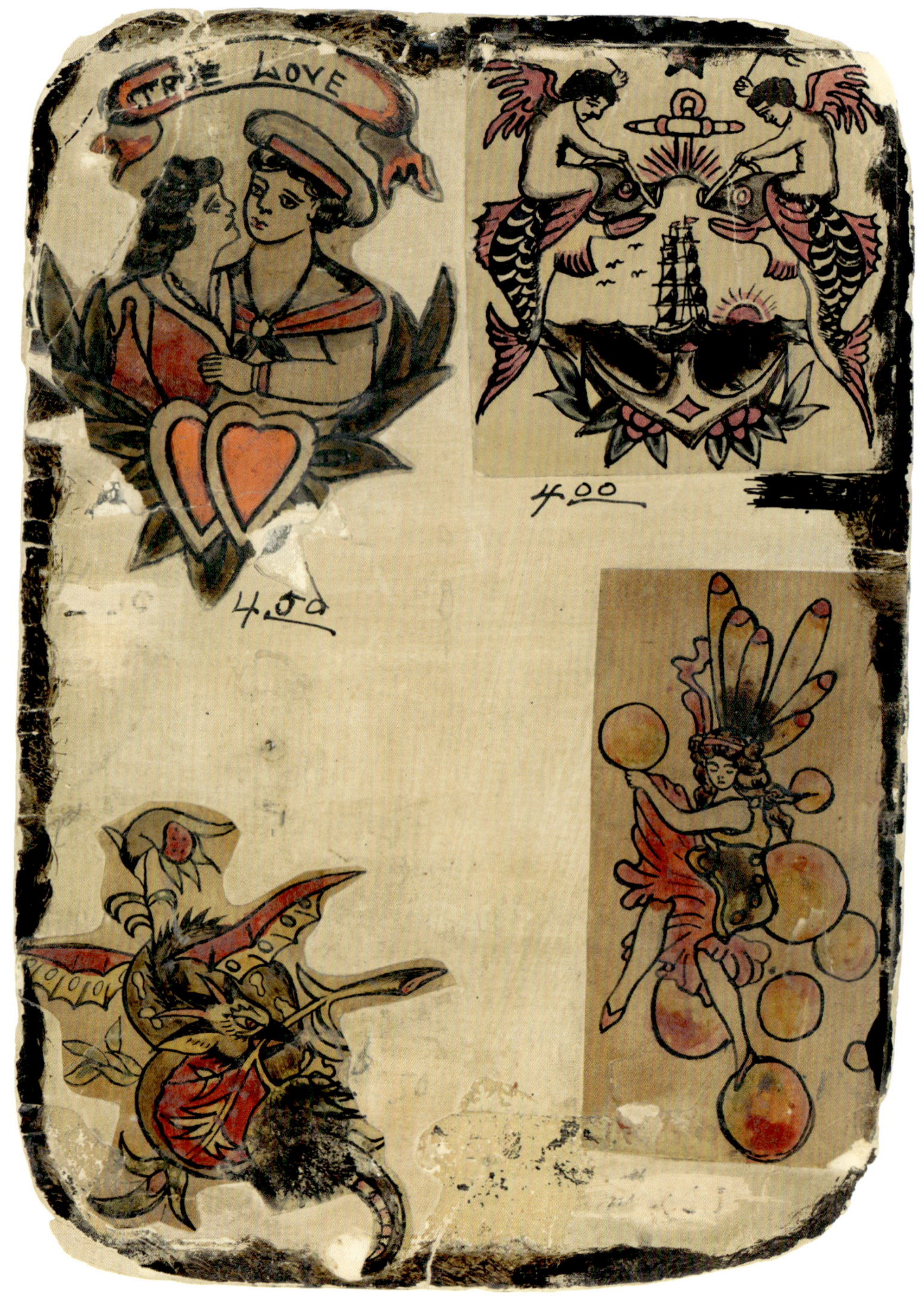
TRUE LOVE
4.00
4.50

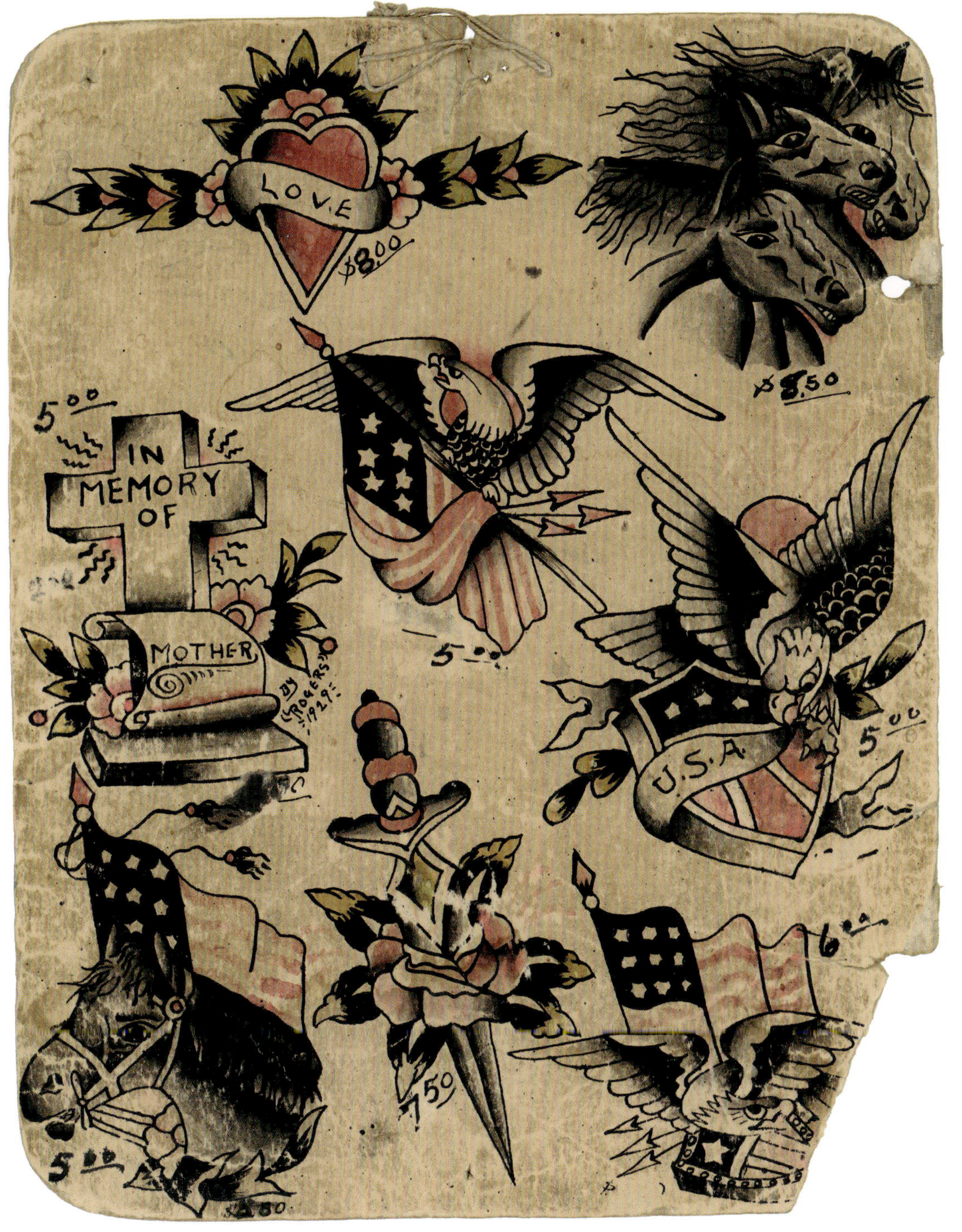

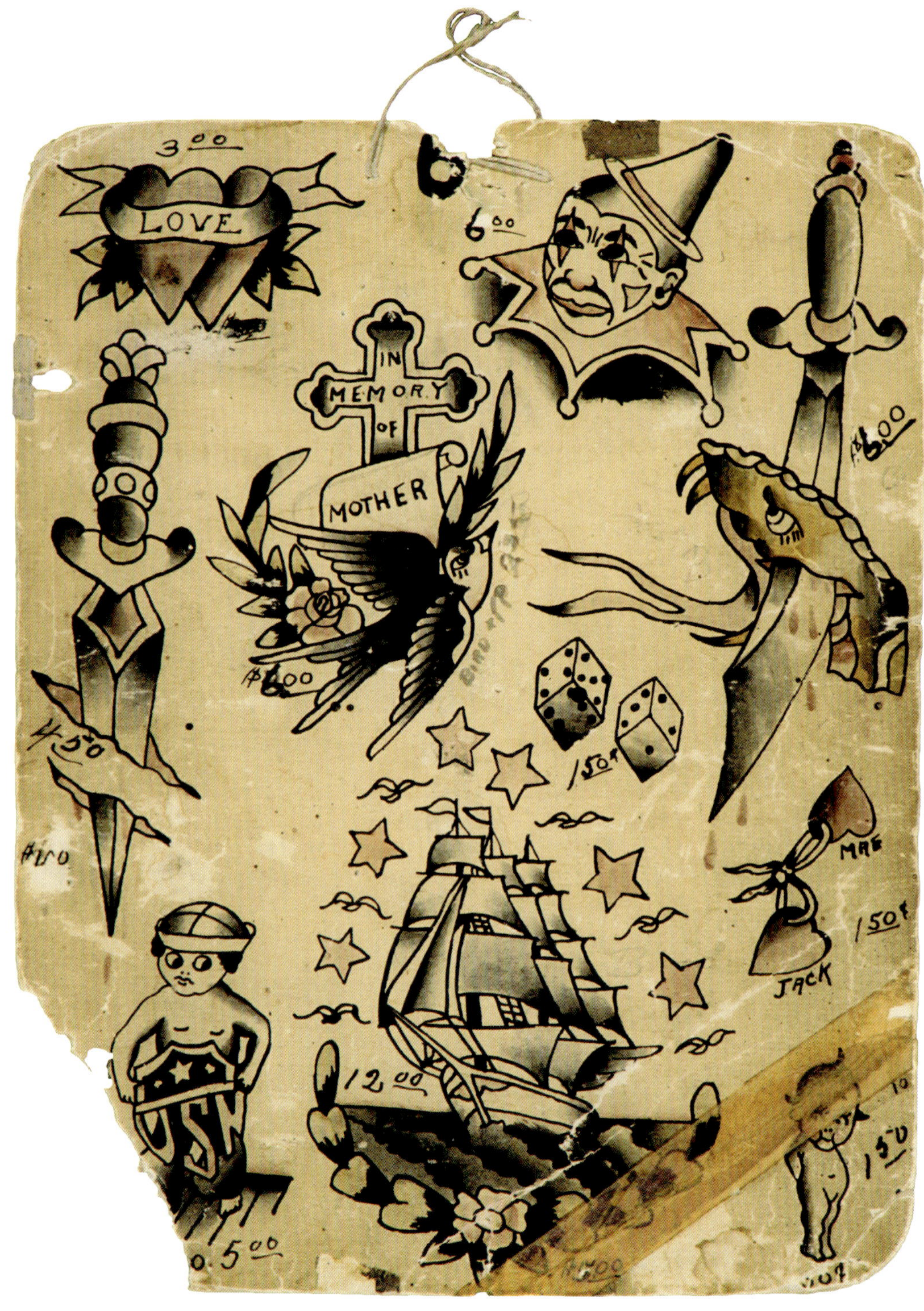

 Flash in Gus Wagner's Collection

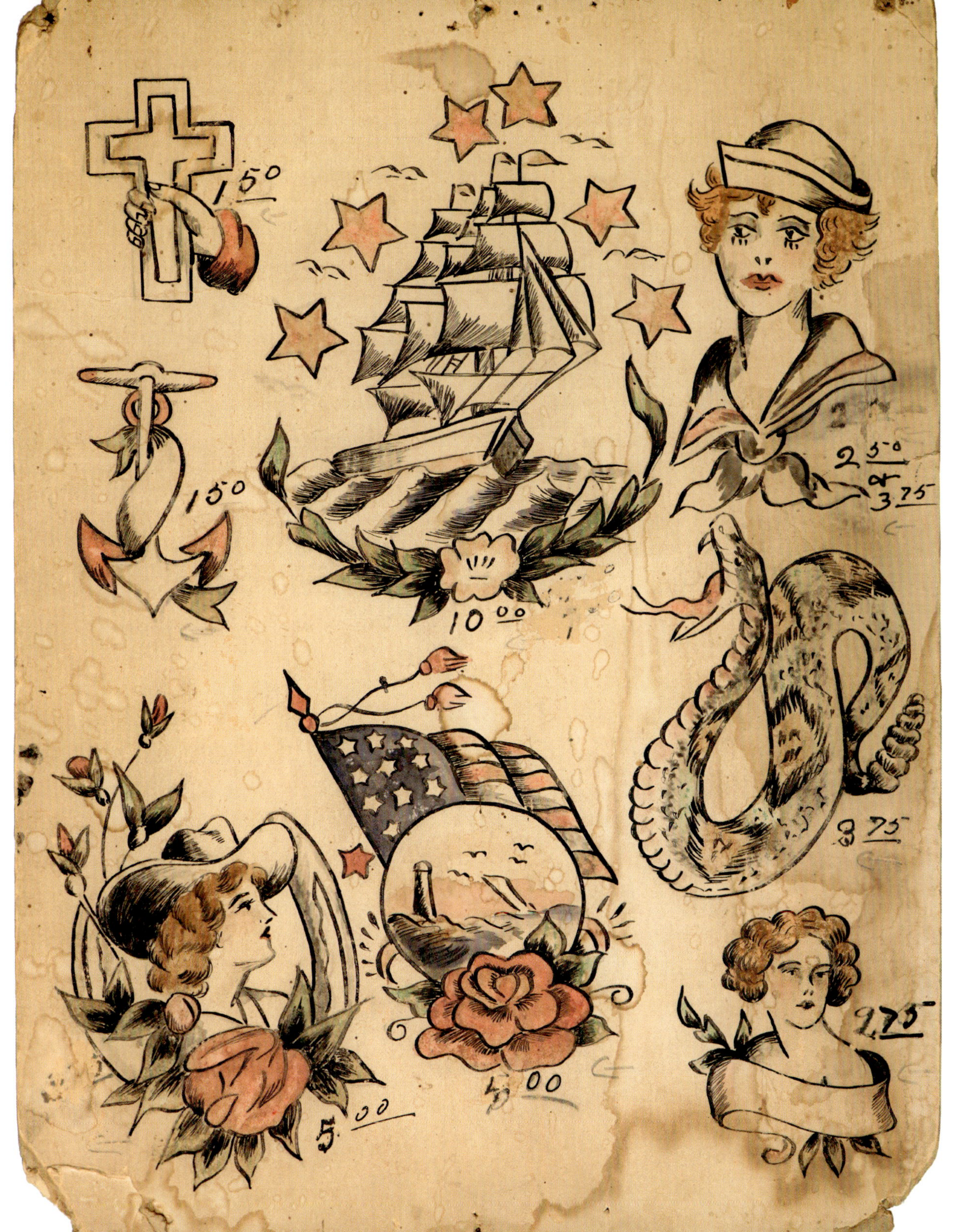

1.50
1.50
10.00
2.5-0 or 3.75
3.75
5.00
4.00
2.75

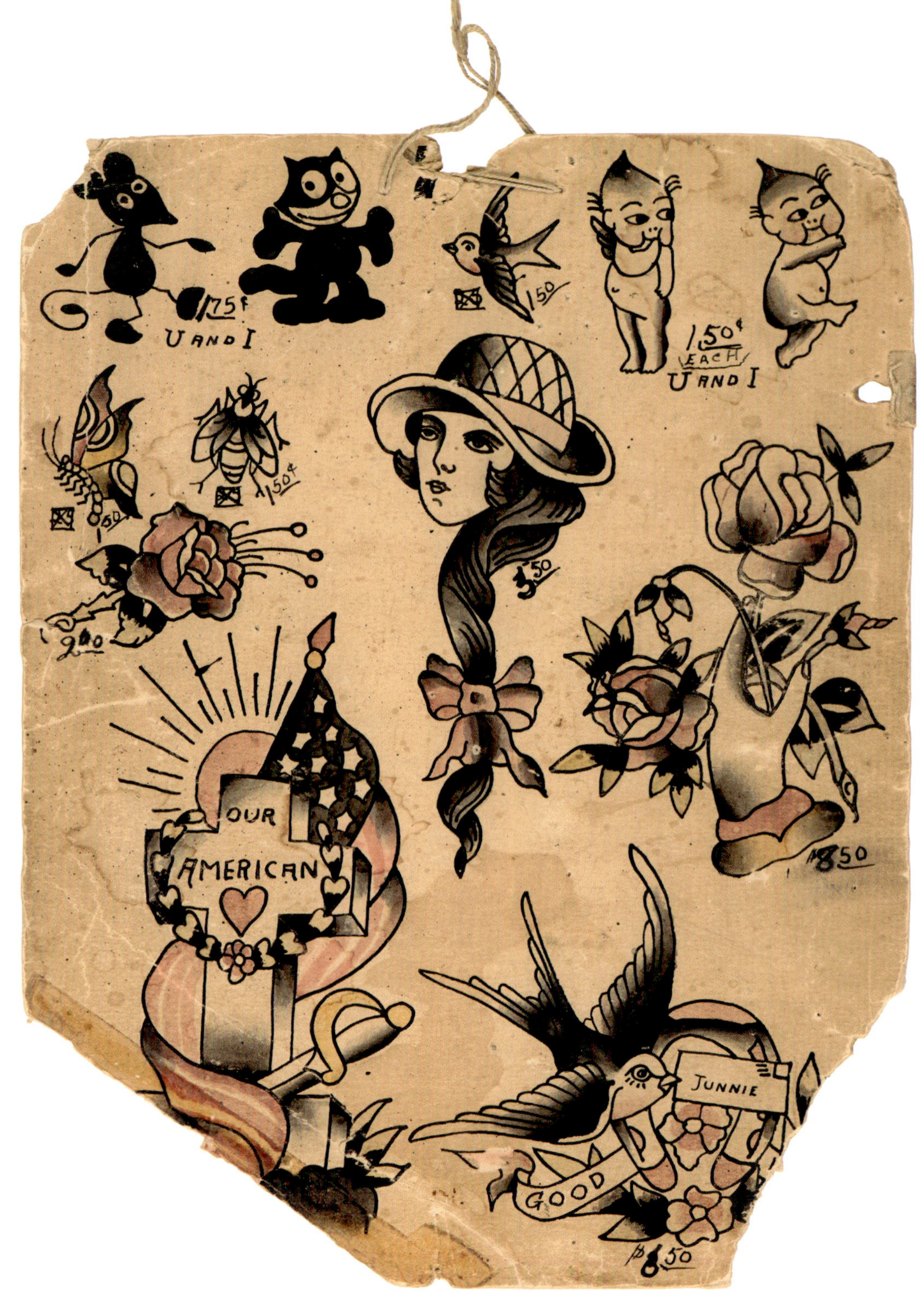
75f
U AND I
1.50
1.50¢
EACH
U AND I
1.50
OUR
AMERICAN
GOOD
JUNNIE
8.50
8.50

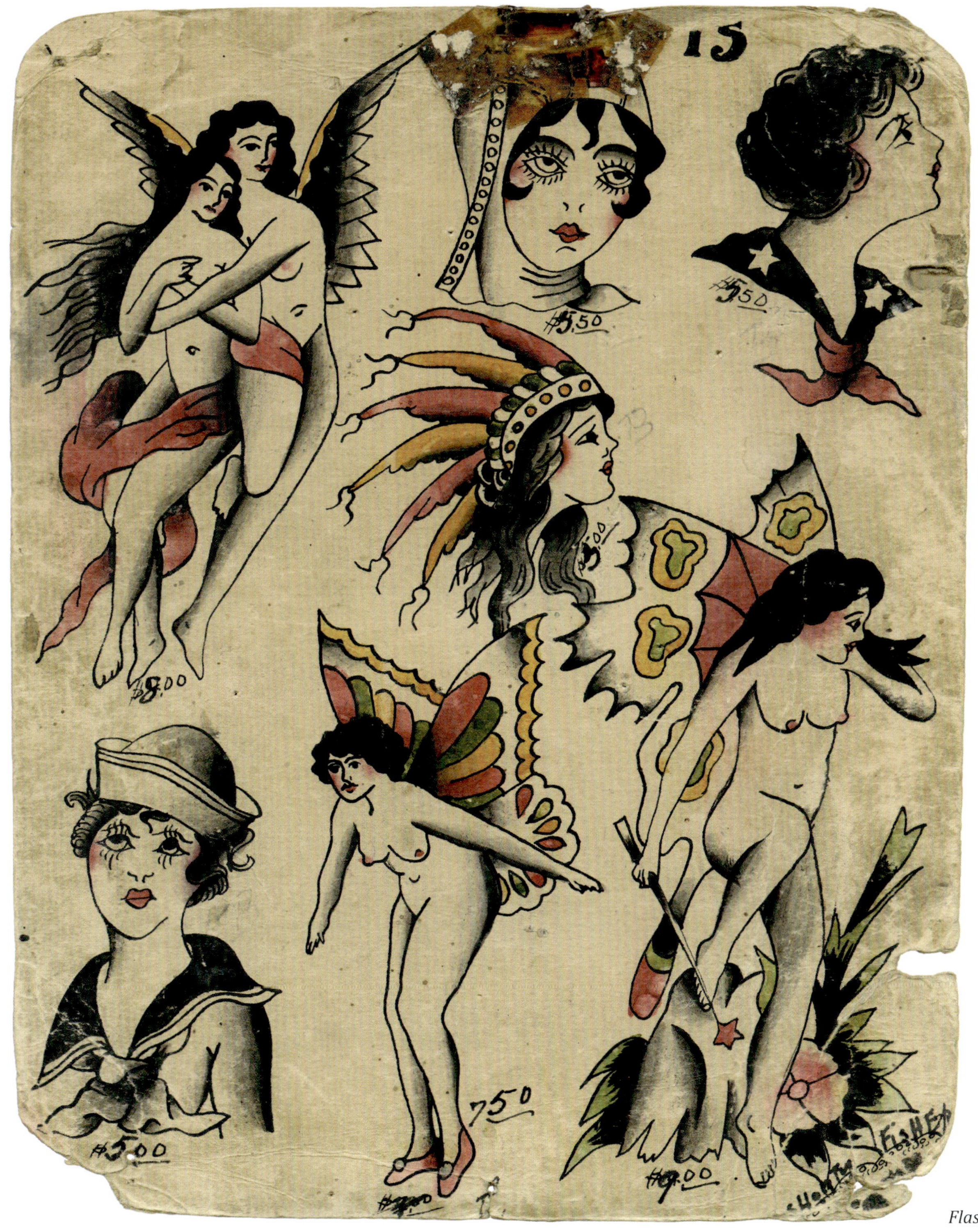

15
$5.50
$5.50
$5.00
$5.00
750
$5.00

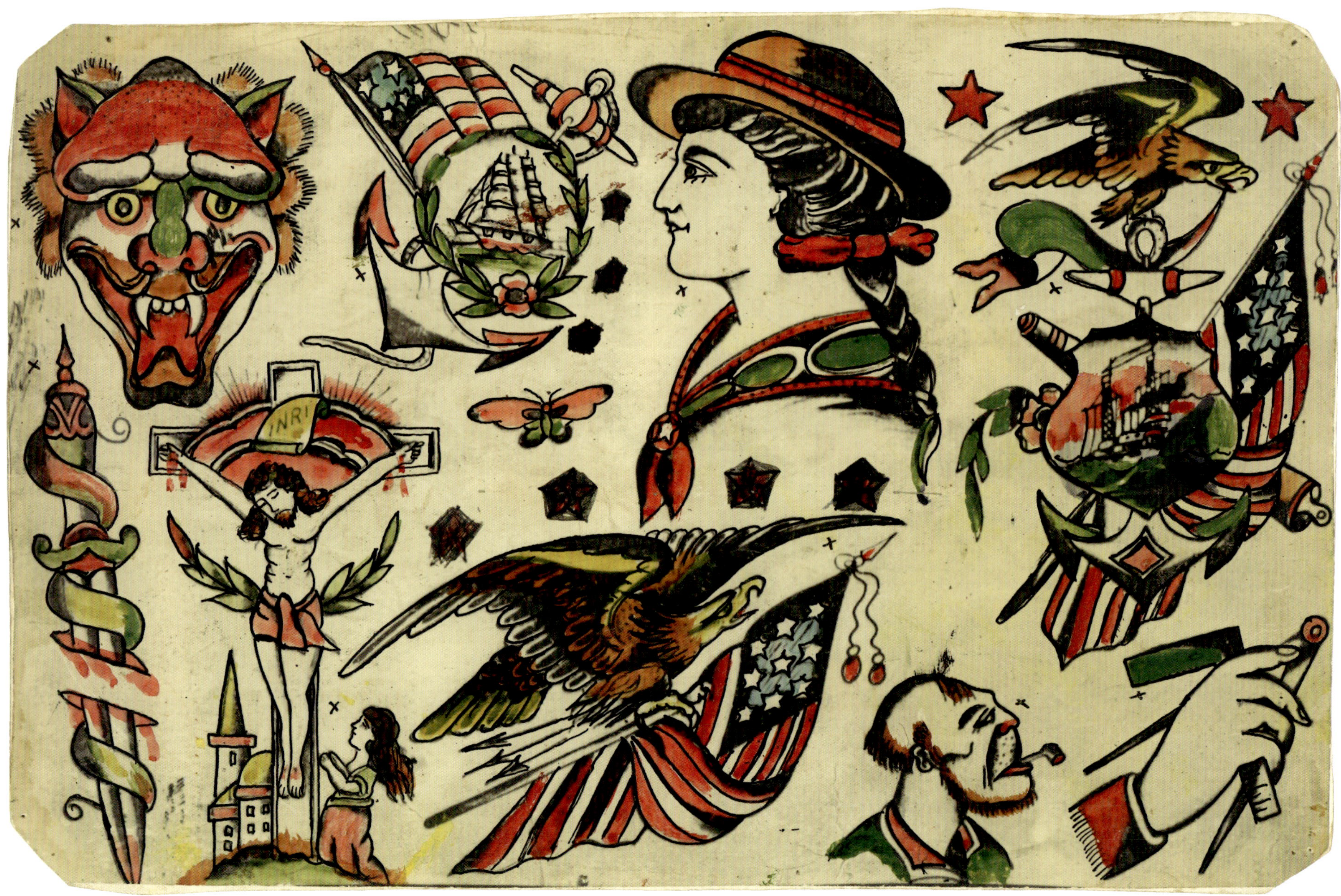

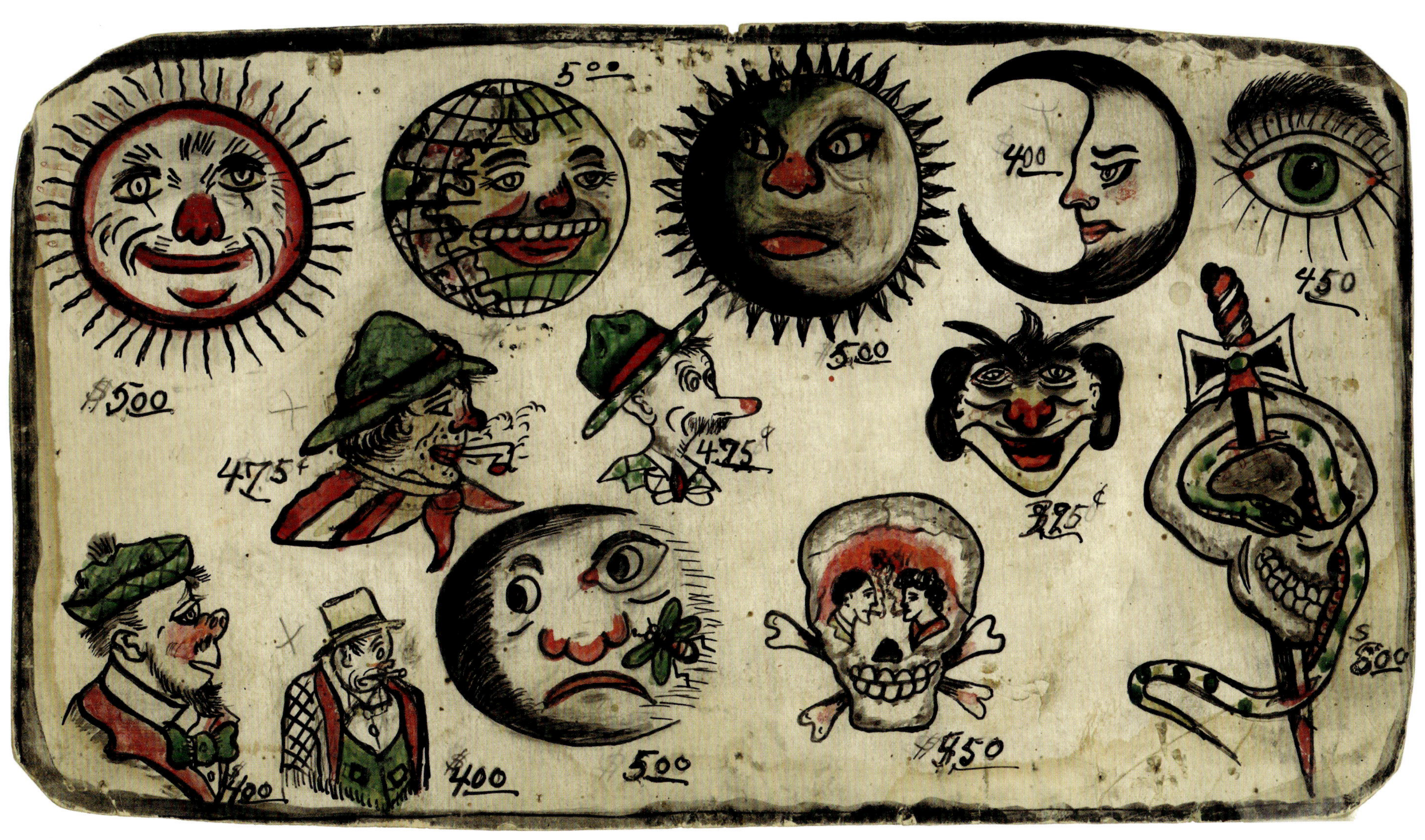

5.00
400
450
$5.00
475¢
4.75¢
85¢
500
400
500
$450
S 500

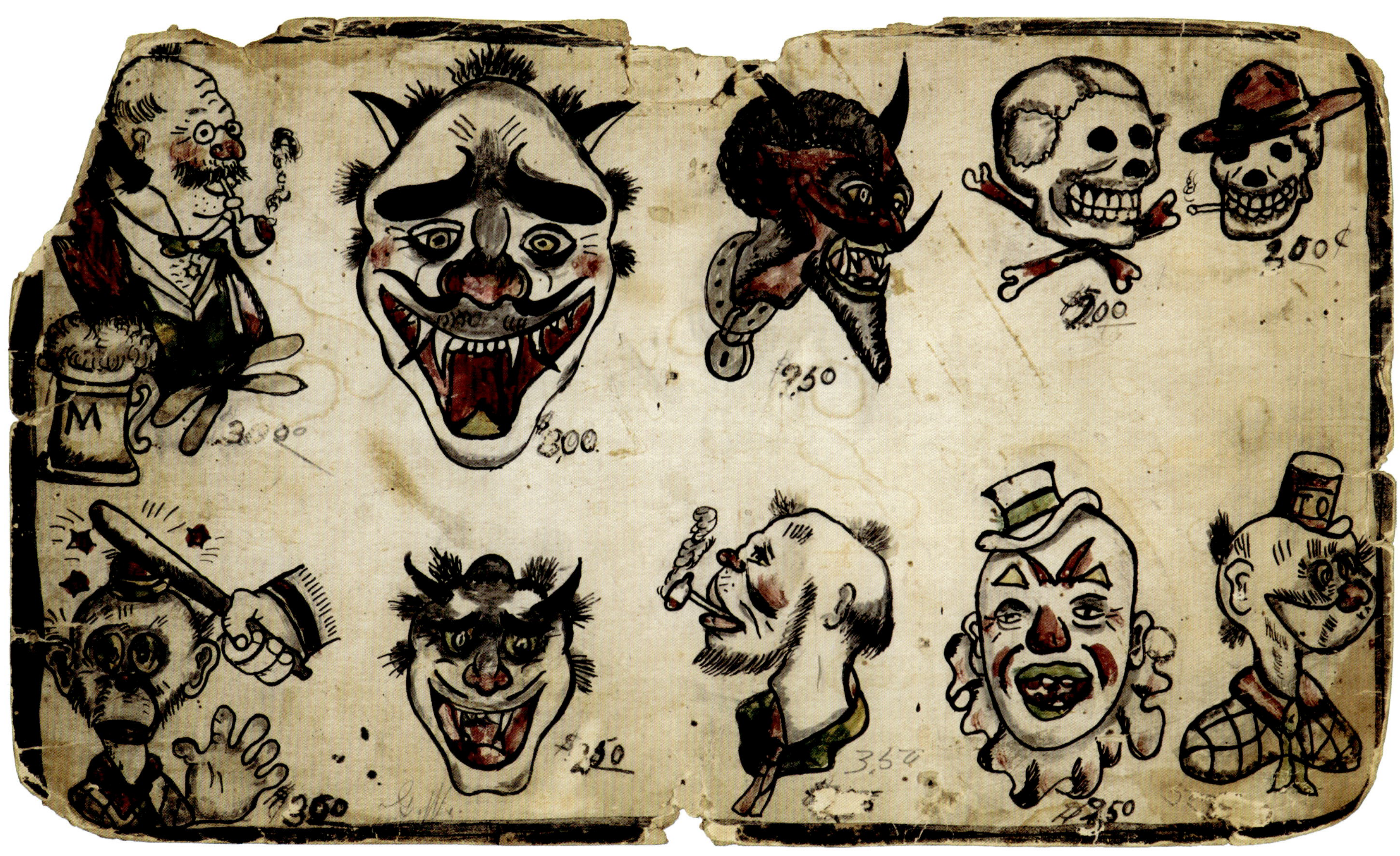

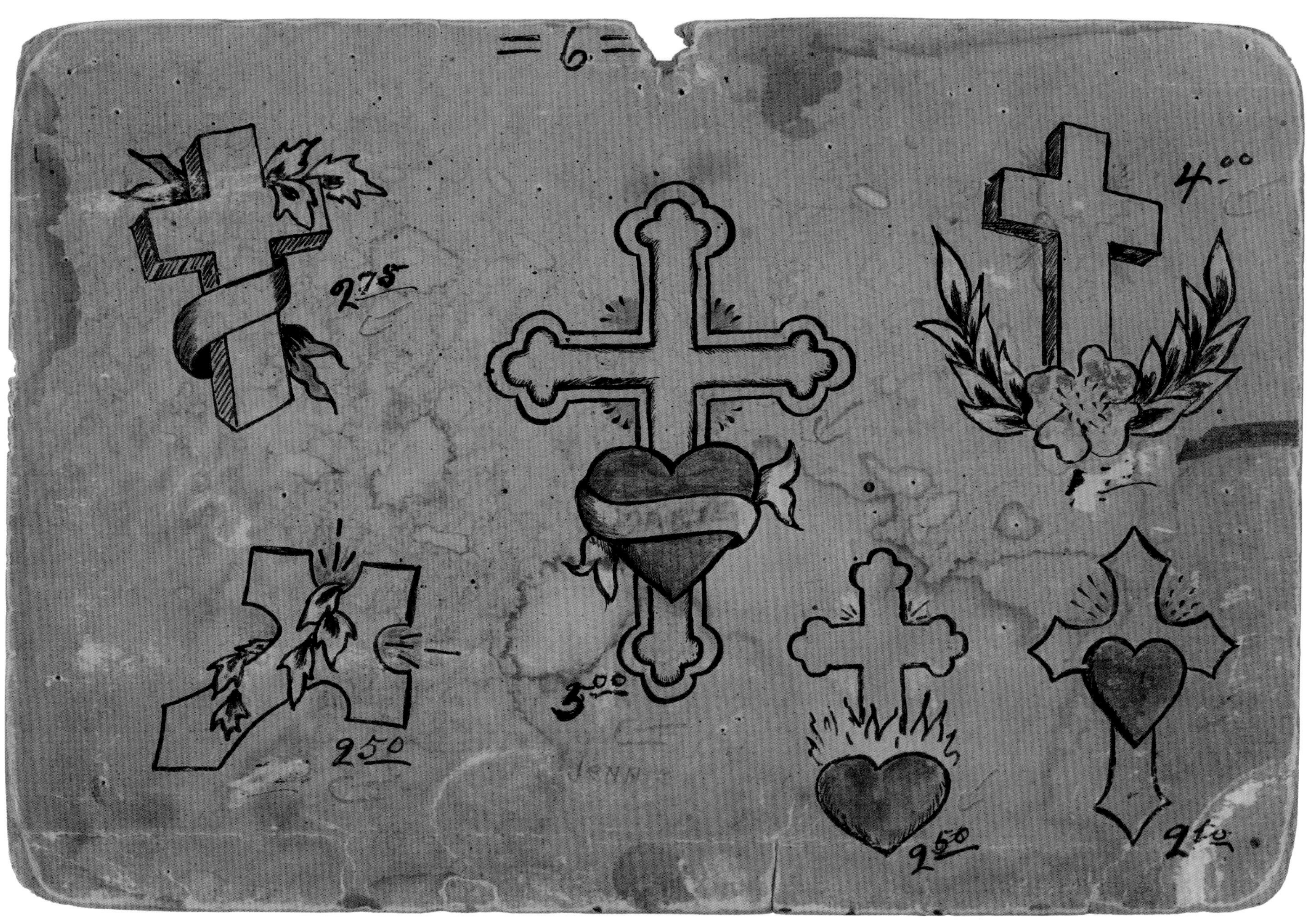
=6=
275
4.00
3.00
250
250
2.00

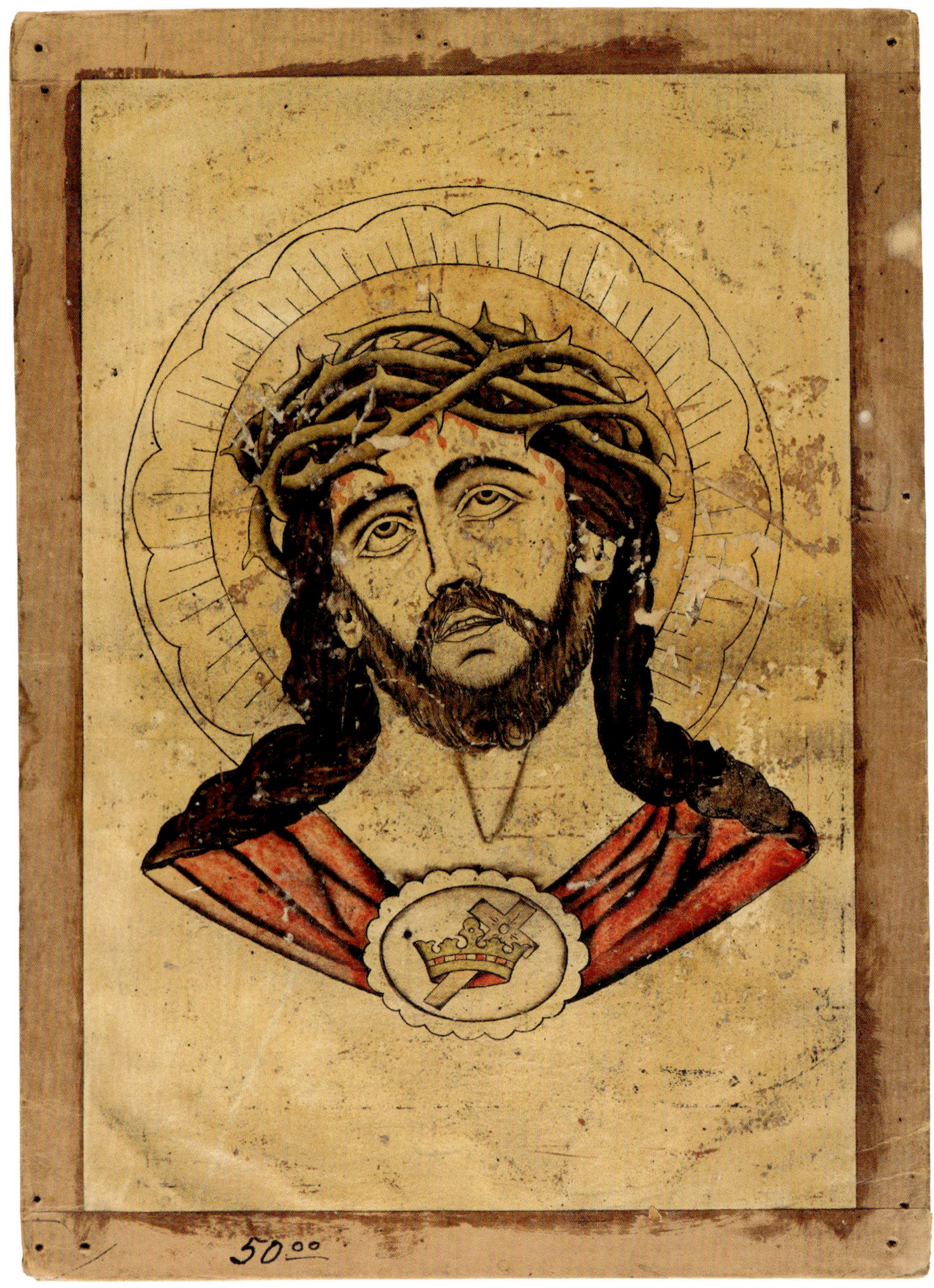

50⁰⁰

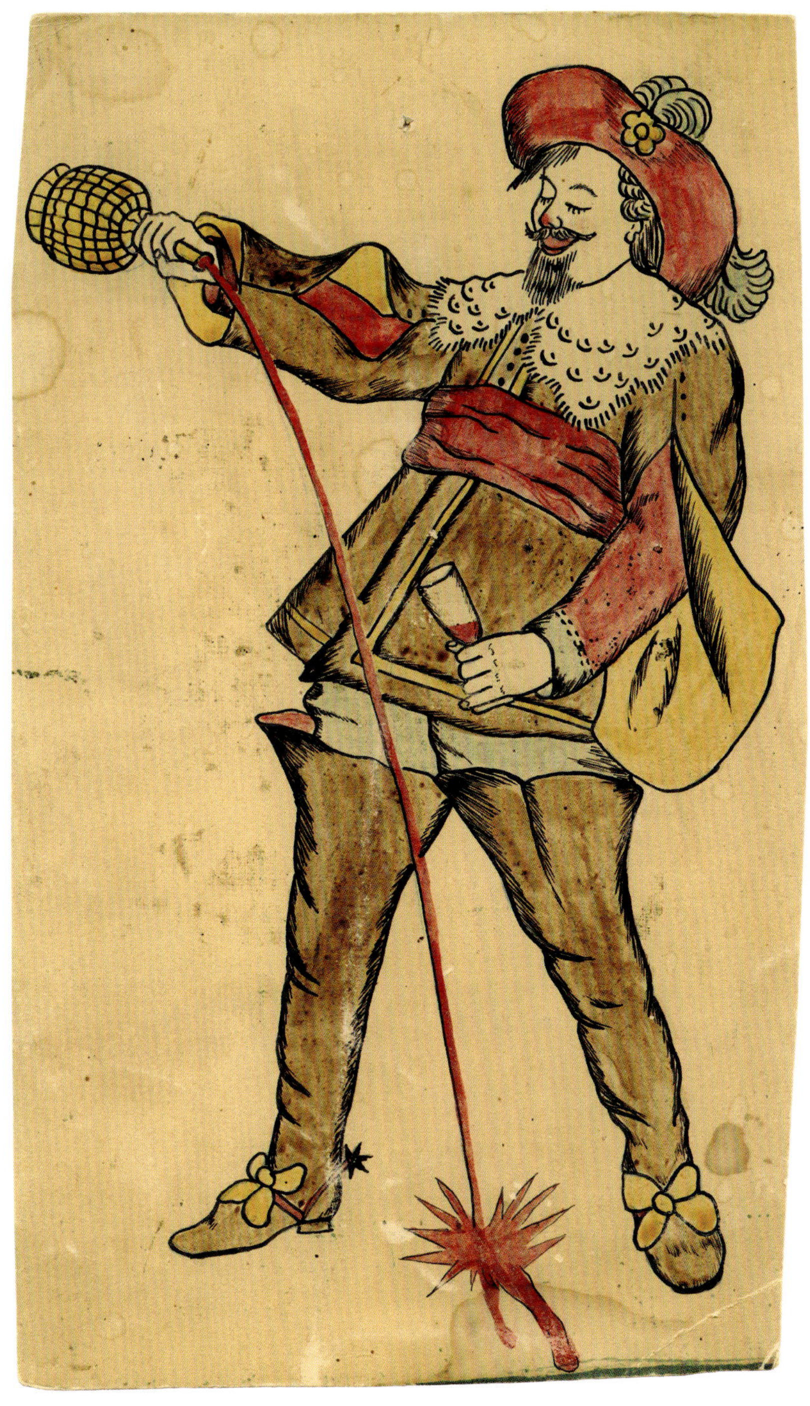

NOTES

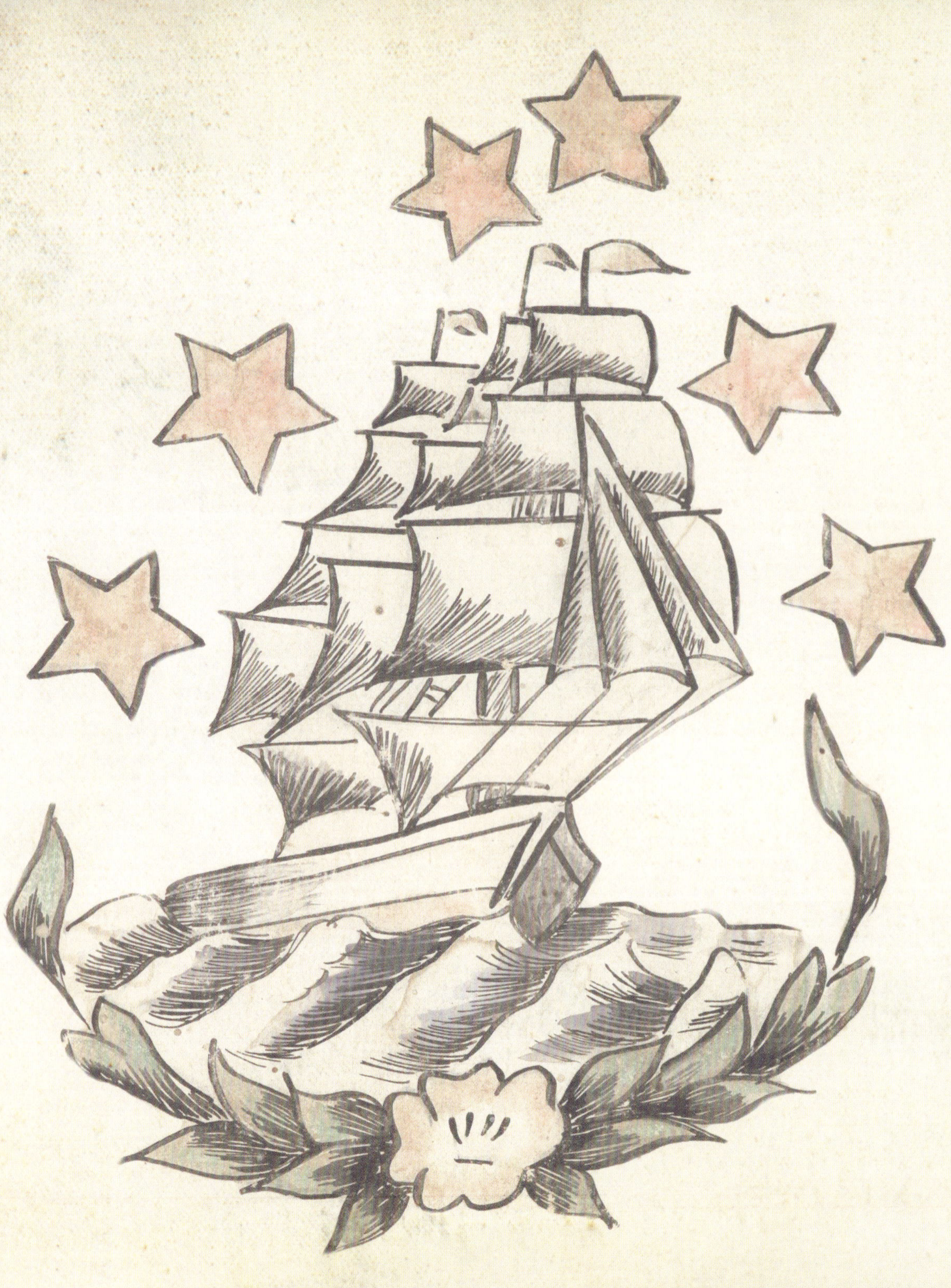

1. Conversation with Patricia "Pat" Waynette Hook, 1992.

2. *St. Louis Dispatch*, December 4, 1904.

3. Conversation with Patricia "Pat" Waynette Hook, 1992.

4. Ibid.

5. Ibid.

6. Ibid.

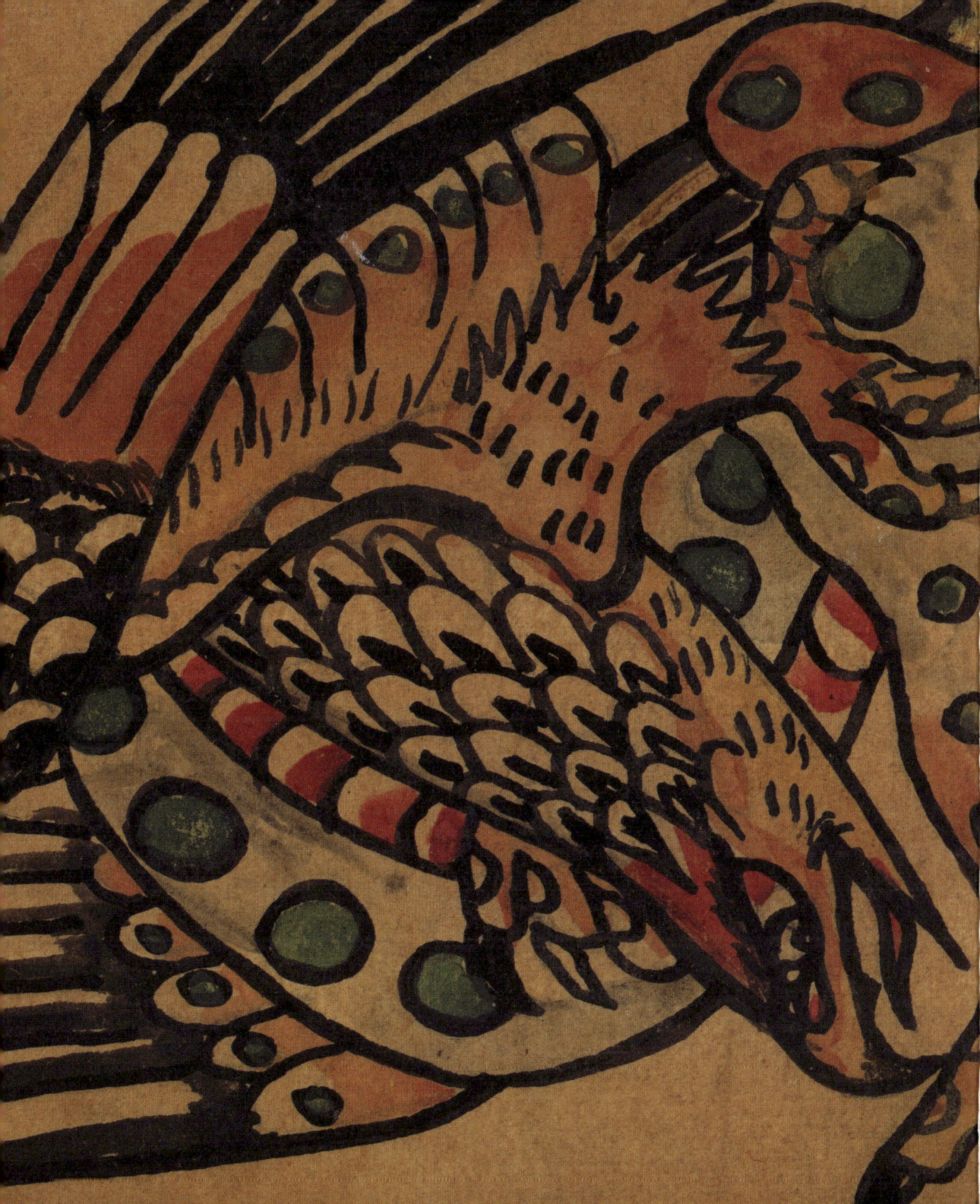

INDEX

INDEX

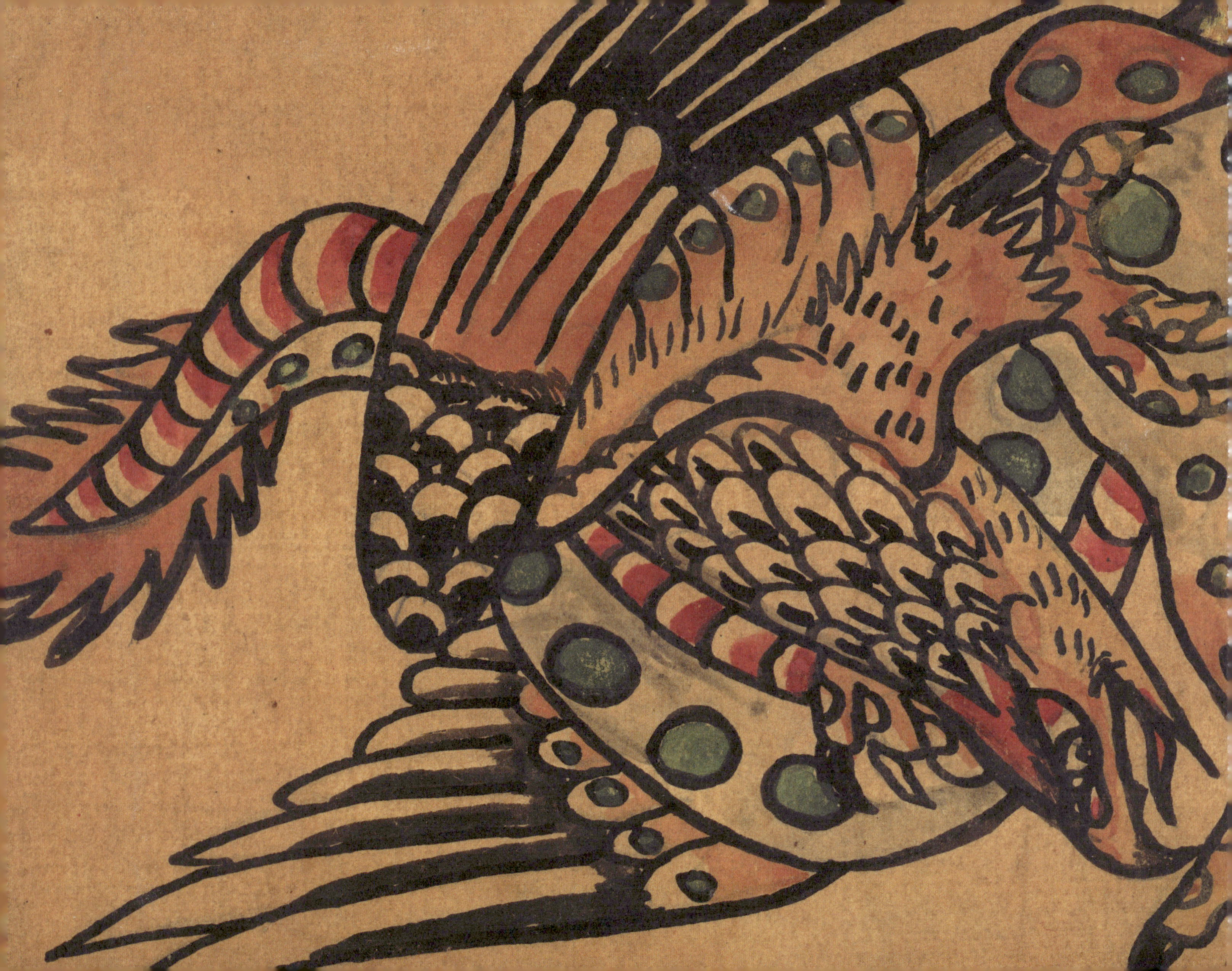